STUDY SKILLS FOR HIGHER EDUCATION

A Use of English Course

by Jean Floyd, M.A.

LONGMAN GROUP UK LIMITED,
Longman House, Burnt Mill, Harlow,
Essex CM20 2JE, England
and Associated Companies throughout the world

First published by Collins Educational 1984
This edition published by Longman Group UK Ltd. 1988

Produced by Longman Singapore Publishers Pte Ltd
Printed in Singapore

ISBN 0 582 03499 X

Contents

Unit 7: Organizing Information

Unit 8: Giving Information

Unit 9: Seeing Connections and Making Judgements

Unit 10: Writing to Convince

Acknowledgements

The author wishes to thank the Use of English students and staff, University of Calabar, 1978–82, for their gratifying enthusiasm and invaluable feedback; the University of Calabar Senate Research Grants Committee, for sponsoring a study of Use of English programmes in other Nigerian universities; and Professor Barry Floyd, for his example and support in a wide variety of roles over many years – not least as an admirable Director of General Studies.

The author and the publishers are grateful to the following for permission to use copyright material in this book:

Organised English 4, extracts reproduced by kind permission of African Universities Press, who allowed the author to draw on her own material for this book; *Unpopular Essays* by Bertrand Russell, extract reproduced by kind permission of George Allen and Unwin (Publishers) Ltd; *Reading a Novel* by Walter E. Allen, extract reproduced by kind permission of Arden Library; 'Imagining a Character' (Unit 9, p. 147) derived from ideas by Paul Baker, formerly Director, Dallas Theatre, Texas and Trinity University Theatre, Texas; Letter on *Psychobabble* reproduced by permission of Dr. K. D. Bardhan; *Use Your Head* by Tony Buzan, extracts and diagrams reproduced by kind permission of BBC Publications; *Memory Matters* by Mark Brown, figure on p. 86 reproduced by kind permission of the author; *Scientists Must Write: A Guide to Better Writing for Scientists, Engineers and Students* by Robert Barrass, extract reproduced by kind permission of Chapman and Hall; *Enjoy Books* by Phyllis Bentley, extract reproduced by kind permission of Victor Gollancz Ltd; *The Story of My Life* by Helen Keller, extract reproduced by kind permission of Hodder & Stoughton Ltd; *How to Study* by Harry Maddox, extract reproduced by kind permission of Pan Books; *Read Better, Read Faster* by Manya and Eric de Leeuw, extract reproduced by kind permission of Penguin Books Ltd; *Psychology in Teaching Reading* by Henry P. Smith and E. V. Dechant, extracts reproduced by kind permission of Prentice-Hall Inc., Englewood Cliffs, N.J.; *The Brain Book* by Peter Russell, two extracts and an illustration reproduced by kind permission of Routledge and Kegan Paul Ltd.

Every effort has been made by the publishers to contact all the copyright owners, but in some cases this has been impossible. It is hoped that any such omissions from this list will be excused.

About This Book

Who it is for

Study Skills for Higher Education is mainly for students who are preparing for or just beginning higher level studies through the medium of English. Normally, students will have a Credit in 'O' Level English, or the local equivalent and be enrolled in a Study Skills or Use of English course.

The book is also suitable for well-motivated students working independently or in a study group.

What it is

This is a text and workbook for a structured, developmental, individualized course which develops the language and learning skills required for independent study and academic work in any discipline at tertiary level. For beginning university students, this would typically be a one-year course worth 3 credits each semester and taught in sections of 25 students each. Regular assignments could replace the third meeting per week. It is recommended that the coursework file count for half the course grade.

Why it works

Course content and method are based on up-to-date research, extensive classroom experience and detailed feedback from several thousand students who used earlier versions of the material. These features are built into the course:

—clear instructions and guided practice in each skill
—active participation by the learner throughout
—reinforcement in each unit of what has gone before
—application of the skills to other courses and adaptation to individual needs
—self-motivation through the setting of ever-higher individual goals and the satisfaction of achieving them.

What you will learn to do

—read faster and understand more
—get more from lectures
—remember more for longer
—use libraries effectively
—take better notes
—plan time sensibly
—write effective essays
—detect and avoid fallacies
—detect and correct language faults
—document sources
—assess your own progress
—tackle exams with confidence

What else you will need

—a file folder for classwork and assignments
—a good dictionary (see Unit 3, p. 37)
—two African novels for reading practice (see Unit 2, p. 27)
—pens or pencils of different colours

How to begin

Put your name and other identification in this book and get acquainted with it:

—Examine the table of contents and leaf through the pages.
—Work out what the marginal symbols mean, e.g. Ⓚ = See Answer Key.
—Decide how the writer's reference section and index might help you.

Get to know your coursemates. There are many ways you can help one another speed the learning process.

Think about some specific personal benefits that doubling (or tripling) your present reading and study efficiency could bring to you.

How to go on

Attend class regularly, taking everything needed with you, e.g. this book.

Set aside regular times for practice and assignments. Frequent practice of techniques is the key to developing a skill of any kind.

Always follow directions exactly. This proves you have understood them and is good preparation for examinations. It is a useful habit to work out the probable reasons for particular instructions and exercises.

Do not be discouraged by initial difficulties. Success will come if you keep trying, and you will soon realize that the time and effort invested in mastering the skills do 'pay off'.

Keep competing against your *own* previous performances. Set yourself realistic goals and plan your strategy for meeting them.

Learn from your mistakes.

—Correct errors, preferably in a different colour.
—If you commit many language errors, concentrate on eliminating one type at a time.
—Use your lecturer's (and coursemates') comments on written work to help you improve next time.

Keep up with the work. Falling behind not only gives you the burden of catching up, but also deprives you of techniques which should be making your other work easier and more rewarding. When you keep up, you get many times more value from the course because it is always working for you.

Likely results

This book presents ideas and techniques that work—if they are used. How well they work for you is up to you. If you take the time to master the techniques and make daily practice a habit, you can get astonishingly quick results in improved study efficiency in all your subjects. Most of your practising can be done on studying you need to do or on a novel you want to read anyway.

You will soon find that the time and effort invested are beginning to 'pay off' and that both the quantity and the quality of what you can accomplish in a given time has increased. This discovery will lead to greater confidence in your ability to learn and remember—which in turn will lead to still greater improvement—and so on, success breeding success.

Here are some specific results to expect from the course:

—tripled reading and study efficiency
—enhanced critical and creative thinking powers
—the elimination of major writing faults and careless errors from your work
—increased command of the English language
—an appreciation of the interrelationships among all forms of knowledge
—satisfaction in achieving ever higher standards
—more pleasure in learning
—greater control over your learning, your language and your life

N.B. Despite the enormous number of English words, there are no satisfactory single words to mean 'he or she' or 'him or her'. To save using these clumsy expressions, 'he' will be used in this book in the same way that 'mankind' is used to mean 'human beings' and should not prevent you from imagining female students or lecturers, where this is appropriate, as easily as male ones.

Unit One Setting Goals

Timed Reading Passage 1: The Reader You Can Become

In order to set goals, you must know where you are now. One of the assignments for this unit will ask you to assess your present ability in a number of study skills required for work at the college and university level. The first task, however, is to get an idea of your present reading efficiency.

Follow directions exactly, to prove that you have understood.

Instructions

1 Your lecturer will provide a simple table, from which you can check your reading time, by writing this on the blackboard:

Minutes	Seconds
	10
	20
	30
	40
	50

He will then give a signal for you to begin reading the passage.

2 Read in your normal way at your normal speed. While you are reading, your lecturer will be using a watch with a second hand to keep track of the time. When one minute has passed, he will enter a **1** in the Minutes column, and then point in turn to the numbers in the Seconds column, until it is time to enter a **2** in the Minutes column, and so on until everyone has finished reading.

3 As soon as you finish the passage, look up at the board and jot down the time your lecturer is pointing to (e.g. 2 min. 40 sec.).

The efficient reader gets what he wants from his reading without wasting time and effort. His speed and his method vary with his purpose. Sometimes he wants to read fairly slowly in order to understand material thoroughly, but he is able to read quickly when he wishes. He can grasp the main ideas accurately and skip details when he chooses. We can say that the chief characteristic of the efficient reader is flexibility.

Perhaps you have a test tomorrow on the first chapter of your chemistry text. Or, for a literature course, you are to read a short story and decide why a certain character behaved as he did. Or you need to collect information for an essay on 'Problems of Palm Oil Production'. You may find that there are ten minutes before your next class and decide to get a general idea of the day's news from the paper. A friend has mentioned an article on 'Today's Educated Woman' and you wonder if it says anything new on the subject. Before sleeping, you decide to relax with a detective story . . .

It is obvious that these situations call for different kinds of reading. The efficient reader is able to read at different speeds and knows different ways of reading.

Furthermore, he is able to choose the most appropriate speeds and methods for the particular reading he is doing.

The efficient reader is also intent on achieving a particular purpose, which means that his mind is alert and questioning: 'Are there any facts here not covered in today's lecture?' 'Will this article explain the government's policy on agriculture?' 'How will the author support such a claim?' Such questions give a reason for reading on. In addition, they help the reader decide when he can go quickly and when he should slow down.

He not only thinks ahead about what he wants to find out; he also relates what he is reading to what he already knows or has just read. He thinks: 'That explanation was confusing, but this example makes the point clear.' Or, 'The author's opinion on this issue is the opposite of my history lecturer's.'

The reader who forms the habit of thinking ahead and looking for relationships can often anticipate what the author will say next. This speeds up comprehension and gives the reader a sense of satisfaction. Finding out that he has made a wrong guess encourages him to pay more attention. Whether he is right or wrong, he is reacting to his reading.

Another important fact about this reader is that he reads meanings rather than individual words. He is always looking for key words and ideas and trying to pick out essentials from what is less important. He is much too busy asking questions and reacting to his reading to say every word to himself as the poor reader may do.

It should be easy now to see why the efficient reader can read a passage faster than the inefficient one, and still understand and remember more of it. And why he can concentrate, and read for long periods without getting tired and frustrated. He enjoys reading because he knows how to get what he wants or needs both easily and accurately.

Since he finds reading rewarding, he probably does more of it. He has the time and interest to move beyond textbooks to books of his own choosing. His vocabulary, his use of English, his general knowledge and his critical judgement all improve in the best and most natural way: while he reads for his own interest and pleasure.

It is a major purpose of this course to help you become more like the reader described in this passage.

(615 words)

Look up at the board. Record the time it took you to read the passage. Then, without looking back at the passage, choose what you think is the best answer to each question below and put a circle around the appropriate letter.

1 This passage is mainly about methods of reading more
a rapidly. *b* effectively. *c* carefully. *d* widely.

2 It emphasizes reading for
a various purposes. *b* literature classes. *c* study purposes. *d* relaxation.

3 The most important thing influencing the way we read should be our
a reactions. *b* education. *c* reward. *d* purpose.

4 Saying each word to ourselves as we read is a sign of
a attentive reading. *b* efficient reading. *c* poor reading.
d scientific reading.

5 The efficient reader is one who reads
a fairly slowly. *b* flexibly. *c* quickly. *d* very carefully.

6 The efficient reader understands accurately
a everything he reads. *b* all the facts he reads. *c* about half of what he reads.
d as much as he requires.

7 In his reading, he usually
a agrees with the author. *b* relates his reading to what he already knows.
c. studies unusual words. *d* rereads interesting sentences.

8 The efficient reader normally concentrates on
a key words and ideas. *b* paragraph development. *c* important details.
d individual words.

9 He probably reads more than the poor reader, because he
a wants to improve his English. *b* reacts critically. *c* finds reading rewarding.
d has a better vocabulary.

10 A major purpose of this course is
K *a* stated at the beginning of the passage. *b* stated at the end of the passage.
c stated many times in the passage. *d* not stated in the passage.

WORDS PER MINUTE CHART: Timed Reading Passage 1 *(615 words)*									
Time	WPM	Time	WPM	Time	WPM	Time	WPM	Time	WPM
1.00	615	2.00	310	3.00	205	4.00	155	5.00	125
10	525	10	285	10	195	10	150	10	120
20	460	20	265	20	185	20	145	20	115
30	410	30	245	30	175	30	140	30	110
40	370	40	230	40	170	40	135	40	110
50	335	50	215	50	160	50	130	50	105

Follow-up

A. Record your progress

1 Prepare a sheet with headings like those in the example on page 4 for keeping track of your reading and comprehension scores and your own evaluation of your progress.

2 Use the Words Per Minute Chart to find out your WPM for the passage read.*
Now fill in the first four columns of your record sheet.

3 When the answers to the comprehension questions have been gone over in class, record the number of questions you answered correctly. For any questions which you answered incorrectly, make sure you understand what the correct answer is and why it is better than the one you chose.

---

* The formula for calculations is $\frac{\text{Number of words in passage} \times 60}{\text{Reading time in seconds}}$ = WPM. Figures have been rounded off to the nearest multiple of 5.

4 Evaluate your performance and record your criticism or your next goal. (See B below).

EXAMPLE

Record of Progress in Timed Readings

Passage	No. Words	Time	WPM	Comprehension	Comments
1	615	4.00	154	8	Too slow!
1 repeat	615	3.00	205		Skipped over familiar parts Looked for main points
2	710	3.30	195	8	Aim for 225 next time.

B. Set new goals

1 Each time you achieve a comprehension score of 7 or more on a timed reading, set your mind to thrust up the speed on the next passage. If you scored 9 or 10 on this passage, you should be reading very much faster!

DISCUSSION QUESTION Which is more efficient and why do you think so?
a reading speed of 200 WPM with 100% comprehension
a reading speed of 400 WPM with 70% comprehension.

2 A recommended minimum long-term goal is to *double your reading efficiency* by the end of this semester. (Many students are able to *triple* their speed.) This means doubling your speed and maintaining a comprehension level of 70%. The relatively easy practice material of the early stages will build up speed and confidence which will help you read any kind of material at a faster rate than you would read it now. For example:

Kind of reading	Rate now	Goal
'Normal' reading	200 WPM	400 WPM
Easy reading, e.g. detective	300 WPM	600 WPM
Study reading, e.g. textbook chapter to be tested	100 WPM	200 WPM

Some students can learn to read non-study material at 700 WPM or higher and still understand as much of it as they need.

C. Read faster

1 *You can push up your reading speed immediately* just by deciding to do so. To prove it, you will reread Passage 1, beginning on the signal. Your aims are:
a to increase your speed,
b to find all the characteristics of an efficient reader mentioned in the passage.

Turn these aims into specific goals:
a to cut a minute off the reading time,
b to be able to list the chief characteristics when you finish.
Think of these goals as you wait for the signal to start.

2 Record your WPM for this second reading and compare it with the first.

D. Test recall

1 Without looking back, list as many characteristics of an efficient reader as you can remember. Give each answer the same form by beginning each one with a verb. The list is started for you:

An efficient reader: can read quickly
adjusts speed to purpose

2 Check to see how complete and accurate your list is. It may help to circle the key words and ideas in the passage and then see how many are on your list. Make additions or corrections in pencil or a different coloured pen.

E. Start the review habit

1 Some students consider this the most helpful study hint of them all:

Study hint: Always review immediately after learning.

It means that you never consider a reading or study session over until you have completed these three steps:
a Attempt to recall *from memory* the main points and as much detail as you need.
b Check up on the completeness and accuracy of your recall.
c Test yourself again on the points you missed the first time.

2 A few minutes spent this way can save hours of relearning as examinations approach. This is because immediate review
a reinforces learning,
b prevents forgetting,
c strengthens memory for related items already learnt.

Related Skills

A. Matching reading speed to reading purpose

1 The speed at which you read any material should be determined primarily by the purpose for which you are reading it. Two additional influences on both purpose and speed are
a the difficulty of the material,
b how much you already know about the topic.

2 A good reader has at his command *at least four speeds* and can move easily from one to the other as needed:
a study *b* normal *c* rapid *d* skimming

AN ANALOGY A car has four gears (plus reverse) for a driver to use. There are many times when first gear, the slowest one, is the right one to use. But to travel in first gear on a splendid motorway with little traffic and in good weather would be absurd. The inefficient reader is like a driver who doesn't know how to get out of first gear when first gear is no longer appropriate.
(Try to define the word *analogy*. Then compare your definition with your dictionary's.)

3 Decide which reading speed, or combination of speeds (study, normal, rapid, skimming) would be most appropriate for each of the following reading purposes:
a To get the main idea or central thought ----------
b To master content, including details ----------
c To keep up with current events ----------
d To review familiar material ----------
e To read a novel, primarily for the plot ----------
f To grasp the relation of details to main ideas ----------
g To be able to retell the story later ----------
h To evaluate how well an author succeeds in achieving his purpose ----------
i To locate specific details ----------
j To outline, summarize or paraphrase ----------
k To solve a problem ----------
l To appreciate the literary style ----------

Study hint: Always consider your reading purpose before you start reading. Choose and adjust your speed accordingly.

B. Assessing reading difficulty

1 In order to tackle study reading effectively, it is necessary to get some idea first of its level of difficulty. A quick glance through, or 'preview', provides information about:
a the familiarity of the topic,
b the length and complexity of the sentences,
c the number of multi-syllable and unfamiliar words,
d how well the material is organized,
e how clearly the author expresses himself.

2 You will be given one minute to assess the probable reading difficulty of the article which begins on the next page. For this practice exercise, it is suggested that you use your one minute this way:
a Read the *first sentence only* of the first paragraph as quickly as you can. Then skip to the first sentence of paragraph two, and as soon as you reach the full stop, jump to paragraph three—and so on, reading first sentences only, as speedily as you can manage, to the end of the article.

b Spend any remaining seconds running your eyes quickly down the pages, trying to get some idea of word length, whether any sections look harder than others, etc.

c At the end of the minute, make a brief assessment of the article's difficulty. How will this influence your speed and approach when you read the article more closely? Jot down your thoughts or discuss them with classmates.

Reading Practice: Your Mind Is Better Than You Think

Instructions:

1 Think for a moment of what you already know from the previous exercise about the article you are going to read. Try to anticipate what the author may say.

2 Then look at Figures 1 and 2 on page 9 and read the captions. What do you think, is the point being made? One of your purposes when you read the passage will be to find out how accurate you are.

3 Next, read the passage as quickly as you can manage for the purpose of finding the author's arguments in support of his claim that 'the mind is better than you think'. How are Figures 1 and 2 related to any of the arguments?

4 Finally, summarize briefly, in your own words, three arguments used by the author to support his claim. Begin 'The first argument is that ......

It is only in very recent years that any real progress has been made in man's understanding of his own mind. Even that progress has shown us little in comparison to what there is to be known. At the moment, despite the fact that we know the various parts of the brain, know much about the way in which chemicals change inside it, know about DNA and RNA, and know about certain experimental results under restricted conditions, we are still struggling with what must be the most elusive quarry man has ever chased.

Sometimes we think we have located areas where activities such as thinking, remembering and speaking are based. Then up pops a situation which proves that the answer is by no means so certain. And just when tests seem to prove that the mind works in a given way, along comes another test which seems to prove it doesn't work that way at all, or along comes a human being with a brain which manages to make the test meaningless.

What we are gathering from our efforts at the moment is a knowledge that the mind is infinitely more subtle than we previously thought. It seems that everyone who has what is ironically called a 'normal' mind has a much larger ability and potential than was previously thought.

A few examples will help to make this clear:

Most of the more scientific disciplines, despite their apparent differences of direction, are all being drawn into a whirlpool, the centre of which is the mind. Chemists are now involved with the intricate chemical structures that exist and interact inside our heads; biologists are struggling with the brain's biological functions; physicists are finding parallels with their investigations into the farthest reaches of space; psychologists are trying to pin the mind down and are finding the experience frustratingly like trying to place a finger on a little globule of mercury; and mathematicians who have constructed models for complex computers and even for the Universe itself, still can't come up with a formula for the operations that go on regularly inside each of our heads every day of our lives.

Dr. David Samuels of the Weizmann Institute recently estimated that in one average brain there are between 100,000 to 1,000,000 different chemical reactions taking place every minute!

We also know that in an average brain there are 10,000,000,000 (ten thousand million) individual neurons or nerve cells. This figure becomes even more astounding when it is realised that each neuron can interact with other neurons in not just one, but many ways: in the late 1960s it was estimated that the number of interconnections might be as many as 10 with *eight hundred noughts after it*. To realise just how enormous this number is, compare it with a mathematical fact about the Universe: one of the smallest items in the Universe is the atom, yet there are billions of atoms in the tip of a person's finger. The number of atoms in the Universe is predictably enormous: 10 with *one hundred noughts after it*. The number of interconnections in one human brain makes even this number seem tiny (see Figs. 1 and 2) especially since we have now learned that even 10 with eight hundred noughts after it is a gross underestimate.

Other examples of the mind's abilities abound. There are examples of extraordinary memory feats, feats of superhuman-strength, and of unusual control of body functions defying the 'laws of science'. Such examples are becoming better documented, more generally recognised and more usefully applied.

Even with this mounting evidence, a number of people still remain sceptical about the mind's potential. They point to the performance of most of us and suggest that we hardly fit a description of mental excellence! In response to this objection, the following questionnaire was given to people from all areas of life. As you read, ask yourself the questions.

In school, were you taught anything about

1 your brain and how understanding its functions can help you learn, memorize, think, etc.?
2 how your memory functions?
3 special and advanced memory techniques?
4 how your eyes function when you are reading, and how you can use this knowledge to advantage?
5 different study techniques and how they can be applied to different disciplines?
6 the nature of concentration and how to maintain it when necessary?
7 motivation, how it affects your abilities, and how you can use it to your advantage?
8 the nature of key words and key concepts, and how they relate to note-taking, imagination, etc.?
9 thinking?
10 creativity?

It may not surprise you to learn that at least ninety-five percent of the replies to each question were 'No'. By now the answer to the original objection should be clear: The reason why our performance does not match even our minimum potential is that we are given no information about how we can best utilize our inherent capacities.

Another, and perhaps the most convincing, case for the excellence of the human brain is the human baby. Far from being the 'helpless and incapable little thing' that many people assume, it is the most extraordinary learning, remembering and intellectually advanced being. Even in its earliest stages it surpasses the performance of the most sophisticated computers.

With very few exceptions, babies learn to speak by the time they are two, and many even earlier. Because this is so universal it is taken for granted, but if the process is examined more closely it is seen to be extremely complex. Try listening to someone speaking while pretending that you have no knowledge of language and very little knowledge of the objects and ideas the language discusses. Not only will this task be difficult, but because of the way sounds run into each other, the distinction between different words will often be totally unclear. Every baby who has learned to talk has overcome not only these difficulties but also the difficulties of sorting out what makes sense and what doesn't.

The young child's ability to learn language engages him in processes which involve rhythm, mathematics, music, physics, linguistics, spatial relations, memory, integration, creativity, logical reasoning, thinking, and more.

The reader who still doubts his own abilities has himself learned to talk and read. He should therefore find it difficult to attack a position of which he himself is evidence for the defence!

There really is no doubt that the mind is far more capable than has been thought. This course will attempt to shed light on a number of the areas in which higher performance and greater self-realisation can be achieved.

(Adapted from Tony Buzan, *Use Your Head*,
British Broadcasting Corporation, 1982)

10,000,000,000,000,000,000,000,000,000,000,000,000,000,
000,000,000,000,000,000,000,000,000,000,000,000,000,000,
000,000,000,000,000,000,000

Figure 1: The number of atoms in the known universe. (An atom is one of the smallest particles we know of; the universe is the largest thing we know of.)

10,000,000,000,000,000,000,000,000,000,000,000,000,000,
000,000,000,000,000,000,000,000,000,000,000,000,000,000,
000,000,000,000,000,000,000,000,000,000,000,000,000,000,
000,000,000,000,000,000,000,000,000,000,000,000,000,000,
000,000,000,000,000,000,000,000,000,000,000,000,000,000,
000,000,000,000,000,000,000,000,000,000,000,000,000,000,
000,000,000,000,000,000,000,000,000,000,000,000,000,000,
000,000,000,000,000,000,000,000,000,000,000,000,000,000,
000,000,000,000,000,000,000,000,000,000,000,000,000,000,
000,000,000,000,000,000,000,000,000,000,000,000,000,000,
000,000,000,000,000,000,000,000,000,000,000,000,000,000,
000,000,000,000,000,000,000,000,000,000,000,000,000,000,
000,000,000,000,000,000,000,000,000,000,000,000,000,000,
000,000,000,000,000,000,000,000,000,000,000,000,000,000,
000,000,000,000,000,000,000,000,000,000,000,000,000,000,
000,000,000,000,000,000,000,000,000,000,000,000,000,000,
000,000,000,000,000,000,000,000,000,000,000,000,000,000,
000,000,000,000,000,000,000,000,000,000,000,000,000,000,
000,000,000,000,000,000,000,000,000,000,000,000,000,000,
000,000

Figure 2: Late 1960s estimate of the different interconnections and patterns which the 10,000,000,000 individual neurons of one brain can make. Calculations with more sophisticated instruments show this number to be far too small!

Assignments

A. Introduce yourself to your lecturer

So far as possible, this course is tailored to the individual needs and interests of the students who take it. Thus it is helpful for your lecturer to know something about you as an individual.

1 At the top of a sheet of file paper, give identifying information as in this example:

Femi Ogunde	*GS 101 Use of English*
Dept. of Sociology	*Section 9*
25th October, 198-	*Unit 1 Assignment A*

2 Letter of Introduction: Using one sheet of file paper only, write a letter introducing yourself to your lecturer. You may use both sides of the paper. Observe the conventions of letter writing by giving your address and date at the upper right and using an appropriate salutation and close. The topics listed below indicate the kinds of information you might include.
Personal data: home, family, children; what kind of person you are.
Education: school(s) and subjects; likes and dislikes; other courses and training; the benefits and shortcomings of your education so far.
Experience: e.g. work, travel, and what you think you have gained from such experience.
Hobbies/Interests: how you like to spend your leisure time; what you would like to know more about purely for your own interest.
Reading tastes: what you read of your own choice; particular titles and authors you have enjoyed.
Plans and ambitions: personal, academic, career.

Check over the essay to eliminate errors of grammar, spelling and punctuation. In particular, make sure you write in complete sentences, avoiding both sentence fragments and run-together sentences.

B. Assess the difficulty of your textbooks

1 Prepare a sheet of file paper as for assignment A. The heading will be 'Comparing Textbooks'. Under it record the titles of three textbooks, including this one, which you will be using for courses.

2 Examine and compare the books. Decide which will be easiest and which hardest to learn from and say briefly how you have come to your conclusions.

3 Set out your comparison clearly. Be concise.

4 A suggestion: Compare your conclusions about each book with those of other students taking the same courses. Use a different coloured pen or pencil to add further points arising from your discussion.

C. Self-assessment

1 Turn to the Self-Assessment Form at the end of this unit. It lists a number of study skills required for college or university work. Judge your present level of

ability regarding each skill. The exercise will be repeated toward the end of the course and improvements noted.

2 Keeping in mind your answers on the Self-Assessment Form, examine the Table of Contents for this book and pick out some sections or topics which might be worth referring to on your own before they are dealt with in class, e.g. 'Detecting faults of grammar and style'. Compare your choices with those of classmates. Remember to use these sections when you need them.

D. Recall and review by making a key word pattern

1 Use a sheet of file paper. In the middle of the page print the key words EFFICIENT READER in large capital letters.

2 Spend a minute trying to recall as many facts and suggestions about efficient reading as you can from this chapter.

3 Once the ideas start coming, start printing *key words* to represent them. Key words are usually verbs and nouns; sometimes they are adjectives and occasionally adverbs.

4 Arrange these key words on lines around the central idea. When one idea leads to another, draw a line between them to show the connection. Try to put the most important points nearest the centre and sub-points nearer the edges.

5 It is more important to keep letting the ideas come and get each key word down *somewhere* on the page than to have a totally satisfactory arrangement on the page. You will improve with training and practice.

6 Check over the pattern and make more lines and arrows to show relationships. Enclose main points in boxes. Use colour.

E. Plan your reading

First, set out a chart with five columns, like the one on page 12.

1 In the first column, list all the reading you intend to do this week, both for your courses and for other reasons. (You will add to the list as the week progresses.)

2 In the second column, give the purpose of each reading. Do not write in the third column yet.

3 Jot down answers to these questions:
a Which will take the most time?
b Which will be hardest to concentrate on?
c Which is the most urgent?
d Which can be done in odd moments?
e Which can be saved as a reward at the end of a day's work?

4 Use your answers to help plan your time. Then, in the third column, say when you are going to do the reading for each purpose listed.

5 Place a tick after each reading which you actually do. Put two ticks if you do it when you planned to.

Keep your purpose in mind when you read.

6 At the bottom of the chart note any ways in which the plan has helped you read more efficiently than usual, and any changes you intend to make in next week's plan as a result of your first attempt.

EXAMPLE

READING PLAN: Week of 27th October

Reading	Purpose	Time Planned	Done	Comments
History	Collect facts for essay on Hausa states. Due next Tues.	Tues & Thurs 10-noon in lib	✓	Lib full, but borrowed books
Pol. Sci notes & ref books	Get meanings of key terms, e.g. Pol science, politics, culture, socialization... Before Fri lect 10 a.m.	Wed & Fri 8-9 in lib		Read notes in room Wed. Books all in use, Fri 8-9. Lect at 9 – assignment not done.
Education	Select pts for class disc on Friday. Should Education be a Marketable Commodity? For Fri 4 p.m.	Wed after Educ class Wed 9-10 p.m.	✓	No empty classrooms. Hostel too noisy. Skipped Fri lunch to finish.
Amadi, The Great Ponds	Own interest & reading practice	Sun a.m. & after evening studies	✓✓	Skipped Thurs only: welcome party for first yrs.
New Nigerian	Reading prac & general interest esp. politics & educ	After lunch		

FOR THOUGHT AND DISCUSSION

This student's first attempt was not very successful. Make some suggestions for increasing his/her chances of success in the future.

NOTE-MAKING HINT

For any *personal* notes (e.g. from lectures or reading, or for planning time and work) abbreviate where possible. Punctuate only to separate different points. Just make sure you will know what the abbreviation means when you see it again!

By way of example, abbreviations for the following have been used in the Reading Plan above:

(days of the week)	lecture	years
political science	library	especially
education	points	reading practice
reference books	discussion	

Self-Assessment Form

Below is a list of study skills required for university or college level work. Look at each item and decide which of the four possible responses best expresses your present situation regarding that skill. Circle the appropriate number:

1 'I can't do this (or I don't know how). Help needed urgently!'
2 'I'm not very good at this. Improvement necessary.'
3 'There is room for improvement, but this is not a big problem for me.'
4 'I feel I am quite good at this.'

The ability to:

a	read efficiently: at a normal speed of at least 300 WPM with about 70% comprehension	1	2	3	4
b	concentrate when reading or studying	1	2	3	4
c	understand what has been read	1	2	3	4
d	remember what has been read	1	2	3	4
e	assess reading difficulty	1	2	3	4
f	preview effectively	1	2	3	4
g	select key ideas quickly	1	2	3	4
h	recognize and use a wide vocabulary	1	2	3	4
i	get the most from a dictionary	1	2	3	4
j	make useful notes from books	1	2	3	4
k	enjoy reading	1	2	3	4
l	plan a week's study	1	2	3	4
m	stick to a plan	1	2	3	4
n	get the most from a library	1	2	3	4
o	get to the right place on time with the right books and equipment	1	2	3	4
p	remember names, dates, assignments	1	2	3	4
q	meet deadlines for assignments	1	2	3	4
r	understand and follow written instructions (e.g. on assignments, exams)	1	2	3	4
s	understand and remember lectures	1	2	3	4
t	make useful notes from lectures	1	2	3	4
u	make an outline or summary	1	2	3	4
v	ask and predict questions (e.g. on course content)	1	2	3	4
w	write clear, grammatical English	1	2	3	4
x	write effective essays	1	2	3	4
y	revise systematically	1	2	3	4
z	perform well in exams	1	2	3	4

Unit Two Increasing Reading Speed

Timed Reading Passage 2: Getting Rid of Bad Habits

Instructions: Your reading purpose for this passage is to go much faster than you did on the first reading of Passage 1, and to get a score of 7 on the Comprehension Test. Begin at the signal, record your time when you finish, then answer the questions without looking back.

1 You do not need every word to understand the meaning of what you read. In fact, too much emphasis on individual words both slows your speed and reduces your comprehension. You will be given the chance to prove this to yourself, but meanwhile, let us look at the implications.

2 First, any habit which slows down your silent reading to the speed at which you speak, or read aloud, is inefficient. If you point to each word as you read, or move your head, or form the words with your lips, you read poorly. Less obvious habits also hold back reading efficiency. One is 'saying' each word silently by moving your tongue or throat or vocal cords; another is 'hearing' each word as you read.

3 These are habits which should have been outgrown long ago. The beginning reader is learning how letters can make words, how written words are pronounced, and how sentences are put together. Your reading purpose is quite different; it is to understand meaning.

4 It has been estimated that up to 75% of the words in English sentences are not really necessary for conveying the meaning. The secret of silent reading is to seek out those key words and phrases which carry the thought, and to pay less attention to words which exist only for the sake of grammatical completeness.

5 An efficient reader can grasp the meaning from a page at least twice as fast as he can read the page aloud. Unconsciously perhaps, he takes in a whole phrase or thought unit at a time. If he 'says' or 'hears' words to himself, they are selected ones, said for emphasis.

6 The assurance that not every word is necessary for meaning often helps readers handicapped by another very common fault: regression. A poor reader frequently lets his eyes wander back over what he has just read. This usually indicates a lack of concentration: he was too lazy and inefficient to get the meaning the first time. Or it may mean he lacks confidence in his ability to understand without looking at every word. But regression rarely helps comprehension. It usually makes it worse, because it interrupts the forward-moving train of thought.

7 An efficient reader seldom goes back. He pushes actively forward from one idea to the next, and he usually gets the meaning the first time. He has learned from experience that a missed word or idea can often be deduced from what follows. He also knows that important ideas are usually repeated. If he does go back, it is with a purpose, to find the answer to a definite question.

8 Neither does a good reader interrupt his reading at each unfamiliar word to use the dictionary. He often infers a meaning from the context. Unless a passage depends on the word, he saves his checking up in the dictionary until the end.

9 We have implied that the good reader's eyes see more words at a time. To understand what this means, you need to know that our eyes do not move continuously along a line of print. They move in a series of jerks, and they see only when they stop. About 90% of our reading time is spent on the pauses or 'fixations' between eye movements.

10 It is possible that a good reader and a poor one will spend roughly the same amount of time on a pause. The difference is that the efficient reader needs fewer pauses than the poor reader. Instead of focusing on every word, whether or not it is needed for understanding, he focuses on key words and takes in the words on either side with 'peripheral' vision.

11 This means that in the same number of pauses—the same amount of time—he can cover more material than the poor reader. He goes faster and gets less tired because he is concentrating on meaning rather than on individual words. He also comprehends better.

12 The exercises which follow will help you discover whether your reading is being held back by undesirable habits. They will also suggest ways to curb those habits. However, it is important to remember that the best remedy for most reading problems is to concentrate on reading for meaning.

13 As you learn to move ahead more purposefully, the wasteful habits will weaken and your speed and efficiency will increase.

(735 words)

Look up at the board. Record your time. Then, without looking back, choose what you think is the best answer to each question and circle the appropriate letter.

1 This passage is mainly about
a improving eye movements.
b reading more widely.
c eliminating poor reading habits.
d concentrating while reading.

2 Saying each word to yourself as you read
a improves comprehension.
b increases reading speed.
c prevents regression.
d hinders reading efficiency.

3 Your reading purpose should be
a to understand all the words.
b to make fewer eye movements.
c to understand meaning.
d to understand the grammatical construction.

4 It has been estimated that up to 75% of words in English sentences are
a grammatically unnecessary.
b essential to the meaning.
c not absolutely essential to the meaning.
d read more than once by poor readers.

5 Efficient readers usually
a move their heads quickly.
b take in whole phrases at a time.
c point at key words.
d miss some important points for the sake of speed.

6 Regression is often a sign of
a lack of confidence.
b efficient eye movements.
c concentration.
d rapid reading.

7 An efficient reader can read a page silently and grasp the meaning __________ as he could read the page aloud.
a almost as fast *b* at least twice as fast
c at the same speed *d* not nearly as fast

8 When he meets an unfamiliar word, the efficient reader will
a ignore it. *b* reread the passage.
c stop immediately and look it up in his dictionary.
d try to infer the meaning from the context, and read on.

9 When we read, our eyes see
a only when they are moving. *b* only when they are not moving.
c at all times. *d* only key words.

K 10 Pauses or fixations take about __________ of our reading time.
a 60% *b* 10% *c* 90% *d* 50%

WORDS PER MINUTE CHART: Timed Reading Passage 2 *(735 words)*									
Time	WPM	Time	WPM	Time	WPM	Time	WPM	Time	WPM
1.00	—	2.00	370	3.00	245	4.00	185	5.00	150
10	630	10	340	10	235	10	175	10	145
20	550	20	315	20	220	20	170	20	140
30	490	30	295	30	210	30	165	30	135
40	440	40	275	40	200	40	160	40	130
50	400	50	260	50	190	50	155	50	125

Record your WPM and comprehension scores on the chart you prepared last week. For any questions which you answered incorrectly, make sure you understand what the correct answer is and why it is better than the one you chose.

Follow-up

A. Observe a reader's eyes

1 Choose a partner and take turns watching each other re-read the first five paragraphs of Passage 2. Hold the book high so that your partner can see how your eyes move.

2 When you watch him, note how many pauses he makes per line. Does he move his head? his lips? Do his eyes linger at the end of a line? Or do they sweep quickly to the beginning of the next one? Do his eyes ever seem to skip back over what he has already read?

3 Discuss with your partner what each of you has noticed.

B. Check yourself for bad habits

Now check yourself for any further bad habits by re-reading the rest of Passage 2. For example, if you put your thumb and fingers on either side of your throat, can you feel any movement as you read? Are you conscious of 'hearing' many words? Record what you notice.

C. Get rid of bad habits

Read through the following hints for curbing common bad habits. Place a tick in the margin for any hints you think you should practise.

HEAD MOVEMENT Read with your elbows propped on the desk, your chin in the V formed by your hands, and your palms holding your head in position.

VOCALIZATION (sounding out words by moving your lips) Read with a pencil held between your lips. You will soon get tired of having it fall out!

THROAT VOCALIZATION Place your thumb and forefinger at the sides of your throat as you read. Try not to feel any movement except for the occasional very important word.

SILENTLY 'SAYING' AND 'HEARING' WHAT YOU READ

1 Talk to yourself *about* the reading and your reaction to it.
2 Read faster.

These activities will keep you too busy trying to understand meaning quickly to say or hear individual words, except for key words.

BACK-SKIPPING AND REGRESSION Going back over what has already been read, whether done as an unconscious habit (back-skipping) or deliberately, because you realize you have not understood (regression), is the most common reading fault among students.

1 Some people find this advice helpful: Push a card or ruler down the page, covering up each line as soon as you have read it so that you cannot go back. Push faster and faster. You may be surprised at how much you understand *without* going back.
2 Another method, very highly recommended, will be introduced later in this unit.

D. Note how punctuation aids clarity

The purpose of punctuation is to help the reader understand quickly and correctly. Read aloud some of the examples you find in Reading Passage 2 in answer to this exercise, noting when the punctuation tells you how to group the words in silent reading and when to pause in reading aloud. The easiest way to do most parts of the exercise is to circle the punctuation and put the letter of the question in the adjacent margin. The paragraphs are numbered for easier reference in discussion.

1 Find three examples of commas used to mark off an introductory phrase.

2 Find three examples of commas used to separate items in a series.

3 Find three examples of commas used to help the reader group words in a fairly long sentence. (N.B. When a sentence is short and the meaning is clear without commas, omit them.)

4 Note the commas in paragraph 10, sentence 3. They are used to mark off a clause that *interrupts* the main clause; the sentence would still make sense if the

clause were removed. N.B. Commas must never be used to mark off a clause which is *essential* to the meaning of the word it relates to. To punctuate the first sentence of paragraph 3 like this would be *wrong*:

These are habits, which should have been outgrown long ago.

5 Find two examples of colons. What purpose does each serve?

6 Find a semicolon used in place of a full stop to show that two sentences are closely related.

7 Find examples of quotation marks used to show that a word is being used in a special sense.

8 How do the dashes used in paragraph 11 help to clarify the relationship of the ideas?

Related Skills

Faster readers usually comprehend better than slow ones. If you are aware of certain facts about the way your eyes work when you read, you will see why this is true. You will also realize why the exercises to be suggested are well worth doing. Minutes spent in practice can prevent hours of inefficient reading.

A. Eye movements

1 Try this series of experiments with a partner:

a Hold a finger motionless in front of his eyes and watch his eyes as he looks at it.

b Next, move the finger up, down and around, and watch what his eyes do.

c Finally, tell him to hold his eyes still, then move your finger about in front of them. Does he obey? If so, ask him how clearly he sees.

2 As you have just confirmed, if an object is still, the eyes must be still in order to see it; and if an object is moving, the eyes must move with the object in order to see it clearly.

The words on a page are still. Therefore the eyes have to stop moving in order to see them clearly. You have already seen how the eyes move across a line in a series of jumps and pauses.

3 Practice in using information: Examine the following facts. Think about what they imply, separately and together, for better reading. List briefly as many implications as you can. (You might tackle this task in groups and compare results.)

a It takes about $\frac{1}{4}$ second to move from one fixation to the next. This seems to vary little from person to person.

b The length of a fixation varies from $\frac{1}{4}$ second to $1\frac{1}{2}$ seconds, depending on the material being read and the reader's skill.

c The eyes can register from three to five words in 1/100th of a second.

d The brain needs between $\frac{1}{4}$ and $\frac{1}{2}$ second to process and recognize an item the eyes have sent.

B. Using peripheral vision

1 Focus your eyes on a point several feet away: a mark on the wall, the nose of a person across the room. . . Note how much else you are aware of around the focal point.

2 Now look at a printed page. Focus on the middle of a word in the middle of a paragraph. Without changing your focus, note how many other words or parts of words you can recognize above, below and to either side. How many more can you guess at? (*After* you have noted the number of words you can recognize or guess at, check on the accuracy of your recognition.)

What clues helped you guess?
a The shape of the word?
b The first or last letters?
c Knowing what words often appear together?
d Knowing what words are likely to be used in discussing the topic?

3 One reason you can recognize words with peripheral vision is that written English, like other languages, contains much *redundancy*.
a Passage 2 referred to the great number of words in a piece of writing which are unnecessary for conveying the meaning.

It is al unnec t se cle ly al th let in a wor t
kn wh th wo is.

You do not even need to see all the parts of letters to know what they are.

Just __ prove that you ___ grasp ___ meaning __ _ sentence with ___ reading _____ word, fill __ ___ blanks ____ ___ words which ____ ____ left ___.

b You will understand even better how redundancy helps if you continue reading this page without turning it around. *The lines are deliberately printed upside down, and that is the way you should read them.*

Your brain is able to put together an extraordinary amount of information from just a few clues sent by your eyes. One purpose of this exercise is to show that your eyes and your brain are able to take in the meaning from a printed page at a faster rate than you may have thought possible. It will also show how quickly your brain can adapt to new ways of receiving information—in this case, through upside-down reading.

You have probably begun very, very slowly, syllable by syllable, like a small child just learning to read his first words. But as you continue, you should find that you can recognize whole words and even simple phrases without much hesitation. As you read on, you will pick up speed, and reading upside-down will feel less strange.

By this time, you are likely to be aware that you are not reading the whole of every word before deciding what the word is. You are probably seeing the first few letters and using these as clues to help you guess the rest. Or you may recognize a common phrase from a key word in it. You may also notice that your eyes are seeking out and focusing on the most distinctive features of a word, or the strangest-looking word in a phrase, and paying less attention to easily recognized words such as *the* and *and*. By directing your attention where it is most needed, you may be able to read whole clauses quite smoothly because you know that certain words or ideas 'go with' the ones you have deciphered. Occasionally you may discover from the rest of a sentence that you have made a wrong guess, which needs correcting, but most of the time you will be right.

Reading upside down should help you appreciate the importance of *context* in reading. The general meaning and grammatical construction limit the possibilities as to what can come next. What we have called guesses are therefore really choices from the small range of words which would make sense in the particular situation. Often you need to see only enough letters to recognize which of the two or three possible words has actually been used. The necessary information can usually be gained from peripheral vision, without having to focus on the word itself.

If you continue practising this upside-down reading, you will find that you are taking in larger chunks of meaning at a time—and, of course, your speed will keep increasing. To prove this point, re-read this section. Since you know what to expect, you will need even fewer clues to decipher the meaning. Notice how much easier and faster the second reading is.

Having learned so quickly to cope with upside-down reading, you can certainly learn to absorb meaning more and more quickly from pages printed the right way up.

C. Contrasting patterns of eye movement

1 Study the two eye movement patterns below, ignoring the accompanying text for the time being.

2 State as clearly as possible the differences between the two patterns and the implications of these differences for reading efficiency.

3 Compare the observations you have made with those listed under each pattern, making a mental note of points you omitted.

4 Recall immediately by seeing how many points under each analysis you can remember without looking back. Which ones did you miss?

5 For further practice in fluent speaking or writing, organize and link the points to form two effective paragraphs.

PATTERN A: EYE MOVEMENTS OF A VERY POOR READER

Analysis:

1 The poor reader reads one word at a time.

2 By failing to relate a word to its neighbours, he misses clues as to which meaning of the word applies here. A single word can have many possible meanings.

3 Since he does not understand what he has read, he keeps going back.

4 He still doesn't understand, and he becomes anxious. The more anxious he becomes, the more he goes back. This only makes things worse.

5 Since he cannot find the train of thought he should be following, his eyes and mind start wandering.

6 His 'pattern' consists of erratic stops, starts and regressions. An erratic pattern is tiring and gives little chance of understanding.

7 His speed is probably 100 WPM or less; his comprehension is almost nil.

8 Yet his eyes have made eighteen stops on this one line alone.

9 He has put in a great deal of mental and physical effort and accomplished nothing.

10 He will soon stop reading because his eyes are tired, he 'can't concentrate', or the book is 'boring'.

PATTERN B: EYE MOVEMENTS OF A GOOD READER

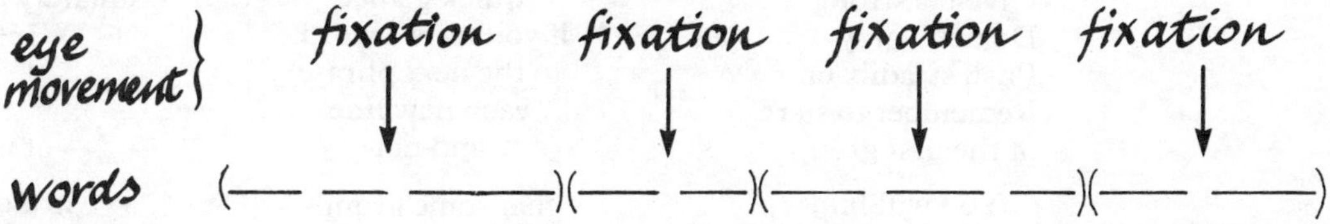

Analysis:

1 The good reader takes in more words at a fixation by focusing on the middle of a word group and using peripheral vision to see the rest.

2 Because he groups words, he has only four units of meaning to deal with, instead of ten different words with all their possible associations.

3 His eyes do less physical work. He has made four fixations, not eighteen. (By the end of a page, he may have made as few as 100, to the poor reader's 500.)

4 By adding each new thought unit to those which have gone before, he is soon following a train of thought and can anticipate what is coming next.

5 He establishes a rhythm of regular eye movements. Regular movements are less muscularly fatiguing than erratic ones.

6 He doesn't regress. To do so would break the rhythm.

7 The rhythm and the train of thought will help him through more difficult sections.

8 Because he is actively pursuing meaning, he is in control of his reading and can adjust his speed and method when necessary.

9 His average speed is unlikely to be less than 300 WPM and may be 600 WPM or higher, depending, of course, on his purpose and the type of material.

10 Because he is comprehending, anticipating and reading rhythmically, he finds his reading satisfying and will feel motivated to continue.

Reading Practice

If you are convinced that you do not need to look at every word to get meaning off the printed page, you are mentally prepared to practise techniques which will train your eyes and brain to read, understand and remember at an even faster rate.

A. Eye training

> Note your starting and finishing times in the table on page 23.

The purpose of this exercise is to encourage
your eyes to move quickly from left to right
in rhythmic leaps without ever regressing. As you read,
try to focus on the middle of each group of words,
taking in the words on either side with peripheral vision.
Do not allow your eyes to slide along a phrase.
Give it a strong quick glance squarely in the middle.
Do not worry if you miss a word. Just keep going.
Push steadily on to the next phrase and the next.
Remember to start each new line in the middle
of the first group and not at the beginning.

You will find that some groups stretch your vision
while others seem too short. This is because
the length of a group is determined largely by the meaning.
In reading a normal printed page, the good reader
unconsciously picks up clues through peripheral vision
as to which words in the line ahead belong together.
Using this information, his eyes move automatically
to key words and the middle of natural groupings.
Having some notion of what to expect, he is prepared
for what he finds, and recognizes the thoughts more quickly.
In this way he speeds along the lines, taking in a unit
of meaning with each glance.

It is possible that you will feel a slight tug
on the six little muscles that move each eye from left
to right. This is because poor reading habits
have made these muscles lazy and inefficient. The point
of this drill is to discipline them so that they learn
how to make more efficient movements. Keep repeating
this drill until the rhythm of sweeping steadily
from group to group feels natural to you. Each practice
should take less time than the one before.

Once your eyes have learned to make the correct
physical movements, you can forget about eye movements!
After all, having mastered the art of walking,
you no longer think about how to make your feet step
correctly so that you get where you want to go.
In fact, undue concern about eye movements
can slow down your reading. Having learned the correct
pattern of movement across and down the page, your eyes
will automatically make fewer and shorter steps if you are
concentrating on getting as much meaning as possible
as quickly as possible from page after page.

From now on, the best way to improve your eye movements
is to keep practising faster reading.

Reading No.	Start	Stop	Time Taken
1			
2			
3			
4			
5			
6			

B. Drawing inferences

Try to read the following extract from Helen Keller's *The Story of My Life* in the same rhythmic way you have been reading Exercise A. Take in as much meaning as you can in one glance. The questions you will be asked to answer or discuss afterwards are listed first. Knowing ahead of time what they are will help you know what to look for and to comprehend more quickly.

1 What clues are there in this account by the teacher that Helen is not an ordinary child? In what ways is she probably different? (Note that you are never directly told.) What makes you think so?

2 Why do you think this extract has been included here? In what ways is it related to the theme of this unit?

She reads books such as ordinary children of her age read and enjoy . . . I remember distinctly when she first attempted to read a little story. She had learned the printed letters, using slips on which the words were printed in raised letters; but these sentences had no special relation to one another. One morning we caught a mouse, and it occurred to me, with a live mouse and a live cat to stimulate her interest, that I might arrange some sentences to form a little story, and thus give her a new conception of the use of language.

So I put the following sentences in the frame, and gave it to Helen: The cat is on the box. A mouse is in the box. That cat can see the mouse. The cat would like to eat the mouse. Do not let the cat get the mouse! The cat can have some milk, and the mouse can have some cake.

The word *the* she did not know, and of course she wished it explained. At that stage of her advancement it would have been impossible to explain its use, and so I did not try, but moved her finger on to the next word, which she recognized with a bright smile. Then, as I put her hand upon puss sitting on the box, she made a little exclamation of surprise, and the rest of the sentence became perfectly clear to her.

When she had read the words of the second sentence, I showed her that there really was a mouse in the box. She then moved her finger to the next line with an expression of eager interest. 'The cat can see the mouse.' Here I made the cat look at the mouse and let Helen feel the cat. Her expression showed that she was perplexed.

I called her attention to the following line, and although she knew only the three words, *cat, eat* and *mouse*, she caught the idea. She pulled the cat away and put her on the floor, at the same time covering the box with the frame. When she read 'Do not let the cat get the mouse!' she recognized the negation in the sentence and seemed to know that the cat must not get the mouse. *Get* and *let* were new words.

She was familiar with the words of the last sentence, and was delighted when allowed to act them out. By signs she made me understand that she wished another story, and I gave her a book containing very simple stories. She ran her fingers

K along the lines of raised letters, finding the words she knew and guessing at the meaning of others . . .

C. The high speed technique (and a cure for regression)

HOW THE TECHNIQUE WORKS

1 The technique you are about to learn takes advantage of the eyes' natural tendency to follow a moving object. It requires you to use your index finger (or the wrong end of a pen or pencil) *not* as a pointer—for that is a bad habit which slows you down—but *as a visual guide to lead the eyes more and more quickly along the lines of print*.*

a To get an idea of your finger's usefulness as a *guide*, ask a friend to imagine a large circle about a foot in front of him, and then to look slowly and carefully around the circumference of his imaginary circle. Watch his eyes.

Next, ask your friend to follow your finger tip as you trace a circle in the air. Watch his eyes again.

What conclusion can you draw from the difference between the unaided and the aided eye movement patterns?

b To get an idea of your finger's potential as a *pacesetter*, stop reading for a moment and move your index finger back and forth across the page as quickly as you can.

You can see that your finger is able to move many times faster than your eyes ever move in normal reading.

2 The method is simple:

a You train your eyes to follow the finger.

b You move the finger swiftly along the lines—*always faster than you think you can read.*

c You make your eyes keep up.

3 The results are impressive:

a Your eyes have to move faster to keep up with the guide (which means also that they can't regress).

b Your eyes learn to take in more—and more—at a glance.

c Your brain learns to 'understand' at a faster rate.

d Your 'normal' reading-with-comprehension speed keeps increasing.

e In addition, you have a means of speeding up your reading whenever you want to.

LEARNING THE TECHNIQUE

1 Like most complex skills, high speed reading is best learned in stages and under supervision. A series of drills will help you perfect the technique. Each drill should be mastered before you attempt the next one. It usually helps to team up with a classmate for some of your out-of-class practice.

---

* This method of increasing reading speed has been developed by the International Learning Methods Group for its courses in advanced reading. The founder, Tony Buzan, reports that students read on average 50 per cent faster when they use a visual guide than they do without one.

2 Please note that in the early stages you are *not expected to comprehend anything at all* during a drill. If you do, then you are not doing the drill properly! If you use a drill as a warming-up exercise, however, you will notice an improvement in the 'normal' reading and studying you do after it.

3 It is suggested that your practice sessions include three to five minutes of high speed drill, *followed immediately by 'normal' reading* of the same material. Here are the first two drills:

HIGH SPEED DRILL 1: FOLLOWING THE GUIDE

The purpose of this drill is to teach your finger and eyes what they have to do. Concentrate on the physical movements required and forget all about comprehension. (Would you expect someone who hadn't learned to stop and start a car, or to change gears, to cope with rush hour traffic in Lagos or Ibadan?)

1 Open the book you are going to read from and place your index finger underneath the second word on the page. Focus your eyes on the very tip of the finger. Move the finger along the line, eyes following. Then jump to the front of the next line, move along . . . jump to the next line . . . and so forth.

2 As you get the knack of it, gradually increase the speed, always making the eyes keep pace with the finger. Don't linger at the end of a line; jump smartly to the next one. Try to establish a rhythm of even sweeps and returns. This is most easily done if your lecturer, a coursemate or you tap out the rhythm and you make your eyes move on to the next line on each successive 'beat'.

3 Build up speed until you are covering about two pages a minute, and keep guiding your eyes across the lines and down the pages until you have been practising for at least three minutes.

4 Then stop, return to your starting point and slow your finger to a speed at which you can just manage to understand, if you concentrate, i.e. to a speed slightly faster than comfortable. *Begin to read for comprehension.*

Stop and practise the drill once before you continue with this page. If you are interested in estimating your WPM for the drills, see Table 1 below.

5 Spend two or three minutes recalling what you have just read at 'normal' speed. Then try to answer this question:
The 'normal' reading you did at the end of the drill was almost certainly accomplished at a faster-than-normal rate, with a normal level of comprehension. Can you suggest why?

6 Practise Drill 1 until you feel you have mastered it, then progress to Drill 2.

HIGH SPEED DRILL 2: SEEING THE WORDS

1 This time you will pay less conscious attention to the finger itself and concentrate more on trying to see the words under which it is passing. *You are still not expected to understand the meaning of what you see.* Simply try to *see* the words as your eyes move swiftly by.

2 Begin at 'normal' reading pace, then increase steadily and rapidly *beyond* the point where you can comprehend—but still trying to look at all the words. Build up to about two pages per minute.

3 After a few minutes of drill, return to your starting place, slow your finger to a speed at which you can just comprehend, and *read for understanding*.

> **Study hint:** Warm up to your study reading by beginning each session with one of these drills. You will discover that you are reading faster and understanding more.

Table 1

WORDS PER MINUTE CHART FOR HIGH SPEED DRILLS	
Beats/lines per minute*	Words per minute
30 (=1 beat per 2 seconds)	300
60 (=1 beat per second)	600
90 (=3 beats per 2 seconds)	900
120 (=2 beats per second)	1200
150 (=5 beats per 2 seconds)	1500
180 (=3 beats per second)	1800

* An average of 10 words per line is assumed.

Assignments

A. Make a new reading plan. (See page 12)

Try to improve on last week's.

B. Practise faster reading and better study techniques

Keep a diary of the various types of practising you do. Some suggestions:

1 Repeat Exercises A and B (Eye Training) from time to time. Adapt to other reading material.
2 Use a High Speed Drill to begin a reading or study session (for any subject).
3 Read faster, with the intention of understanding.
4 Test yourself on the content of this course so far.
5 Recall and review at the end of each study session.
6 Stay behind a minute or two after a lecture (in any subject) while you mentally recall the main points.

Keep the diary simple, e.g.

28/10 Ex. 1 (Eye Training) Twice. Pleased with improvement over attempt in class.

C. Check your punctuation

Go over any piece of writing you have done. See whether each punctuation mark is necessary and aids the sense or the rhythm. Remove, add or change punctuation as necessary to make your meaning clear and each sentence easy to read. If the work you are correcting is for this course, make your corrections in a different colour.

D. Begin a programme to triple your reading rate

The purpose of this programme is to help you double, then triple, your reading rate in the course of reading two novels. You will use the first novel daily for 1) high speed reading practice and 2) reading for comprehension, aiming to double your rate by the time you finish. You should improve still further with the second novel.

PRELIMINARIES

1 Examine some novels for the purpose of selecting one of them to read now. Read the cover, the 'blurb' and any introductory sections which tell you about the book or its author. Look at chapter titles and illustrations. Assess the level of difficulty. The book you finally choose should look interesting to you and not too difficult. (If the books have been set, take the easier one first).

2 Plan a regular time each day for reading in the book, e.g. before the evening's study or when you wake up in the morning.

3 Decide which of the following methods of assessing progress will be most convenient for you and prepare a record page. (See the examples on pages 31–2.) The first method is the one your lecturer is likely to use for class practice, but for out-of-class practice it requires either an alarm clock or a co-operative roommate to call time. For this reason, you may find Method 2 more satisfactory for your independent practice sessions.

Method 1: Increasing the Pages
This method requires you to read for the same length of time each day, e.g. 5 minutes, always trying to increase the number of pages read within the time limit. For quick rough estimates of your WPM on these 5 minute readings, see Table 2.

Development of the ability to read at a forced pace for longer and longer periods can be encouraged by occasionally increasing the number of minutes, e.g. to 6, then 8, then 10 minutes—and setting higher and higher targets as to the number of pages to be read.

Method 2: Cutting the Time
For this method, you set yourself a given number of pages to read, e.g. four. Note your starting time, read the required number of pages and then note your finishing time. Each day you try to cut the time it takes to read the quota. (If a page ends in an awkward place, finish the sentence, do the record-keeping, then carry on until you reach a more convenient place to start next time.) You can build up your stamina for sustained reading at a forced pace by increasing the number of pages from time to time.

4 Determine your starting rate. Ideally you will do this in class with your lecturer keeping time for you.

a Read for 5 minutes (or read three or four pages) in your normal way at your normal speed. For this first reading you should not use your finger as a visual guide or try to go abnormally fast.

b Think about what you have just read. How would you assess your comprehension? Give yourself a mark out of ten and fill in the record columns.

Table 2

WORDS PER MINUTE CHART FOR 5 MINUTE READING-FOR-COMPREHENSION PRACTICE

First deal with the number of whole pages read. If part of an additional page has been read, add on the appropriate number from Part B of the table. An average of 10 words per line is assumed, allowing for paragraphing and dialogue.

A. Number of whole pages read in 5 minutes		WORDS PER MINUTE Book with 30 lines per page	Book with 36 lines per page	Book with 40 lines per page
2		120	144	160
3		180	216	240
4		240	288	320
5		300	360	400
6		360	432	480
7		420	504	560
8		480	576	640
9		540	648	720
10		600	720	800
11		660	792	880
12		720	864	960
13		780	936	1040
14		840	1008	1120
15		900	1080	1200
16		960	1152	1280
17		1020	1224	1360
18		1080	1296	1440
19		1140	1368	1520
20		1200	1440	1600
B. Fraction of page read				
for: 1/4	add:	15	18	20
1/3		20	24	27
1/2		30	36	40
2/3		40	48	53
3/4		45	54	60

Optional Calculations

Whether you choose Method 1 or Method 2 for keeping track of your progress, you will want to compare your approximate WPM at the beginning and end of the book. Many students also like to work out the daily WPM. If you are number-shy, Table 2 will give you enough of an idea of how you are progressing, but if you want more exact estimates, the following instructions will help you to make them.

1 How to estimate the number of words per page:

a Choose an average looking page, i.e. not the first page of a chapter, which usually has fewer words than average, and not a page with an unusual amount of dialogue.

b Count the number of words in a 10 line section. Then divide by 10 to get the average number of words per line, to the nearest whole number, e.g.

$$\frac{113 \text{ words}}{10 \text{ lines}} = 11 \text{ words per line.}$$

c Count the number of lines on the page and multiply the average number of words per line to get the average number of words per page. Round off to the nearest 5 or 0, e.g. 385 (not 383) or 410 (not 408). Use this figure when you want to work out your WPM.

2 How to estimate words per minute (WPM)

a Use this formula:

$$\frac{\text{Pages read} \times \text{words per page}}{\text{Minutes of reading}} = \text{Rate in WPM}$$

Example:

$$\frac{3 \text{ pages} \times 440 \text{ words}}{5 \text{ minutes}} = \frac{1320}{5} = 264 \text{ WPM.}$$

b If you stop in the middle of a page, or part of the page is illustration, or the chapter ends part-way down, or most of the page is dialogue, you will want to allow for this. It is easiest to deal first with the whole pages and then to add on the fractions or leftover words;

Example:

$$\frac{(3 \text{ pages} \times 440 \text{ words}) + (15 \text{ lines} \times 11 \text{ words})}{5 \text{ minutes}} =$$

$$\frac{1320 + 165 \text{ words}}{5 \text{ minutes}} = 297 \text{ WPM.}$$

While even these results can only be approximate, they will give you a clear enough indication of your progress and will provide incentive for surpassing each previous record.

E. How to ensure success

1 Make the daily comparisons as fair as possible by working every day at about the same time and under the same conditions. You may wish to experiment at the beginning by trying morning and evening practices and deciding whether one generally gives a better result than the other.

2 Always work through these five steps:

a *Review* what you read yesterday. First try to remember, then run your eyes quickly over yesterday's pages to check on your memory and get mentally 'set' for today's reading.

b *Do a High Speed Drill*, beginning from where you stopped reading yesterday. Work up to a good speed and establish an even rhythm. (Put a marker at the first page so you can find it quickly again later.) Drill for about three minutes.

c Then return to your starting place to begin the reading for comprehension which you will record. Quickly note your starting time. Then *read to understand, using your finger as a guide* to lead your eyes at the fastest pace you can go and still get meaning. You should feel that the pace is forced but that you can just keep up if you work hard to do so.

d At the end of the set time or number of pages, *stop and record*. Then *try to recall* what you have read. Judge your level of comprehension and record that too.

e *Check up on your comprehension* and clear up any difficulties. Apply what you learn in this course by choosing whatever techniques seem most appropriate. Here are some examples:

—Run your eyes swiftly down the pages, searching for key words and ideas.
—Look for answers to specific questions.
—Reread selected paragraphs to grasp more details or savour the language.
—Look up in the dictionary a word which keeps recurring but whose meaning you are still not sure of.

In such ways you can develop your increasing range of reading and study skills at the same time as you improve your comprehension and appreciation of the novel.

3 Aim to improve each day on your achievement of the day before. Don't give up or slow down because you feel strained or comprehension has dropped. Both are normal for some people at the beginning. Just keep on practising—and your eyes and your brain will learn to cope. Push up your speed first; then learn to comprehend at the faster rate.

4 Keep an accurate record so that you will have a true picture of your achievement. While you should not worry about occasional setbacks—they happen—it is always worth thinking about possible reasons for them because you may be able to change something which is adversely affecting your reading: Are you following instructions correctly? Would you do better at another time of the day? In another place?

5 There is nothing to stop you recording several practices in a day, or reading a bit further in the novel when you have finished the recorded practice. There are many other books to enjoy when you finish this one!

Two examples of Reading Records: the first five days

Days 1–5 of a Reading Record: Method 1 (5-minute sessions)

READING RECORD: African Novel

Mongo Beti: MISSION TO KALA, Words per page: 380

Bad habit: Regression

Time planned: Before evening's study (Room mate keeping time for me and I for him)

Date	Time	Min.	Pages	Est. wpm	Compr.	Comments
27/10	In Class	5	2¼	170	7	'Normal' speed. No High Speed Drill. Very slow.
	In Class	5	3	228	6	HSD with lecturer checking. Then slowed pace, using finger. Drop in compr. but v. pleased at better speed.
	7:25-7:30	5	2½	190	6	Disappointing. HSD didn't go well. Harder w/o lecturer. Forgot to keep finger moving.
28/10	7:30-7:35	5	3¼	240	6	Spent longer on HSD first. Forced pace with finger. Reading felt better. Should push up next time.
29/10	In Class	5	3¾	285	7	Really tried. Amazed at result. Compr. a bit better.
	7:22-7:27	5	3½	265	7	Must keep up to std. achieved in class.
30/10	7:25-7:30	5	4	304	6	Success! Better review and drill helped I think. Making finger lead eyes.
31/10	7:30-7:35	5	4	304	8	Speed same but better compr. Concentrating better.

Days 1–5 of a Reading Record: Method 2 (4 pages each time)

Reading Record: African Novel
Chinua Achebe, ARROW OF GOD,
Av. Wds per Pg. 385

Date	No. Pages	Time Start	Time Stop	Min.	WPM	Compr.	Comments
5/11	4	7:15	7:25	10	153	7	Normal speed.
5/11	4	7:40	7:48:30	8.5	181	7	Practised HSD first. Still feel awkward, eyes a bit strained but some improvement.
6/11	4	7:10	7:18	8	192	5	Thinking about finger instead of meaning. Clumsy method still seems strange.
7/11	4	7:20	7·28	8	192	5	No change. Discouraging.
8/11	4	7:15	7:23	8	192	5	Depressing. What am I doing wrong?
8/11	4	9:10	9:16	6	256	8	Reread same pages after noting instructions again: e.g. recalled, skimmed, did longer HSD, made finger guide faster. Much better result!
9/11	4	7:12	7:17:30	5.5	280	6	I'm catching on. V. pleasing speed and Comp. still fair!

Unit Three Increasing Word Power

Timed Reading Passage 3: Developing Vocabulary

Instructions: This passage is divided into two parts which will be timed separately. The questions cover both parts together. Think about the title and about what the passage is likely to say. Warm up with a High Speed Drill. Then, at the signal, begin reading for comprehension at the fastest speed you can manage. Record your time for Part A and wait for the signal to begin Part B.

Part A

You cannot grasp the meaning of whole groups of words if too many individual ones are difficult. If you stop continually to puzzle out meanings or to use the dictionary, you interrupt the trend of thought. Both speed and comprehension suffer; reading becomes a tiring chore.

Yet, if you skip over too many strange words, you may miss the point of the reading. Then the time spent has been wasted.

To be efficient, therefore, you need a wide basic vocabulary so that you can instantly recognize most of the words you meet and keep moving with the author's thought. You must also know how to deal confidently with new words and add those you need to your own vocabulary.

How can you acquire a large stock of words? And what should you do when you meet an unfamiliar word?

Most new words are learned by meeting them in use. A child learns what a word means by hearing it repeated often. If it is a word he needs so that he can ask for something he wants, or understand something he wishes to know, or express his own ideas, he learns to use it himself.

When he can read, he has a second way of meeting words. A reader's vocabulary grows when he wants or needs new words in order to understand or discuss new ideas. If a student finds that his English vocabulary is so poor that he cannot cope with his university work or enjoy other kinds of reading, the reason is likely to be that he has not read enough to develop an adequate vocabulary.

A person who reads widely and has many interests usually has a good vocabulary simply because he is continually meeting new words in use. Each time he encounters a particular word he develops a better idea of its meaning and one day, when the need arises, he uses the word correctly himself.

Besides a wide general vocabulary, an efficient reader has a stock of special words used in particular fields. For example, it is essential to understand certain terms in each university subject in order to understand what is being discussed in the text or in lectures. *Sedimentary* is such a word in geology. World and national affairs, student life, sports and hobbies involve other special vocabularies.

The easiest and best way to broaden both your general and special vocabularies is simply to meet more words in use—by listening carefully to people who use words well and by regular reading of newspapers, worthwhile magazines and books on varied topics.

This natural way of learning new words is better than memorizing lists of dictionary definitions. First, it means that you concentrate on the words you *need* to know. Second, you develop a better idea of shades of meaning and of which word is most appropriate in a particular sentence. By paying attention to the way other speakers and writers use words, you add not only to the number of words you can recognize but also to the number you can use correctly yourself.

(510 words)

Look up. Record your time and WPM. Make up one sentence expressing the main point of Part A. Try to recall other points made in Part A.

Think of a question you expect Part B to answer. At the signal, begin to read Part B, as quickly as you can manage.

Part B

When you are looking for meaning, you often get it despite an unfamiliar word. Sometimes, however, a strange word makes you slow down or even stop because you have lost the author's meaning. Such a word deserves attention. How much attention it deserves depends mostly on your reading purpose.

The first step is to note the word mentally, or make a pencil mark in the margin, and *read on*. Going on prevents further interruption of the author's thought. It also gives you a chance to find out whether the rest of the passage makes the meaning clear enough for your purposes. When reading for pleasure, you can usually learn enough about a word from its context. It is more important to go on enjoying the book than to find out how the dictionary defines every new word.

The second step is to return to troublesome words, after completing a passage, and try to work out what each one means; the need for this step increases with the amount of comprehension required. Saying the word aloud may help you to recognize it as one you have heard and then to recall how it was used. If this fails, you can often make an intelligent guess based on what you have learned from reading the whole passage; another look at the context may confirm or improve upon the guess.

A knowledge of common prefixes, roots and suffixes helps too. By analyzing the parts of a word, you can often work out the whole meaning. With practice you can learn to recognize new words as 'relatives' of familiar ones: e.g. *family—familiar* and *dictionary—dictate—predict—contradict.*

When you make a real effort in these various ways to work out the meaning for yourself, you not only understand the word better, but you remember it better too. Even if you decide to look up the word, the thinking you have done will help you to get maximum benefit from consulting the dictionary.

The third step, using the dictionary, is important for two kinds of words. The first group consists of words which *must* be understood to understand the rest of the passage adequately. Basic terms in a textbook belong to this group. The second group consists of words you know you have met before but still do not fully understand. If you come across a word three times, then clearly it is a word you should master.

Your main aim when you have located the word is to find the definition which fits the context in which you have met it. You should compare this with your own definition and note the difference. Having looked up the word, however, you should learn all you can about it. This small extra effort may save you the trouble of looking it up again, and may yield information which will help you attack other words.

For example, note other meanings of the word. Check on the pronunciation, for you may hesitate to use the word if you are unsure of how to say it. If the word has synonyms you know, try to discover the slight differences in meaning. Note how the word can be changed to form some other part of speech, e.g. *appropriate—appropriately*.

Finally, record important words and terms, with sample sentences using each one correctly. You can keep a glossary at the back of each subject notebook, or make a collection of vocabulary slips. Use odd moments to test yourself on these words.

Improving your vocabulary and word-attack skills in all these ways should bring significant improvement also in reading speed and comprehension.

(610 words)

Record your time and WPM for Part B. Then, without looking back at the passage, choose what you think is the best answer to each question below and put a circle around the appropriate letter.

1 To be efficient, a reader must
a skip unfamiliar words.
b recognize all the words he meets.
c never skip an unfamiliar word
d easily recognize many words.

2 The best way to learn new words is to
a read worthwhile novels.
b read and listen more.
c spend more time with the dictionary.
d study vocabulary lists.

3 The passage implies that a student may find university level work difficult if he
a has too many outside interests.
b has not read widely enough.
c does not use a dictionary.
d has a poor memory for words.

4 The passage suggests that such a student might improve by
a substituting reading for outside activities.
b spending more time on his studies.
c finding ways to meet more words in use.
d memorizing more definitions.

5 The importance of a word to the reader is determined mostly by
a its context.
b the number of meanings it can have.
c its pronunciation.
d how badly the reader needs the word.

6 When we first meet a strange word in our reading we should
a ignore it.
b notice it and read on.
c analyze it.
d look it up in the dictionary.

7 The steps mentioned in the passage should be used
a for all new words.
b for all new words in textbooks.
c selectively, according to need.
d for all special words in particular fields.

8 Working out a meaning for oneself
a wastes valuable time.
b helps fix the word in one's mind.
c always eliminates the need for a dictionary.
d is wrong because it calls attention to an individual word.

9 The main consideration when choosing or judging a word is whether it is
a the most appropriate word for the particular sentence.
b a general or a special word.
c the most impressive word.
d pronounceable.

10 A reader who uses the suggestions in the passage should increase his ability to
a use the dictionary intelligently.
b master the words he needs.
c use words more appropriately.
d make use of context clues.
e do all of the above.
f do none of the above.

K

WORDS PER MINUTE CHART:
Timed Reading Passages 3A and 3B *(510 and 610 words)*

Time	WPM 3A	WPM 3B	Time	WPM 3A	WPM 3B	Time	WPM 3A	WPM 3B	Time	WPM 3A	WPM 3B
1.00	510	610	2.00	255	305	3.00	170	205	4.00	130	155
10	435	525	10	235	280	10	160	195	10	125	150
20	385	460	20	220	260	20	155	185	20	120	140
30	340	410	30	205	245	30	145	175	30	115	135
40	305	365	40	190	230	40	140	170	40	110	130
50	280	335	50	180	215	50	135	160	50	105	120

Record your WPM scores for A and B. Then add them together and divide by two to find your average for the entire passage. Record this too, along with your comprehension score.

Follow-up

A. Factors in efficient reading

For which part, A or B, was your WPM higher? Can you suggest why? Jot down as many factors as you can think of which may influence your reading speed and comprehension (e.g. difficulty of vocabulary).

B. Recall and review

Part B suggests some steps which may be used in dealing with new words encountered while reading. Try to answer the following questions by using key words only: the fewest possible to convey the meaning.

1 What are the steps?
2 What reasons are given for Step 1?
3 List three ways of working out the meaning of a word without using the dictionary.
4 For what types of word should Step 3 be used?
5 What, specifically, might one find out in Step 3?

Related Skills

A. Listening and remembering

Your lecturer will read some short passages about choosing a dictionary. Listen carefully to each one without writing anything. When your lecturer stops, try to express in your own words the most important points you have heard. Then decide what key words would remind you of this point in future and jot them down.

B. Getting to know your dictionary

1 For which of these purposes have you ever used your dictionary?
—to find out how to spell a word or where to divide it at the end of a line
—to find out how to pronounce a word
—to find out a word's usual function in a sentence (part of speech) or get an idea of how to use it in a sentence
—to find out the meaning of a word in general or in a certain context
—to learn what other meanings a word can have
—to find out about special idioms associated with the word
—to find out the origin or history of the word
—to find out about words formed from the basic word, e.g. *educate, education, educational, educator*
—to find out how to form the past tense or past participle of a verb, e.g. *choose*: *chose, chosen*
—to look up spelling rules
—to answer a question about numerical expressions, metric conversion, weights and measures, or money
—to find out what an abbreviation stands for, e.g. WHO (World Health Organization)
—to find out about common affixes (word parts added at the beginning or end)
e.g. *intra-* (inside) e.g. *intravenous*
gram (something written down or drawn) e.g. *telegram, monogram, diagram*

You may agree that you have not been getting full value from dictionaries, even though you probably own at least one. The purpose of the following exercises is to make any dictionary more useful to you, but it is recommended that for practice you use a dictionary intended for students of English as a second or foreign language (*Collins English Learner's Dictionary, Oxford Advanced Learner's Dictionary, Chambers Universal Learners' Dictionary)*. Compare these dictionaries if you can.

2 Preview the dictionary

a Note what information appears on the inside covers and examine the table of contents.

b Thumb through the front matter (all the pages before the dictionary itself begins). Note the headings and any illustrations. Mentally note any questions you should find the answers to, e.g. What is the meaning of a key term or a certain symbol or abbreviation?

c Run your eyes down the columns of a sample page or two within the dictionary. What can you observe about, e.g. the order and types of information, varying lengths of entry, different kinds of type, abbreviations used etc.? Have you more questions?

d Most dictionaries have appendices at the back. What kinds of information are included in the dictionary you are using?

e Now mentally review what you have already learned about the dictionary that you didn't know before.

3 Return to the introductory pages

Make sure you understand the meaning of the following terms and can give an example of each:

entry	phonetic symbol
headword	syllable
phrase/phrasal verb	part of speech
idiom	etymology
usage label/stylistic value	derivative

Set aside some time for learning more about how to use your dictionary—and set yourself some specific learning tasks, e.g. how to use the phonetic symbols to check the pronunciation of any word; what the labels and abbreviations used in the dictionary mean; how to use the tables of verb patterns.

4 Examine the appendices at the back more carefully. Which do you think will be of most use to you?

5 For each of the words below, do the following:

a Find the word as fast as you possibly can. Look only at the guide words at the top, as you turn the pages, until you get to the right page: (For example, the word *speed* in one dictionary is on a page headed *specs/spell.*) Then run your eyes quickly down the page until the word you are searching for 'jumps out' of the page at you.

b Read the entire entry. Make sure you understand all the information given about the word, including the meaning of all the symbols and abbreviations used. What you don't know, find out.

read	humour	efficient
study	educate	lousy
dictionary	education	much

6 Check that you can now answer these questions about your dictionary.

a How is the stressed syllable of a word indicated?

b What help is given with irregular plurals? With past tense forms?

c Where and how is information given about pronouncing and spelling derivatives of a headword?

d What help is offered for using verbs correctly in sentences? Is special attention paid to phrasal verbs (verb+preposition or adverb)?

e How are American pronunciation and spelling indicated?
f Some words and sentences appear in italics. Why?
g What do the following mean? vt sl pl n usu
Give the meaning of any other three abbreviations or symbols used in the entries.

C. Practice in using the dictionary

ALPHABETICAL ORDER

Thorough familiarity with the alphabet is essential for efficient use of a dictionary or for any other reference book. The greater the familiarity, the greater the speed with which you can locate information.

Race to see how quickly you can put the following lists in alphabetical order. Then use the dictionary to confirm that the order is correct and that you know what each word means.

A	B
dictionary	sensitivity
diagram	sensory
didactic	sacrilege
diction	scene
diatribe	sardonic
dictator	sensuous
dialectic	scrutinize
diametrically	selection
dictation	script
dialogue	sceptical
diagnose	science
diaphragm	sanction
dictum	separable
diaphonous	scarcely
	sensibility

Study hint: Continue to improve this important skill by looking up alphabetically arranged items at speed and by rearranging vocabulary and other lists into alphabetical order—again at speed.

PRONUNCIATION

There are many irregularities in the pronunciation of English words. One sound may be represented by different spellings and the same letter or group of letters may be pronounced differently in different words. Further, British and American pronunciation may differ. For these reasons, a knowledge of phonetic symbols can be invaluable.

The chart on page 41 sets out the pronunciation symbols and key word examples for vowels and diphthongs (vowel combinations) as they appear in the dictionaries most commonly used by students using English as a second or foreign language. Pronounce the key words, trying to associate each vowel sound with the symbol used in your dictionary. The following exercises will reinforce what you have learned.

1 Copy the 20 symbols used in your dictionary and the key word for each. Then choose from the following list a second example for each sound.

heart	said	siege	bough
learn	paid	choice	cough
beer	stare	upon	dough
stop	might	full	rough
act	his	your	through

Choose another example for each from this list.

flow	weighed	weird	away
mud	awe	cow	kite
bled	heir	fill	fury
odd	juice	far	shook
leave	match	term	joy

2 In each of sets A and B below there are only four different vowel sounds. Arrange the words in each set in four columns according to the vowel sounds, with the appropriate symbol for the sound at the top, e.g. *eat* would go in a column headed *i*: (or *i*)

Set A	eat	scene	waive	leave	great
	eight	friend	risen	meant	wit
	fill	prey	guessed	games	grief
	sleep	jest	gist	sick	scent
Set B	whir	whole	wrote	word	nought
	gone	caught	heard	drawl	blur
	called	cold	rough	bird	button

3 Give the correct symbol for each of the vowel sounds printed in italics.

A	B	C	D
l*i*beral	st*a*te	d*e*bt	h*u*m
l*i*bation	st*a*tistics	d*e*duct	h*u*man
l*i*tre	st*a*tic	d*e*mon	h*u*rt

E	F	G	H
s*ou*p	d*ea*r	n*o*vel	chr*o*m*o*some
s*ou*nd	*ea*rn	n*o*ble	*i*nd*i*v*i*dual*i*zed

4 Give the symbols for the letters in italics, noting likenesses and differences in spelling and pronunciation.

A: regre*ss*ion, glo*ss*ary, vi*s*ion, effi*ci*ent, fixa*ti*on
B: *g*ene, *j*eans, *g*arrulous, e*x*aggerate

5 Give the complete phonetic transcription for the following words:

A: decease, disease
B: scheme, schism, schist
C: tough, though, thought
D: lose, loose, lost, lozenge

Vowels and Diphthongs

	Oxford Advanced Learner's Dictionary	Chambers Universal Learners' Dictionary	Collins English Dictionary	The Concise Oxford Dictionary	KEY WORDS				
					OALD	CULD	CED	COD	
1	i	iː	iː	i	see	feel	green	meet	1
2	ɪ	i	ɪi	ɪ	sit	milk	pity	bit	2
3	e	e	e	e	ten	head	set	met	3
4	æ	a	æ	æ	hat	bag	bat	fat	4
5	ɑ	ä	ɑː	ɑ	arm	hath	farm	bah	5
6	ɒ	o	ɒ	ɒ	got	box	rot	got	6
7	ɔ	ö	ɔː	ɔ	saw	hall	board	paw	7
8	ʊ	u	u	ʊ	put	foot	full	book	8
9	u	uː	uː	u	too	blue	root	boot	9
10	ʌ	ʌ	ʌ	ʌ	cup	love	come	dug	10
11	ɜ	äː	əː	ɜ	fur	first	fern	fur	11
12	ə	ə	ə	ə	ago	ribbon	above	token	12
13	eɪ	ei	eɪ	eɪ	page	pain	fate	fate	13
14	əʊ	ou	oʊ	əʊ	home	go	ago	goat	14
15	aɪ	ai	ai	aɪ	five	fine	lie	bite	15
16	aʊ	au	aʊ	aʊ	now	loud	sow	brow	16
17	ɔɪ	oi	ɔɪ	ɔɪ	join	join	toy	boil	17
18	ɪə	iə	ɪə	ɪə	near	here	here	fear	18
19	eə	eə	ɛə	eə	hair	hair	fair	fare	19
20	ʊə	uə	ʊə	ʊə	pure	poor	pure	poor	20

6 Note the difference between the British and American pronunciation of the following:

schedule privacy tomato inquiry either

INFLECTED FORMS

1 Give whichever form is missing:

Singular:	bacterium	basis	focus	________	appendix
Plural:	_______	_____	_____	criteria	_______
Singular:	alumnus	______	thesis	________	
Plural:	_______	alumnae	____	phenomena	
Singular:	mouse	house	goose	________	wife
Plural:	_______	_____	____	sheep	_______

2 Note these examples concerning forms of adjectives:

short, shorter (of two), shortest (of three or more)
helpful, more helpful, most helpful

Give the comparative and superlative forms for these irregular adjectives:

good bad little much

3 Divide each of the following words into syllables and mark the syllable carrying the principal stress. Make sure you can pronounce each word and know its meaning.

abdomen	calumny	harangue	status
advertisement	choreography	incongruous	universality
alias	colloquial	inquiry	victuals
argumentative	familiarize	precedence	voracious
antecedent	frequency	secretive	zenith

4 Give the past tense and past participle of the following infinitives. Then use the dictionary to check on your accuracy. Learn any you missed.

e.g. *arise arose arisen*

awake	come	forgive	lie	steal
bear	do	get	lose	swear
begin	draw	give	mistake	swell
bind	drink	go	outshine	swim
bit	drive	grow	overdo	teach
bleed	eat	hang	pay	throw
blow	fall	hide	ring	thrust
break	feel	hit	run	write
build	flee	kneel	seek	
buy	fly	know	shine	
catch	forbid	lay	slide	
choose	foresee	lead	sow	

ABBREVIATIONS

1 Do you know what each of the following means?

Afr.	cf.	etc.	illus.	q.v.
anon.	ed.	ff.	p.	viz.
b.	e.g.	fig.	pl.	vol.
c. (or ca.)	et al.	i.e.	pp.	v.t.

2 Choose any ten other abbreviations in your dictionary's list which you think you should know and learn them.

D. Using the context

Even when you decide to look up a word in the dictionary, it is essential to consider its context first. These exercises will demonstrate why:

1 Note the differences in meaning among the following:

He was too fat to *run* to the shop.
His parents *run* the shop.
Trains *run* on rails.
He plans to *run* in the next election.
They built a *run* for the chickens.
She lets her children *run* wild.
The robbers have been on the *run* for four months now.
He'll soon *run* through his inheritance.
Please *run* off 100 more copies of that handout.
The clerk in that office is giving me the *run* around.
He said he would *run* the risk.
He is *running* a temperature.
She's going to *run* herself into the ground.

Now look up the word *run* in the dictionary. Note its uses as a noun and as a verb. Check meanings where necessary. Look for further uses of the word you think you should know.

2 How much space does your dictionary devote to each of the following words? How many parts of speech can each be used as? What words are derived from each? What are some of the idiomatic uses of each?

do face foot form get head lead make set

3 How does the context help in the following examples? (Read them aloud.)

Record your WPM. Keep a *record* of your reading *progress*. Try to *progress* each week.
You will have one *minute* to read the passage. Do not worry about *minute* details.
She won the beauty *contest*, but her rival may *contest* the decision.

Make up your own examples for *address*, *content*, *present*.

4 Use the context to help you form a definition of the italicized words. Then compare your definitions with your dictionary's:

Her voice could be heard easily at the back of the room, but his was almost *inaudible*.
The judge was *adamant*; he refused all pleas to review the case.
The burglar escaped unnoticed by slipping *stealthily* through the window.
The new law created so many problems that the government *abrogated* it.
Her statements left us in no doubt; they were *unequivocal*.
The lecturer's drone was *soporific* and several students soon feel asleep.

5 Give the meaning of each italicized word as used in the sentence below. Then use the same word in another sense.

The dress of those men is *peculiar* to the Efiks.
The *sensation* of fear was overpowering.

The barrister claimed that the new evidence was *material* to his client's case.
My French was as *indifferent* as his English.
The English teacher told the class to be careful of *expression.*

E. Using roots and affixes

A knowledge of the most common Latin and Greek roots and affixes makes it possible to ascertain the meaning of many words by breaking them down into their component parts. One writer has estimated that a knowledge of just fourteen Latin and Greek roots can help us to recognize over 14,000 words.

The Greek *tele*, for example, meaning 'far', helps to make nearly 50 words in the *Collins English Dictionary* (e.g. *telescope, telephone*). *Photo* (as in *photograph*) appears almost 90 times, and *phone* almost 30.

An understanding of the affixes listed at the back of the *Oxford Advanced Learner's Dictionary* or the *Chambers Universal Learners' Dictionary* will give you a key to thousands of the new words you read or hear, and further study of the list on pages 49–50 will help you unlock the meaning of hundreds more.

Key Word Patterns Practice

A. Learning from examples

By looking at the two examples on the following pages, you can learn a great deal about making and using Key Word Patterns of your own.

Figure 3 is a pattern summarizing the content of Units 1 and 2 of this course. It was devised by a student trying to recall what she had learned so far. Making the pattern served as a review of what she knew—reinforcing it in her memory—and also as a reminder of what she needed to revise. Note:

1 The eyes are first drawn to the centre of the page where the airplane and large capital letters remind the viewer that Better Reading means both Better Speed and Better Comprehension.

2 Main aspects of the topic radiate out from the centre. Key words for the main aspects (e.g. PRACTICE) are printed in capital letters; linking verbs (e.g. Select) are in smaller letters with an initial capital.

3 Attached to main sub-topics are lines indicating further subdivisions; these words are in lower case letters. In one case these are numbered. Do you see why?

4 The lines and enclosures, the different sizes of print, and the arrangement of ideas on the page all help to show the relationships of the parts of the pattern. Arrows also help; they indicate that this pattern is best read in a clockwise direction.
Think back over Units 1 and 2. Is anything missing from this pattern which you think should be included?

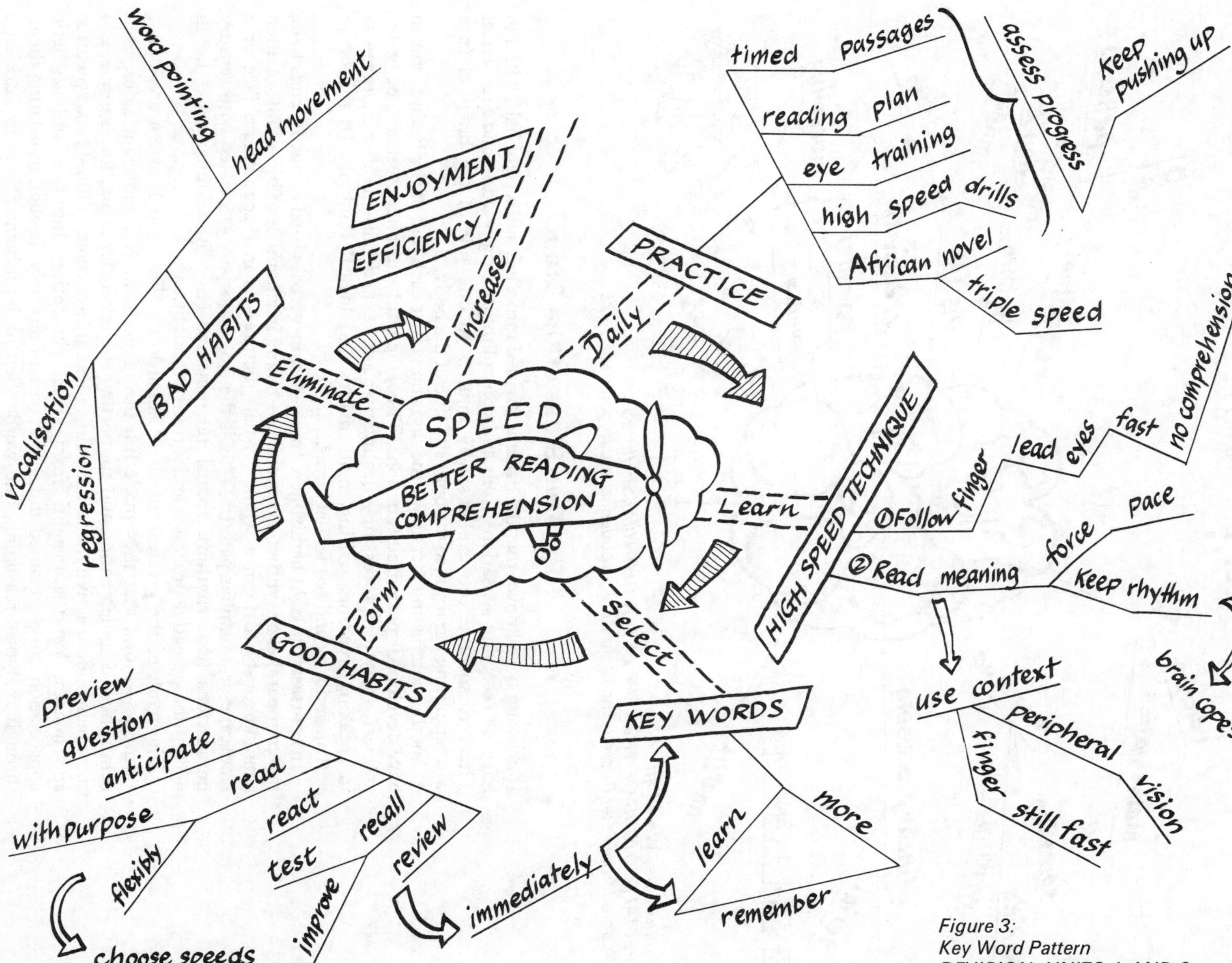

Figure 3:
Key Word Pattern
REVISION: UNITS 1 AND 2

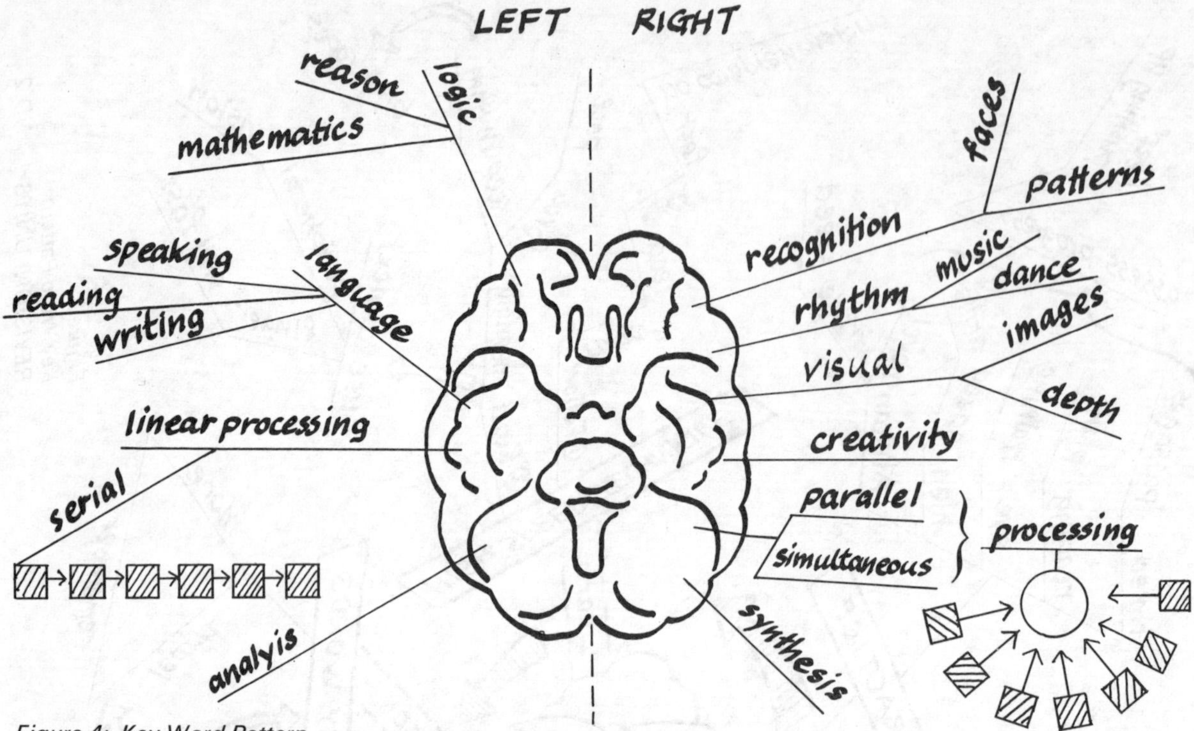

Figure 4: Key Word Pattern
SPECIALIZATIONS OF THE LEFT AND RIGHT HEMISPHERES
(Adapted from Peter Russell, The Brain Book, *Routledge and Kegan Paul, 1979).*

The Two Sides of the Brain

It has long been known that the brain is divided into a left and a right half, with the left side receiving sensations from and controlling the right side—and vice versa. This 'crossover effect' explains why injuries to one side of the brain cause a corresponding paralysis to the opposite side of the body.

Another interesting fact about the division is that each half of the brain seems to have developed specialized functions. Thus, the left hemisphere seems to be better at linear, analytical processing—dealing with a series of details one after another—as in speaking, reading, writing, mathematics and logical thinking. It 'thinks' in verbal, auditory and sequential terms.

In contrast, the right hemisphere thinks in non-verbal visual terms. It tends to be better at parallel or synthetic processing—taking in a number of bits of information simultaneously to form a whole (visual) picture—as in recognizing a face or a landscape or a familiar pattern. This is the side especially associated with sensory impressions (e.g. rhythm), spatial relationships (e.g. three dimensional depth perception), creative processes and intuitive thought.

The work of the greatest minds—Leonardo da Vinci and Einstein are classic examples—shows that they made full use of both the left and right sides, each hemisphere complementing and supporting the other. Drawing, for example, is a right hemisphere activity, and Einstein's ideas always came to him first as pictures and images. Yet the insights from visual perception, intuition and aesthetic appreciation can be retained and shared with others only through translating them, through analytical reasoning, into words. Setting both hemispheres to work on a task and then integrating the two streams of information, effectively increases our mental capacity.

Reading is normally considered a left hemisphere activity, but the High Speed Technique brings into play the abilities of the right hemisphere as well. The result is an overall increase in reading efficiency.

Figure 4 and the accompanying text will help you understand the short passage which you are going to read and summarize in Key Word Pattern form. (The passage will tell you more about the High Speed Technique introduced in Unit 2.) Note:

1 Instead of the word BRAIN in the centre, there is a diagram showing the two sides of the brain. Often a sketch or diagram can replace words to create a more memorable visual impression.

2 This pattern represents only two paragraphs of the text. The scope of a pattern and the amount of detail required will vary with your purpose.

Is there information in any of the other paragraphs which you think should be attached to the pattern? How and where would you add it?

B. Reading and pattern-making

READ

1 Make your eyes follow your fast-moving finger along the lines and down the page of the passage on 'High Speed Training' below. Aim to finish in 30 seconds or less.

2 Repeat. Then, at the signal, begin reading for comprehension, aiming to finish in one minute. (Mark the point you have reached when one minute is called). What can you recall?

3 Repeat if necessary, aiming to cut your reading time and increase your understanding.

High Speed Training

In high-speed training, the reader is forced to scan pages of print at speeds many times faster than normal reading. The reader starts by moving the visual guide as fast as physically possible along each line, not worrying if very little is absorbed. Then he begins moving the guide down the page, increasing the pace every few minutes until he is spending only one second on each page. At this speed very little, if anything, will be absorbed. After about five minutes of high-speed training, the person goes back to reading at what he takes to be a normal speed. He will probably find, however, that he is reading at double his usual speed and yet with the same or even greater comprehension.

The training breaks the habit of reading at a set pace. It is rather like driving down a highway at eighty miles an hour for a long period, and then being asked to slow down to thirty miles an hour. If you try to do this without looking at the speedometer, you will probably think you are at thirty when in fact you are still doing fifty.

High-speed training has two other advantages. It encourages you to see the key words in the text; and it brings the right side of the brain into the reading process.

When you first start high-speed training, spending only a second on each page of the book, everything seems to be a blur and nothing is absorbed. But after a few minutes an interesting phenomenon may occur. You may find that a few of the words are in fact being seen. This by itself is not remarkable. What is significant is that the words that are being picked out are generally the nouns and verbs in the text. Moreover, they are often the key nouns and verbs. The fact that these words are being picked out implies that, although the page of print is not being consciously read in detail, most of the page is nevertheless being processed by the brain. And being processed in only a second! The high-speed training develops this ability to extract the relevant words from a page.

A person learning to read finds it easy to stop saying the words aloud and not difficult to stop subvocalizing (moving the throat); but many people find it difficult to stop hearing the words they are reading and this limits their speed to 250 or so words per minute. High-speed training breaks the habit. At a page a second you cannot hear many of the words, but you can still take in the page visually, for visual processing is many times faster.

This shift in processing corresponds to a shift from the left hemisphere to the right. When you slow down again to 'normal' speeds, the right hemisphere stays enlivened, words continue to be taken in visually, and reading is correspondingly faster. It is only when the shift is made from auditory to visual reading that high speeds become possible. Indeed, it could be said that until you have made this shift, you have not fully learned to read.

(530 words)

(Peter Russell, *The Brain Book*, Routledge and Kegan Paul, 1979, pp. 200–201)

MAKE A PATTERN

1 Go through the passage picking out what you consider to be the Key Words: those which will call back to mind the ideas and related details.

2 In the centre of a sheet of paper, print in capitals the words HIGH SPEED TRAINING. Draw a shape around the words or otherwise highlight them.

3 Select Key Words for the major divisions. Print them in capitals on lines or in boxes linked to the main heading.

4 Take each major division in turn and add subdivisions. You may print lower case letters for these.

5 Add colour, arrows, three-dimensional shapes, diagrams, doodles—whatever will make the pattern more visually memorable.

REVIEW

1 Use your pattern to review the passage. That is, take each key word in turn and try to recall the associated ideas. Check back to see if your recall has been complete and accurate.

2 Make further improvements if necessary.

JUDGE

Look at other students' patterns of the passage you have just reduced to pattern form. Discuss the merits and faults of the patterns. Which do you consider most effective and why? How could any of the patterns be improved? How would you rate the effectiveness of your own pattern?

Lists of Useful Word Parts

LATIN Word Roots and Affixes

Root or Affix	Meaning	Examples
aqua	water	aqualung, aquarium, aquaduct, aquatic
bellum	war	belligerent, rebel, rebellion, bellicose
bene	well	benefit, benediction, benefactor, beneficent, benevolent, benign
circum	around	circumference, circumlocution, circumnavigate circumspect
cogni	know	cognition, cognizance, connoisseur, incognito, recognize, recognition
cor	heart	cardiac, cordial, courage, discord, encourage, record
corpus	body	corpse, corporation, corps, corpulent, corpuscle
cred	believe	credible, incredible, credit, credence, creditable
crux, crucis	cross	crux, crucial, crucify, crusade
cult	care for	cult, cultivate, culture, agriculture, horticulture
curr, curs	run	current, currency, curriculum, courier, course, excursion
dei	god	deity, deify
dent	tooth	dental, dentifrice, denture, indent, trident
dict	say	dictate, diction, edict, indicate, indict, predict, verdict, dictionary
digit	finger, toe	digital (Explanation: fingers and toes are useful in counting)
domin	master, rule over	dominate, domineering, predominate, dominion
dorm	sleep	dormitory, dormant
duc, duct	lead, take	conductor, induction, aquaduct, deduce, duct, duke, educate, product
ego	I	egotism, egocentric
fac, fect	make	facile, fact, factory, faculty, manufacture, affect, effect, perfect
fin	end	define, confine, final, finale, finish, infinite, refine, definite
frater	brother	fraternal, fraternity, fraternize, fratricide
ject	throw	abject, dejected, eject, interject, projectile, reject, trajectory
locus	place	location, locality, local
loqui, locut	talk	colloquial, eloquent, loquacious, ventriloquist, elocution
luc	light	elucidate, illustrate, lucid, translucent, pellucid
mit, miss	send	admit, commit, intermittent, remit, transmit, missile
mor	dead	morbid, moribund, mortal, mortify, mortuary
ped	foot	biped, pedal, impediment, pedestal, pedestrian, pedometer
pel, puls	drive	compel, dispel, expel, impel, propel, pulse, impulse, repulse
pon, posit	place	component, exponent, postpone, position, preposition, transpose
port	carry	porter, deport, export, portfolio, portable, report, support, transport
poss, poten	be able, power	possible, impossibility, potent, impotent, potential
rupt	break	interrupt, rupture, corruption, abrupt, bankrupt, disrupt, erupt
scrib, script	write	circumscribe, inscribe, script, description, scripture, transcribe, manuscript
sent, sens	feeling	sensitive, sensory, senses, sentient, sensibility, sensible, sensitize, sentiment, sentence
spect	look	inspect, introspective, spectacle, spectator, spectacular, speculate, speculum

Root or Affix	Meaning	Examples
spir	breathe	expire, inspiration, respiration, spirit
tain, ten	hold	abstain, contain, detain, retain, tenable, tenacious, tenet, tenant, container, tenure
tang, tact	touch	tangent, tangible, contact, tact, tactual, tactical
temp	time	temporary, tempo, temporize, temporal
tens	stretch	tense, tensile, extend, tension, extension, intense, intensify, intention
ven, vent	come, arrive	advent, convenience, convene, intervene, revenue, adventure, invent
vers, vert	turn	verse, version, reverse, avert, convert, extrovert, invert, vertical, revert, adverse
vid, vis	see	vision, evident, provident, revise, supervise, visor, vista, visible, video
voc	call	vocabulary, vocal, advocate, avocation, convocation, evoke, provoke, evocative

GREEK WORD Roots and Affixes

Root or Affix	Meaning	Examples
amphi	around, both sides	amphitheatre, amphibian
crit	judge	critic, critical, criterion, critique
dys	bad, difficult	dysfunction, dysentery, dyslexia, dyspepsia, dystrophy
endo	inside	endoparasite, endosperm, endocrine, endocardium, endoscope, endogamy
epi	upon, outside	epidermis, epiglottis, epicentre, epigraph, episode, epithelium
gen	birth, race	genesis, genetics, homogeneous, genealogy, eugenics, generation
hypo	under	hypodermic, hypothermia, hypothesis
morph	form	morpheme, amorphous, anthropomorphic, metamorphosis, endomorph, geomorphology
para	beside, beyond	paraphrase, parallel, parabola, paramilitary, parable, paranormal, paradigm, paragraph, parasite, paratyphoid
path	suffering, feeling	pathos, pathetic, sympathy, pathology, psychopath, pathogenesis, telepathy
pneum	breath, wind	pneumatic, pneumonia
soph	become wise	sophomore, sophisticated, sophism

Assignments

A. Plan your time

1 Make another Reading/Study Plan.

2 Record the reasons for *any two* changes or decisions you have made as to what should be done when.

3 Once you have made the plan, make an effort to stick to it. Note any problems which arise. (Is the trouble with you or the plan?) What can you do to make the next plan more workable?

B. Learn useful roots and affixes

1 Go through Appendix 3 of the *Oxford Advanced Learner's Dictionary* or Appendix 9 of *Chambers Universal Learners' Dictionary*. Note the affixes whose meanings or use you do not already know. List those you think would be useful for you to learn.

2 Set yourself to learn, say, five a day. Test yourself by writing down the word, its meaning and some examples without looking.

3 Each day, test your recall of the previous learning before you learn the next set.

4 Follow the same procedure with the lists on pages 49–50.

C. Build vocabulary in your academic subjects

Follow these instructions for making and using vocabulary slips.

Vocabulary slips

Fold, then tear, a sheet of paper so as to get eight slips of equal size. Keep them in an envelope or clip them together.

During the week, be alert for important new words in lectures or reading assignments in your various courses. Select *any eight* words to record in this way:

1 Print the word on one side of the slip. Copy the phonetic transcription of its pronunciation from your dictionary. Then add a sentence which uses the word correctly.

2 In the upper right hand corner indicate how you met the word, e.g. BIO 101 Lect., or SOC 101 Text, or HIS 111 Handout.

3 On the other side, with the help of your dictionary, write the definition of the word which seems most appropriate for the context in which you met it. You may add here anything else you wish to remember about the word.

4 Test yourself on the words.

5 Arrange the slips in alphabetical order. Put your name and section no. on the top one and submit them to your lecturer.

Add to the collection as needed. You will find it easier from now on to keep the slips for each course together. Each set will then become a glossary for a course; you will find the glossaries very useful for examination revision.

D. Improve your spelling

Writer's Reference, section E, makes suggestions for improving your spelling and lists the words most commonly misspelled and confused by students. Work out a programme for eliminating spelling errors from your written work.

E. Make a key word pattern (or two)

Try any of the following:

1 Take notes from a lecture in key word pattern form.

2 Test your recall of a lecture by making a key word pattern. (Clear up difficulties and fill in gaps by comparing your pattern with a coursemate's.)

3 Test your recall of a chapter or a course topic by making a key word pattern. Check back and make additions or improvements.

F. Work at the triple-your- reading-rate programme

1 Do not worry at this stage if comprehension is less than you wish. Just keep on reading at a forced rate; your brain will soon adjust to the higher speeds and comprehension will improve.

2 Check back to the end of Unit 2 to make sure you are following directions properly. You will get best results if you always work through the five steps listed under E.2 on page 30.

G. Begin each study session with a high speed drill

You will find this makes you more alert. You will read and absorb information faster after such a drill than you would without it.

Unit Four Using a Study Method

Timed Reading Passage 4: Thinking Before Reading: Previewing

Instructions

1 Look at the title and try to anticipate what the passage will say.

2 Warm up with a High Speed Drill, taking 25 seconds from the beginning to the end of the passage (an average of 3 seconds per paragraph) and consciously searching out key words and ideas.

3 Stop and think about what you now know on the topic and what you expect to find out.

4 At the signal, begin to read at a faster rate than you have read any previous passage. Your comprehension goal is to achieve a score of 7.

It is surprisingly easy to get around in a strange town or country with the aid of a good map. The map shows what direction a road takes, where it branches off, what towns or markets or other landmarks are along the way, and even the relative size and importance of these landmarks. The traveller, knowing in a general way what lies ahead, is able to anticipate the route, to 'recognize' features and to test his advance notions of them through actual experience.

Similarly, the reader who sets out with a plan of the ground he is to cover will reach his destination more quickly and easily than the one who has no clear idea of where he is going, what he will pass along the way or where the going may be rough. The latter may get lost altogether; at best he is likely to tire himself by taking an unnecessarily long and difficult route, or get bogged down in a swamp of detail, or become bored because he doesn't know what he can look forward to.

The plans provided with non-fiction books and articles vary in the amount of information given. A textbook, for example, often contains a table of contents which is really a complete summary or outline of the book. Within each chapter, there may be headings and sub-headings and captions in different sizes and type-faces and with differing indentations. These indicate how the material is organized and how the parts are related to one another. The reader who does not pay attention to these guide-posts is not only inefficient but foolish!

More often, it is the reader's responsibility to find out where he is going without being explicitly told. The best method for most non-fiction is to make a preliminary survey before beginning intensive reading.

This survey, or *preview*, involves skimming over the material for the purpose of getting an over-all impression. One object is to locate such things as the central idea, the major supporting points, topic sentences and the summary or conclusion. This provides a basic framework to which additional points and details can be attached later. Comprehension during a closer reading becomes easier.

Other preview aims are to find out how relevant, how familiar and how difficult the material is. If a section looks irrelevant to the reader's needs or interests, or if it contains ideas with which he is already thoroughly familiar, he knows that he can skim through or even skip this section during the next reading.

On the other hand, if he sees that an important section contains many ideas, complex sentences, and difficult vocabulary, he knows that he will need to summon up all his powers of concentration when he reads it for fuller understanding. If he notices a particular new word several times during the preview, he can assume it is one he will need for adequate comprehension, and he can pay special attention to its context when he reads.

These are some of the ways in which previewing helps the reader establish an appropriate mental attitude towards a particular piece of reading. His preview impressions help him decide what to look for, what to concentrate on, what to skim over, and sometimes what to skip altogether during a further reading: they help him read more flexibly.

Skimming before reading may be compared to flying over unfamiliar country before exploring it on foot. The aerial survey may reveal a pass through the mountains, a bridge across a river, a swampy area, the location of villages, and other features which make it possible to plan the ground trek intelligently and complete it successfully. Until these major features have been located, details such as the average number of huts in a compound are not very useful.

Thinking about a title before beginning to read, looking at the introduction and conclusion, picking out key sentences and generally keeping a sharp look-out for what is especially significant, are activities which produce impressions, guesses and questions. Testing the accuracy of impressions and deliberately looking for the answers to specific questions make for alert reading; they also help concentration and memory.

Thus time spent on a survey, whether of landscape or reading matter, is time well-spent. Armed with a 'sketch map' or 'air photo' and a list of questions raised by the survey, the efficient reader plunges into a more thorough reading with confidence and purpose, adjusting his speed to his need, finding answers, constructing more questions, thinking ahead, and very likely, shedding bad habits along the way.

(765 words)

Look up. Record your time and WPM. Go on to the questions.

1 This passage emphasizes the value of
a using maps properly.
b skimming before reading.
c locating topic sentences.
d reading books that are worthwhile.

2 The reader is compared to
a a traveller.
b a student.
c a mapmaker.
d a guide.

3 Books are compared to
a good maps.
b landmarks.
c strange countries.
d roads.

4 The ideas in the passage refer mainly to the reading of
a non-fiction.
b poetry and plays.
c short stories and novels.
d maps.

5 Headings and sub-headings are helpful mainly because they
a are in different sizes. *b* always give a complete outline.
c indicate how the material is organized.
d add visual appeal.

6 For most non-fiction, the best method is to begin by
a reading intensively. *b* making a preliminary survey.
c looking up any new words in a dictionary.
d paying attention to sentence context.

7 In skimming over material, we should ignore
a topic sentences. *b* the conclusion.
c the details. *d* the organization.

8 At the preview stage, it is usually *least* necessary to determine the _______ of the ideas.
a complexity *b* validity *c* familiarity *d* gist

9 Preview impressions help a reader to
a avoid difficult parts during the next reading.
b set his mind obstinately.
c pay more attention to the words while reading.
d adjust speed and method to suit the material.

10 The reader who follows the advice in the passage will be able to read more
K *a* thoroughly. *b* relaxedly. *c* purposefully. *d* intensely.

WORDS PER MINUTE CHART: Timed Reading Passage 4 *(765 words)*									
Time	WPM	Time	WPM	Time	WPM	Time	WPM	Time	WPM
1.00	765	2.00	385	3.00	255	4.00	190	5.00	155
10	655	10	355	10	240	10	185	10	150
20	575	20	330	20	230	20	180	20	145
30	510	30	305	30	220	30	170	30	140
40	460	40	290	40	210	40	165	40	135
50	420	50	270	50	200	50	160	50	130

Follow-up

A. Recall and summarize

1 State briefly the main idea of the passage. Check back. Is your answer satisfactory? Rewrite or improve the statement.

2 Suggest three brief rules which might be included in a list headed 'How to Tackle Non-Fiction'.

3 An analogy is often used to make a point more clear. What analogies are used in the passage? (Use key words only.)

4 Justify your answer to Question 8 on the Reading Passage.

B. Increase your vocabulary

Note how each of the following words is used in the passage. Try to define it without using your dictionary.

non-fiction	skimming	landmark	caption
indentation	explicitly	intensive	preliminary

Look up each word in your dictionary. Compare its definition with yours. What else can you find out about it?

C. Preview and anticipate

Did you preview the whole of this unit? What did you find out? Stop and spend 30 seconds looking over the remaining pages again. What else have you discovered about what lies ahead? Repeat if necessary.

D. Note differences in style

The word *style* is a good example of a word with several meanings. Read the discussion below and then select from your dictionary the meaning of *style* intended in the heading you have just read.

> The forms and rules for presenting written work differ according to whether the material is being printed, typed or handwritten, and even from one discipline, publisher or journal to another. Typed papers, for example, are normally double-spaced, while handwritten ones are not. Outline symbols such as I, II and A, B, C, used to distinguish different levels of heading in handouts, may be removed if the material is published because different sizes of type can be used instead. Whereas you have probably been taught to indent all paragraphs, the first paragraph of a chapter or major section in a book usually begins at the left hand margin. In books, words which are underlined in typed or handwritten work are set in italics instead.
>
> If you are aware that such differences exist, you are less likely to be confused by them and more likely to be consistent within a given style when presenting your own work. Find some examples for yourself of differences in style by comparing books with one another and with other forms of written work.

E. Check on tenses and agreement

If you check the verbs in the Reading Passage, you will see that the Present tense is used consistently throughout and that each verb agrees with its subject in number and person, e.g. 'the map shows', 'plans vary', 'aims are'.

1 Go through the passage, picking out the predicate verbs of sentences and their subjects. Underline them and pay particular attention to subject-verb agreement by noting the verb endings.

2 Did you notice that the first sentence of paragraph 2 includes verbs in the Future tense? When the dominant tense is Present, the Future and Present Perfect tenses are used when necessary to indicate time in relation to the present. When the dominant tense is the Past, the Past Perfect and Conditional tenses are used to indicate time further in the past or further in the future than the main events.

The rule is to stay within the chosen 'block' of tenses (Present or Past) unless the meaning demands otherwise, as in this example:

The teacher *said* that lack of agreement *is* a common fault in student writing.

3 Discuss the time relationships within these two passages. How do the tenses clarify the relationships?

Past The last time the teacher had read one of my essays, I had been very proud. This time I was so humiliated I couldn't look anyone in the face for the rest of the day. I vowed that in future I would always read over my work before handing it in.

Present Until now, I have always been proud when a teacher has read one of my essays in class, but this time I am so ashamed I won't be able to look my classmates in the face if I meet them again today. In future, I will always read over my work before handing it in.

4 You can avoid most problems with tenses if you always make a conscious choice between Present and Past and remember what tenses go together, e.g.

Present	goes/has go/have	gone/will go/will have gone
Past	went/had gone/would go/would have gone	

You can eliminate most errors in agreement by always checking your verb endings.

Related Skills

A. Using memory aids: mnemonics and key words

1 Note the mnemonics and the key words for remembering the steps in the following well-known study methods. Then discuss the likenesses and differences among them.

SQ3R:	Survey,	Question,	Read,	Recall,	Review	
PQRST:	Preview,	Question,	Read,	Summarize,	Test	
OK4R:	Overview,	Key points,	Read,	Recall,	Reflect,	Review
3S3R:	Survey,	Study-read,	Speed-read,	Recite,	Review,	Reflect
Organic Method:	Preparation:	Time,	Amount,	Knowledge,	Questions	
	Application:	Overview,	Preview,	Inview,	Review	

2 The study method to be described on the next pages is an updated version of the SQ3R Method. SQ3R is the oldest and probably the best known of the very similar methods outlined above, and has been widely used and adapted in many countries. The adaptation for this course incorporates the strong points of all the methods so that you have to remember the name of only one system: SQ3R. Without looking back: What do the letters stand for?

3 Key Word Patterns are sometimes called Mind Maps, for obvious reasons. They have an extraordinary range of uses.

For example, an author can make a pattern (map) of what he wants to say in a chapter and then use his pattern as a guide while writing. His readers can use it to preview the chapter and later to review it. The pattern on page 59 represents a student's review of SQ3R after he had learned it. You, however, are going to use it to *preview* the SQ3R method.

4 Look at the pattern carefully, trying to decide what the accompanying text might say. Could you write a brief essay or give a short talk on SQ3R by simply referring to the pattern? Try composing a paragraph which introduces the method as a whole, and another well-developed paragraph describing what is involved in any one of the individual steps. Are there any points which are not clear? What will you do about these?

B. Previewing textbooks (or other non-fiction)

Page 69 shows how to record your preview of a *non-fiction* book—either a textbook or a library book covering an assigned topic—for any of your courses. (Do not use a novel or play; these require a slightly different approach.) Work this way:

1 First, learn the ten steps below, How to Preview a Textbook.
   a Spend two minutes reading through the list with the intention of remembering all ten steps.
   b Stop and jot down one key word for each item you remember.
   c Check back to fill in gaps and clear up difficulties.
   d Compare your list with the key words in the pattern on page 68.

2 Preview this book and record the information asked for on page 69.

3 Work through the same steps for other textbooks. Use key words as headings to save time and copying.

4 Practise previewing until it becomes automatic whenever you pick up a new book.

> **Study hint:** While at first the previewing of a textbook may seem like a lot of extra work and effort, the process actually requires only a few minutes once you know what to do. These few minutes could well be the most important ones you spend on the book.

C. Previewing fiction

What are the similarities and the differences between previewing non-fiction and previewing fiction? Which of the ten steps are not applicable to fiction?

How to Preview a Textbook

1 Examine the outside, front and back. Study the title, cover illustration, 'blurb' and comments on the back or the end flaps.

2 Note the author's name and his or her qualifications for writing the book.

3 Check the publishing information: place, publisher, date. In some fields, the date is very important. If it is an older book, has it been revised lately or only reprinted? (What is the difference?)

Figure 5: Key Word Pattern
HOW TO STUDY A TEXTBOOK CHAPTER

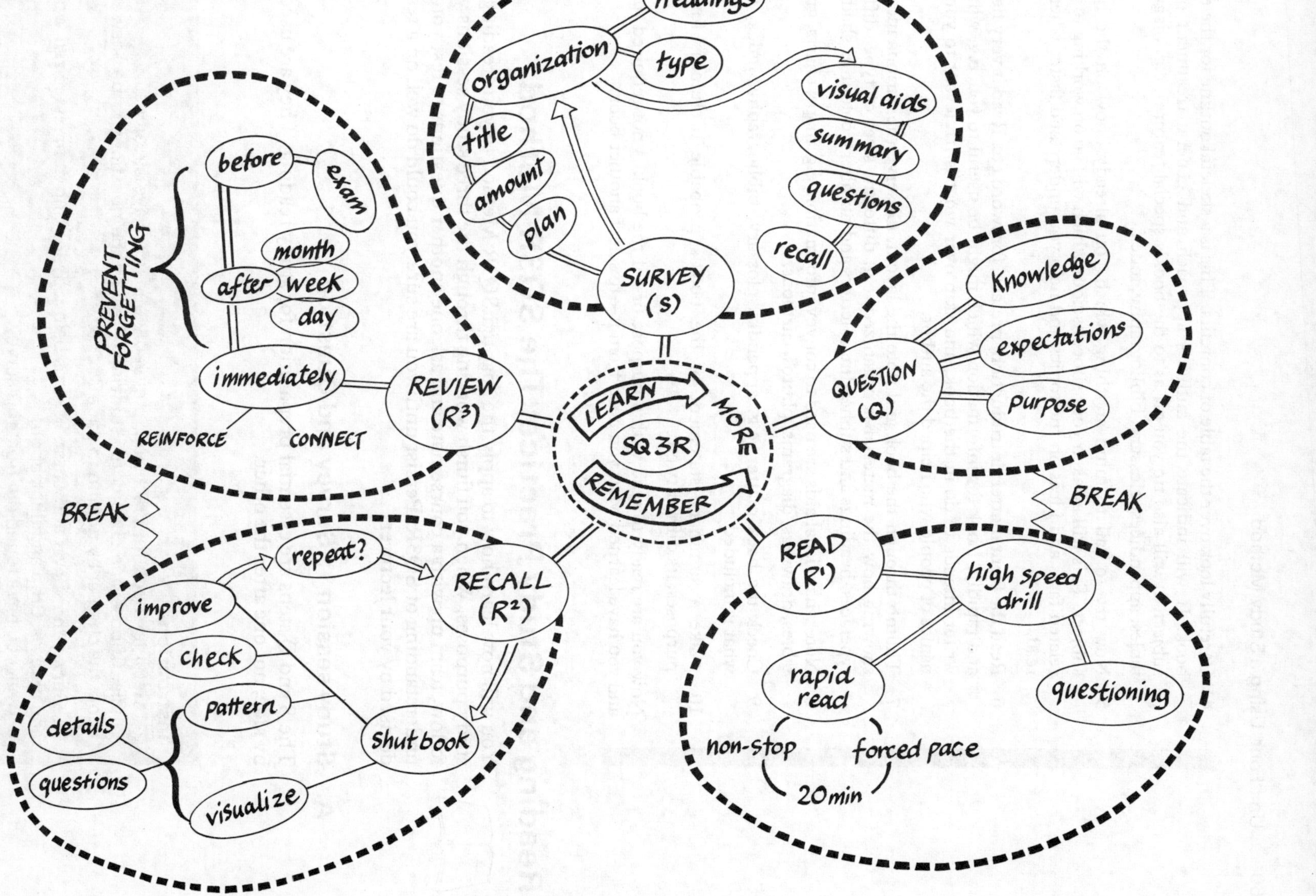

4 Carefully look over the table of contents. This is a skeletal outline for the entire book. It will indicate the author's approach and general treatment of the subject. It will also tip you off as to the book's special features, e.g. diagrams, tables, appendices, glossary, bibliography, index.

5 Now try to call to mind anything which you already know on the book's subject. This will awaken your subconscious which will go on working to recall related facts and ideas on the topics and help you understand faster when you read.

6 Read the front matter: introduction, preface, foreword etc. Read it very flexibly and rapidly. Look for information which might be useful to you, e.g. what the writer intends to do in the book, and skip over what is irrelevant to you, e.g. names of people who helped the author.

7 Thumb through the book and note the layout. Observe the various means of showing how the material is organized, e.g. different sizes of type, different typefaces, headings and subheadings, letters and numbers, colour or shading.

8 Note what visual aids are used to convey information, e.g. maps, charts, graphs, tables, drawings, diagrams, photos, cartoons.

9 Check the back matter, e.g. appendix, glossary, bibliography, index, to see what is included.

10 Make a summary statement of the book's probable usefulness for your purposes, its difficulty etc.

Now you are ready to read with a purpose or—if the book is not required reading and you have learned what you need from it—to select another book.

Reading and Study Practice: The SQ3R Method

You will now learn how to apply the adapted SQ3R Method to your reading for study purposes. When you finish working through the three study sessions which follow, team up with a coursemate and ask one another questions to test your understanding of SQ3R. Persist until you are sure you could do well on a test devised by your lecturer.

A. Study session 1: Survey and Question

The S and Q steps are essential preparation for study reading. They are used side by side, not one after the other.

Instructions

1 Get a textbook for practising, preferably one you have already surveyed as a whole. Choose one chapter for studying. Preview the questions to be answered about the chapter by turning to page 70.

2 Survey the SURVEY and QUESTION steps below by looking at the italicized words and phrases. Stop and think about

a what you have found out from this survey.

b what you expect to find out when you read more thoroughly.

3 Read each instruction in turn and apply it to the selected chapter of your text.

4 Fill in the information called for on page 70. Use key word headings to save time if you record on file paper.

SURVEY

The Survey step may be applied at various levels: to an entire book, an entire chapter, or a section of a chapter. The survey of an entire book—all the material not in the regular body of print—is sometimes called the *overview*. The survey of a chapter is sometimes called the *preview* and sometimes the *survey*. Here is the SQ3R method for surveying a chapter. The same principles apply if you are surveying an article in an encyclopedia or journal.

1 Begin by noting how the chapter (or section) you are to read fits into the book's total plan, e.g. is it one of several equal topics in a large subdivision of the book? Does it provide the background for a series of later chapters? Does it elaborate on a topic introduced in a previous chapter?

2 Locate the exact pages. Count them. Make a preliminary estimate of the time the assignment is likely to take you altogether. Decide how much time you are going to spend on it now.

3 Note the major divisions or the main topics of the chapter and decide the amount you are going to learn now, e.g. the main ideas of the whole chapter? the first major section thoroughly?

4 Study the chapter title. Turn it into a question. Think about
—what the title says or means.
—what you already know about the subject.

5 Read the headings and subheadings. They tell you the key words and ideas of the chapter and how it is organized. Turn the headings into questions.

6 Read the introduction and the summary (or the first and last paragraphs). If there are any questions at the end of the chapter, read them too.

7 Read any sentences, phrases, or words in boldface lettering or in italics.

8 Look at any visual aids, e.g. diagrams, graphs, pictures. Read their captions.

9 Revise your estimate of the time needed, or the amount you should attempt to cover, if necessary.

10 Stop and think about the various questions raised by the Survey. (See the QUESTION step.)

Now stop and think about the details of the SURVEY step. Test your recall by jotting down on the file paper as many of the sub-steps as you can remember. Use key words only.

Check back on the completeness and accuracy of your list. Fill in any gaps and make any necessary corrections.

QUESTION

Three basic questions lead to all the others. (Read the three italicized questions, then return to the examples of related questions for each.)

1 *What do I already know?*

e.g. What does the title of the chapter mean?
What information do I already have on this subject?
What did my lecturer say about this subject?
What questions do the headings and subheadings suggest?
(or: What are the key words in this chapter?)
How are the headings related to the title?
How are the subheadings related to the headings?
Where have I heard this idea/this word before?
Isn't this rather like the idea of X in (some other subject)?
Which section will be the most difficult for me (take the most time)?
How much can I reasonably aim to get done now, considering what I already know/how much of the topic is new to me?

2 *What is the author likely to tell me?*

e.g. What questions is he likely to answer?
Can I predict any of the facts, ideas or examples he will give?
What will he tell me that I don't already know about the subject?
How can he justify his view that . . . ?
Can he clarify this point by giving an example?
Isn't this point of view opposed to my lecturer's? (Which is the more reasonable?)
Can he explain the concept of Y, which I didn't grasp during today's lecture on the topic?

3 *What, specifically, do I need to find out?*

e.g. What instructions did the lecturer give?
What is my purpose? Is it
—to acquire background for understanding the next lecture?
—to make notes I can revise from after the book is returned to the library?
—to prepare for a quiz?
—to memorize all the parts of the Z System?
—to gather information for an essay on the subject?
—to compare the three methods of . . . ?
Are there questions at the end of the chapter?
What am I supposed to know/be able to do when I am finished?

How to complete the preparation stage of SURVEY and QUESTION:

1 Spend two minutes making a mental SURVEY of what you now know about the subject and jot down as many key words as you can to represent what you know. Arrange the key words around the topic and use lines etc. to show relationships.

Why?—to improve concentration and eliminate mind wandering.
—to prove to yourself that you are not starting from scratch.
—to establish a good mental 'set' for receiving new information.

2 Jot down the important QUESTIONS, leaving space for filling in answers (from memory) after reading.
Why?—to establish in your mind what you are looking for.

3 Take a short break, i.e. three to five minutes. When you return, refresh your memory by looking again at your Key Word Pattern and at the questions you wrote down. Then go on to the READ step.

B. Study session 2: Read and Recall

READ (R^1)

The READ step is the *middle* one in SQ3R, and in all the other study methods. Reading without the preparation steps of SURVEY and QUESTION usually means poor comprehension, mind-wandering and much unnecessary rereading. Reading without the follow-up steps of RECALL and REVIEW means that most of what has been read will be forgotten by tomorrow. The READ step can be repeated, in combination with other steps, as often as is necessary to get the level of comprehension required.

1 Begin with a High Speed Drill. From three to five minutes of high speed training will increase your 'normal' reading-with-comprehension rate and encourage the use of the right hand side of the brain. During the drill you will unconsciously absorb a considerable amount of the text so that you will comprehend faster during the actual reading. (You will be taught a third drill later in this unit.)

2 Return to the beginning of the chapter or section and, still using a visual guide, read for comprehension at the fastest pace you can manage (slightly faster than 'comfortable').

3 Read to answer the first main question raised during the SURVEY/QUESTION routine. See tinted box above.
a Actively search for key passages which help to answer the main question.
b Notice how details are related to the main point, e.g. are they reasons? examples? subdivisions?
c Keep a sharp look-out for transition clues, e.g. *on the other hand, the third point is, another reason why.*
d Note especially any italicized or bold-printed words or phrases.

4 Do not stop to reread a difficult passage or to look up unfamiliar words or to go back for some missed detail during the first reading. Keep right on going, reading quite rapidly, to the end of the section.

5 Go on to the RECALL step. This will tell you whether you need to repeat the READ step for all or part of this section, and if so, what you need to look for the second time.

Two study hints

1 In a given amount of time, it is always more efficient to read a passage two or three times quickly than once slowly. In the repeat readings,
—you reinforce what you grasped the first time, and
—you can fit details into the framework you have now acquired.
Thus you both understand and remember better.

2 It is better to move over a particularly difficult point than to batter away at it immediately from one side only.

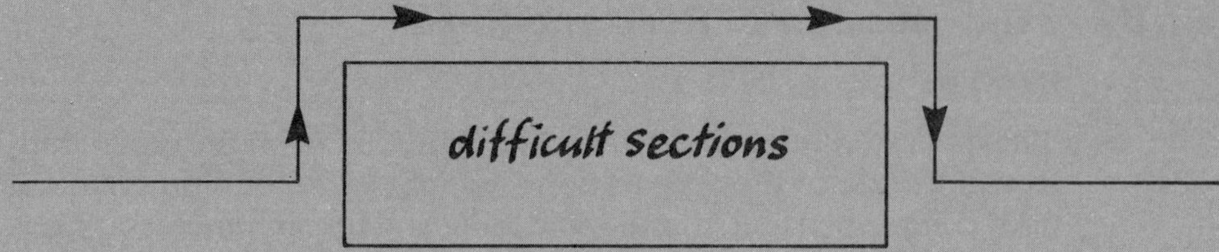

Advantages

1 Moving on relieves tension. Anxiety only makes things worse.

2 The brain has a chance to work on the difficult part subconsciously. (Have you ever returned to an 'impossible' examination question and found that you knew the answer after all?)

3 When you come back later, you will have information from 'the other side' as well which may help you to understand the difficult bit. The brain has an automatic tendency to fill in gaps. Considering a point in context helps.

RECALL (R^2)

Other names for this step include Recite, Record, Summarize and Test. They all involve RECALL—going over in your mind what you have just read or learned—by retelling it orally, by making notes of some type, or by making a summary by answering questions.

Without this step, you will probably have forgotten 80% of what you have read within a day or two. With immediate recall, you may be able to remember 80% or more.

1 Close the book (or put it aside). For some subjects, especially the sciences, your book could profitably be closed for *over half* your study time, while you prove what you have understood and remembered.

2 Try to answer the first main question. Use your own words and try to give examples. Making a pattern is a good way of testing your recall. You can add to it as your understanding and the amount recalled increase.

3 Try to visualize the diagrams, graphs, tables, etc. If they are important, try to draw them from memory.

4 Can you attach any more detail to the main points you remember? (Your subconscious will have found more detail for you.)

5 Jot down any questions which you realize still need answering, or any terms you do not yet fully understand.

6 Open the book again. SURVEY the section or chapter again to check up on the completeness and accuracy of your answers and diagrams. Add to the list of questions which still need answering.

7 Repeat the QUESTION, READ and RECALL steps as needed for this and later sections. Concentrate on:
a clearing up difficulties
b completing your understanding to the required level.

8 RECALL the main points and important details of the entire chapter. A good way to do this is to use two pages in this way:
a On one page reduce the chapter to a key word pattern. Each key word should be capable of bringing back to mind the points or ideas associated with it.
b On the opposite page put any material which does not fit easily into the pattern e.g. formulae, definitions, statistics, graphs, quotations. You can use numbers or symbols to relate these items to points in the pattern.

9 Look for opportunities to RECALL and use what you have learned. Every time you RECALL, you are not only helping yourself remember new information; you are also reinforcing your memory of what you already know. Well remembered items are available when you want them: you can RECALL them at will.

You will have to use your judgement about when to stop and RECALL. Stopping too frequently interrupts the train of thought. Reading too long without stopping leads to reduced concentration, reduced comprehension and fatigue. A stop every 20 minutes for RECALL and a two or three minute break is highly recommended. At the end of an hour, take a longer break.

C. Study session 3: Review

REVIEW (R^3)

Regular review consolidates memory. That is, it transfers initial short-term, easily forgotten information to long-term, even permanent storage. Furthermore, it ensures that the stored information is easily retrieved when it is needed.

If you have used the SQ3R Method up to this point, each review should take you only a few minutes. This is because you will be re-viewing what you have already learned—not learning what you failed to learn in the first place, or re-learning what you have allowed yourself to forget.

1 The first REVIEW should take place almost immediately after learning. It should normally take only two to five minutes, because everything will still be fresh in your mind. This review catches and holds the information before it can slip from your mind. In other words, it prevents forgetting.
a Finish the RECALL step for the section you have been working on and then take a break of five to ten minutes. Stretch, touch your toes, walk about, run on the spot, juggle oranges, get a drink, rest your eyes by cupping them in your palm. . . . While you are resting, your brain will be completing and linking more firmly the inter-connections of what you have been studying.

b When you return, do whichever of the following is appropriate:
—Use your prepared key word pattern. First, without looking at it, see if you can recall the main points. Check back. Then take each main point in turn and see if you can recall the sub-points. Check back. If a key word fails to bring back the required information, it may be that you need a better key word.
—If you are now reviewing an entire chapter which you have worked on section by section, prepare a key word pattern which gives an overall or 'bird's eye' view of the whole. As you put down each point and sub-point, your mind will be re-viewing the associated details which may appear in patterns devoted to specific sub-topics.
—If you have notes on the topic from a lecture or another book, look them over briefly to see how they tie in with what you have just patterned. You can use underlining, numbers, symbols, etc. to relate these notes to your pattern.

2 The second REVIEW should take place the following day. Again, you are reinforcing your memory before the information fades away. This review should also take two to five minutes. *Together, the first two reviews, totalling four to ten minutes, can save you hours during the examination revision period.*

3 The third REVIEW should take place after one week, and the fourth after one month. Not only will they strengthen your memory; they will also give you an idea of your progress in the subject. (In Unit 5 you will learn a system for keeping track of what needs reviewing when.)

4 Obviously, you will need a final REVIEW before taking an examination. The more efficiently you have done the earlier reviews, the less time you will need for examination revision and the more knowledge you will have been able to add in the meantime because of the available 'pegs' for attaching new items.

> Now: REVIEW what you have learned about SQ3R by referring again to p. 68. If you have questions about any of the steps, write them down. You will come back to these questions later to see whether you have discovered the answers to them. How do you think you would score on a test covering the Study Practice section of this unit on the SQ3R Method?

Assignments

A. Continue or repeat previous assignments

1 Improve on previous reading and study plans.

2 Add to your diary of reading practice.

3 Set higher goals in the Triple-Your-Reading-Rate programme.

4 If you finish reading the novel, begin reading it again at a much faster pace by way of review. At the end of each chapter, stop and recall the key characters and events and think about your reactions to the book. (This will help you with a future assignment.)

B. Make up mnemonics

These are examples of mnemonics (memory aids):

1 A litre of water's/A pint and three quarters.
Two and a quarter pounds of jam/Weigh about a kilogram.
A metre measures three foot three./It's longer than a yard you see.
(Used in Britain to help the public change to the metric system.)

2 N*u*merator is *up* as it has a *u* in it.
*D*enominator is *down* as it has a *d* in it.

3 The root of 2? I wish I knew.
$\sqrt{2} = 1.4\ 1\ 4$ (Numbers = number of letters in words.)

4 Period II of Periodic Table of Elements:
Lithium Beryllium Boron Carbon Nitrogen Oxygen Fluorine Neon
*Lit*tle *Beryl bor*rowed a *car* for the *night*. She bumped into an *ox* and *flew* into a *neon* light.

Make up and write out mnemonics for any two items or series of items you want to remember. You can use rhyme, rhythm, key words, associations, mental pictures or any combination of methods.

C. Preview before reading

1 Record your preview of one textbook in addition to this one.

2 Record your preview of at least two textbook chapters in addition to any done for this book.

3 Preview any two novels other than the one you are reading. Say which of the two you would prefer to read, and why.

D. Improve your high speed technique

Here are two more advanced drills. (Record your practice in the diary.)

HIGH SPEED DRILL 3: GETTING THE GIST

1 Begin at 'normal' reading pace, then increase steadily and rapidly but trying to catch as many words and ideas as possible as you increase. Even when you have lost all comprehension, keep on going, until you are covering about four pages per minute.

2 Maintain this rate for two or three minutes, then gradually begin to slow down. Slow only to the point where you realize you are beginning to get a little meaning—the general idea, or gist, of what the passage is about.

3 Then return quickly to your starting point and start reading for whatever comprehension you can get at this speed. Record your time, the number of pages read, etc.

4 Give yourself an additional minute to go back over the pages read to fill in gaps in your understanding. How would you assess your comprehension now?

HIGH SPEED DRILL 4: USING PERIPHERAL VISION

This time you will make zigzag movements down the page and force your eyes to see words with vertical as well as horizontal peripheral vision.

1 Start with line one. When you reach the end, move your hand diagonally to the beginning of line four and along the line, then to line seven, and so forth, trying to see as many words as possible as you move. Build up speed until you are covering a page in this fashion every ten seconds. Make your eyes follow.

2 After several minutes, return to the beginning and read for comprehension at a forced rate.

E. Use the SQ3R method

Use it on any assignments you choose from your other courses. Your lecturer may ask to see some written evidence of your working process, e.g. surveys, questions, key word patterns, when you reviewed what and for how long, a note on difficulties, etc.

F. Adapt SQ3R for listening to lectures

The mnemonic TL3R may help: it stands for TUNE IN, LISTEN, REDUCE, RECORD, REVISE. Think out for yourself what each step should involve.

G. Check your verbs

Return to any piece of written work and examine the verbs. Check that you have stayed within either the Present or the Past block of tenses (Follow-up section E) and that the time relationships within the block are correct. Check the verb endings to make sure each verb agrees with its subject. Make your corrections in a different colour so that you and your lecturer can see what they are. Keep repeating this exercise until you have eliminated faulty tenses and errors of agreement from your writing.

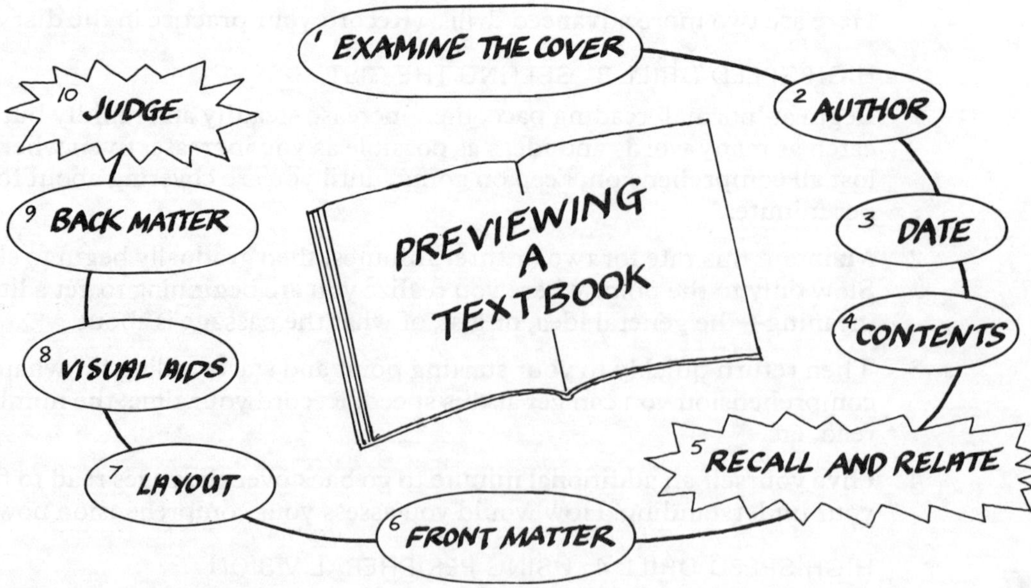

Figure 6: Key Word Pattern
THE TEN STEPS IN PREVIEWING A TEXTBOOK

Previewing a textbook

1 Full title of book: ....

2 Author(s):...

3 Place/Publisher ....

4 Date of first publication: .... Date of latest revision (not reprinting): ....

5 List at least three questions or thoughts which the title and cover material suggest to you:
a...
b...
c...

6 List two major points the author makes in the Introduction (or Preface):
a...
b...

7 Take any five chapter titles listed in the Table of Contents and turn them into questions:
a...
b...
c...
d...
e...

8 What clues to organization and to the relative importance of ideas are provided to make the study task easier? (Tick or record the clues provided.)
headings and subheadings ....
the use of colour for headings ....
different sizes and kinds of type for headings ....
numbered and/or lettered sections ....
italics and/or boldface lettering in the text ....
chapter summaries .... study/examination questions ....

9 Check the back matter. Tick or record what you find. Appendix ....
Glossary .... Bibliography .... Index ....
Anything else (specify):..............
a Of what does the Appendix consist? ....
b Record three words from the Glossary which are new to you and which you think you might need: ....
c Look through the Index for names, concepts or terms you need to find out about and record them. ....
....

10 Write a short summary statement of your expectations (hopes, fears, etc.) about the book. ....
....
....

Surveying a Textbook Chapter

1 Author and title of textbook:...

2 Title of chapter:...

3 Number of pages: ....

4 Total estimated study time: ....

5 How is this chapter related to the rest of the book?...

6 List three questions the title suggests:
a..
b..
c..

7 Read the first paragraph, headings and subheadings, and the last paragraph or two of the chapter. What is the chapter about? (Use key words instead of sentences to save time.) ....
....

8 What study aids does the chapter contain? (Tick or record those it has.)
bold print .... colour .... different type sizes ....
numbered or lettered sections .... italicized words ....
graphs, charts, maps, diagrams .... pictures ....
summary .... questions ....
Other (specify): ....

9 Will you need to divide the chapter into sections to study it? If so, where will you divide it? (Name headings to be covered and inclusive page numbers.)
....

10 List at least four questions for which you are going to read to find answers:
a..
b..
c..
d..

11 What is the major purpose of your reading of this chapter?
....

12 Make a Key Word Pattern of what you know at this moment about the subject/topic. You have three minutes only, so concentrate on the most important ideas. Use a whole sheet of paper so there is plenty of room for the various branches.

13 When you have finished, note how long you actually spent on the chapter .... or the first section ....

Unit Five Organizing Study Time

Timed Reading Passage 5: Remembering More: The Break-and-Review Routine

Instructions: Before you read the passage, which begins on p. 74, you will need to *review*, *preview* and *anticipate*, as outlined in the following steps:

1 Look at the title of this unit and the title of Passage 5. Think about the titles, e.g.

—What do you already know about these topics?
—What ideas, advice, exercises or assignments do you expect to find in this unit?
—What questions are suggested by the titles?
—What questions would you like answered?

Jot down some ideas, guesses, questions etc. suggested by the titles.

2 Review the REVIEW step of SQ3R (Unit 4). Notice any references to breaks as well as to reviews.

3 Now spend several minutes studying the five graphs on this and the next two pages. They illustrate the passage you are going to read.

a Try to understand what each graph is showing and to put the information into words.
b Can you relate any of the graphs to previous information or work in this course?
c Judging from the graphs, what do you expect the passage to explain?
d What questions concerning the graphs do you expect the passage to answer?

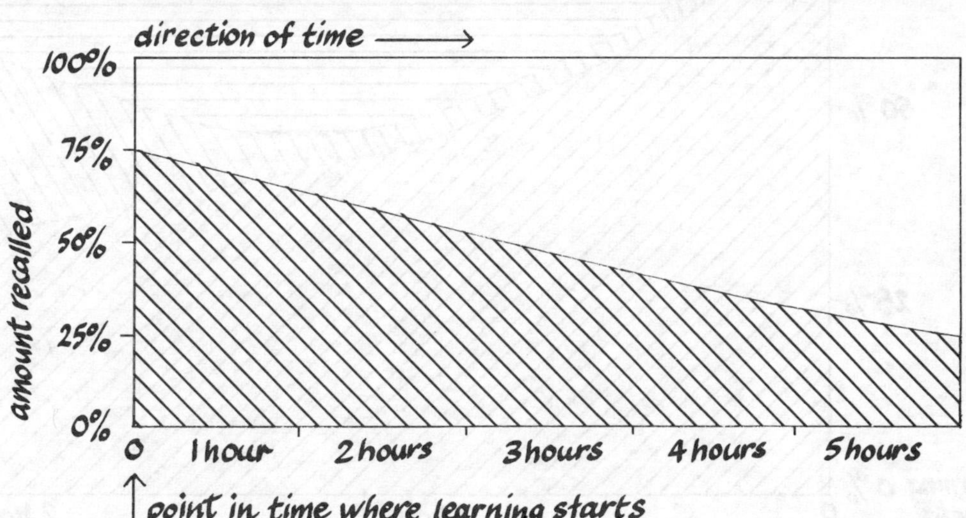

Figure 7: RECALL DURING LEARNING WITHOUT BREAKS. As time goes on, recall of material being learned tends to get progressively worse unless the mind is given proper rests.

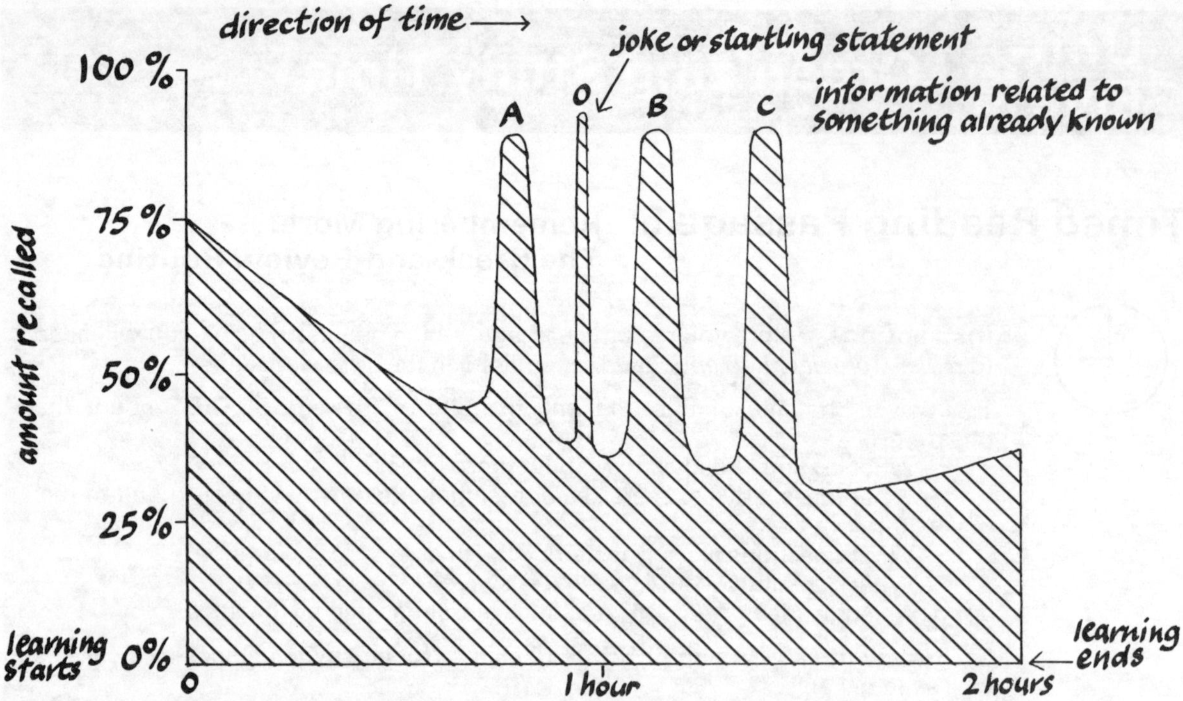

Figure 8: RECALL DURING LEARNING—PATTERN AND EXCEPTIONS. We recall more from the beginning and ends of a learning period. We also recall more when things are associated or linked (A, B and C) and more when things are outstanding or unique (0).

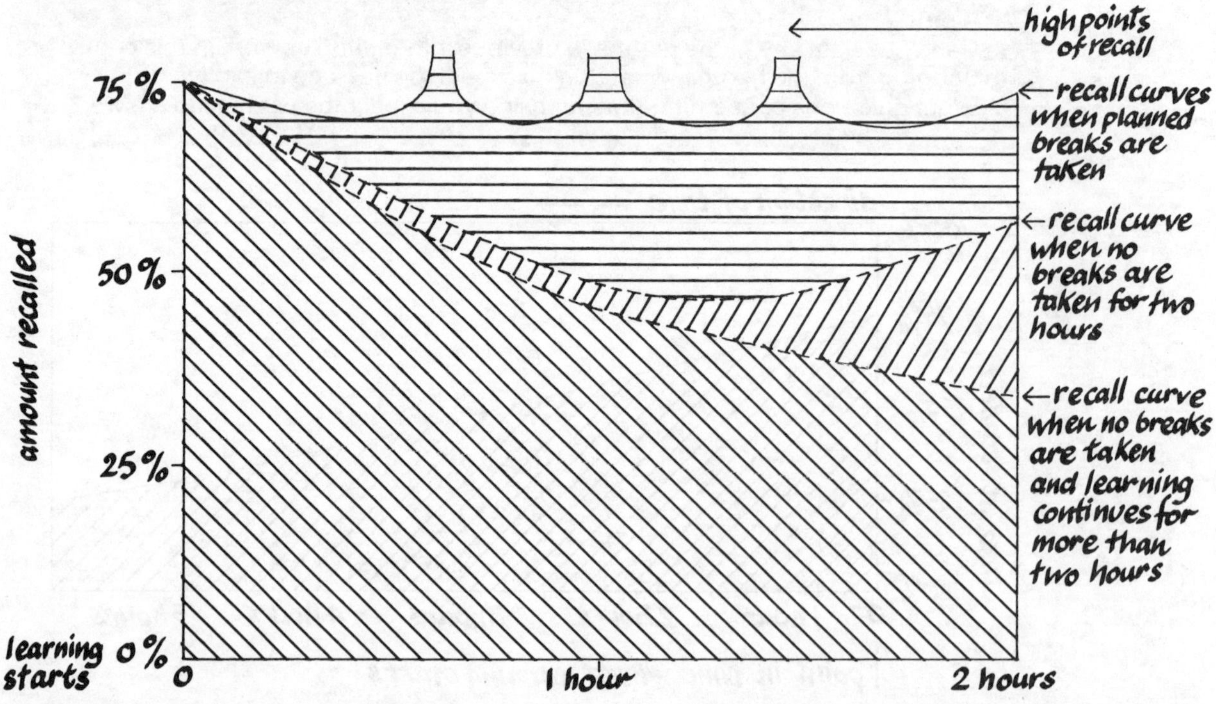

Figure 9: RECALL DURING LEARNING—WITH AND WITHOUT BREAKS. A learning period of between 20 and 40 minutes produces the best relationship between understanding and recalling. Breaks keep the recall level high. Taking a break aids concentration and comprehension after the break.

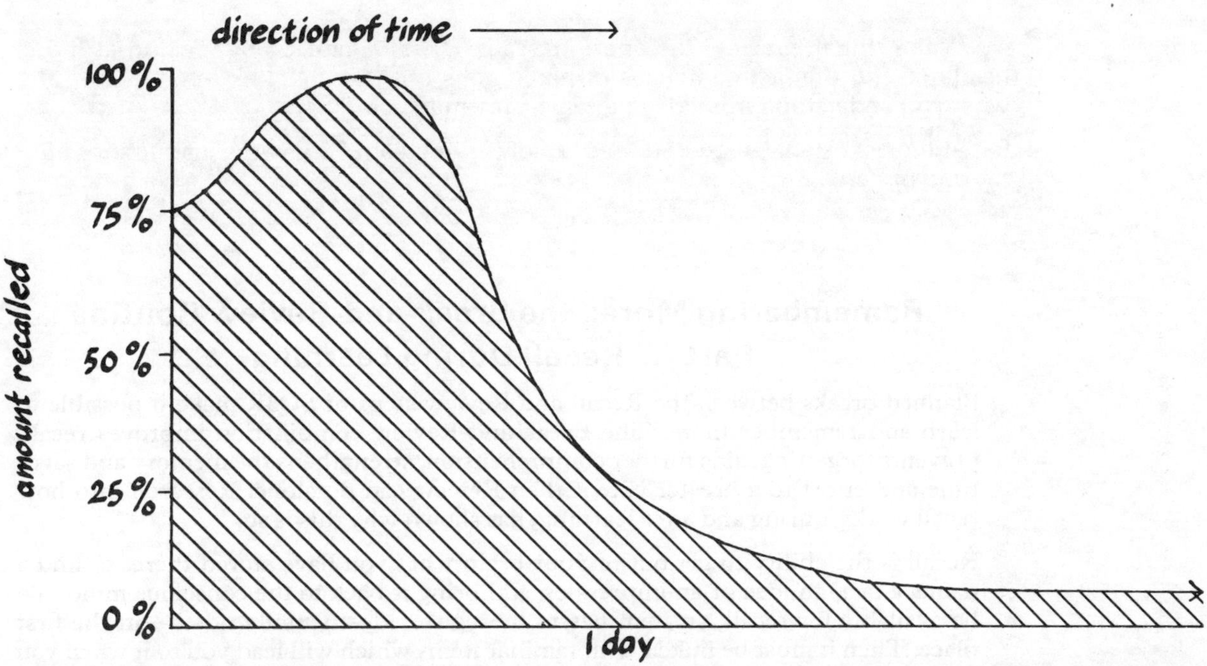

Figure 10: RECALL AFTER LEARNING. Human recall rises for a short while after learning and then falls steeply, with 80% of detail forgotten within 24 hours. Taking a break and then reviewing enables a learner to catch the memory at a high point of recall and to prevent the steep drop from taking place.

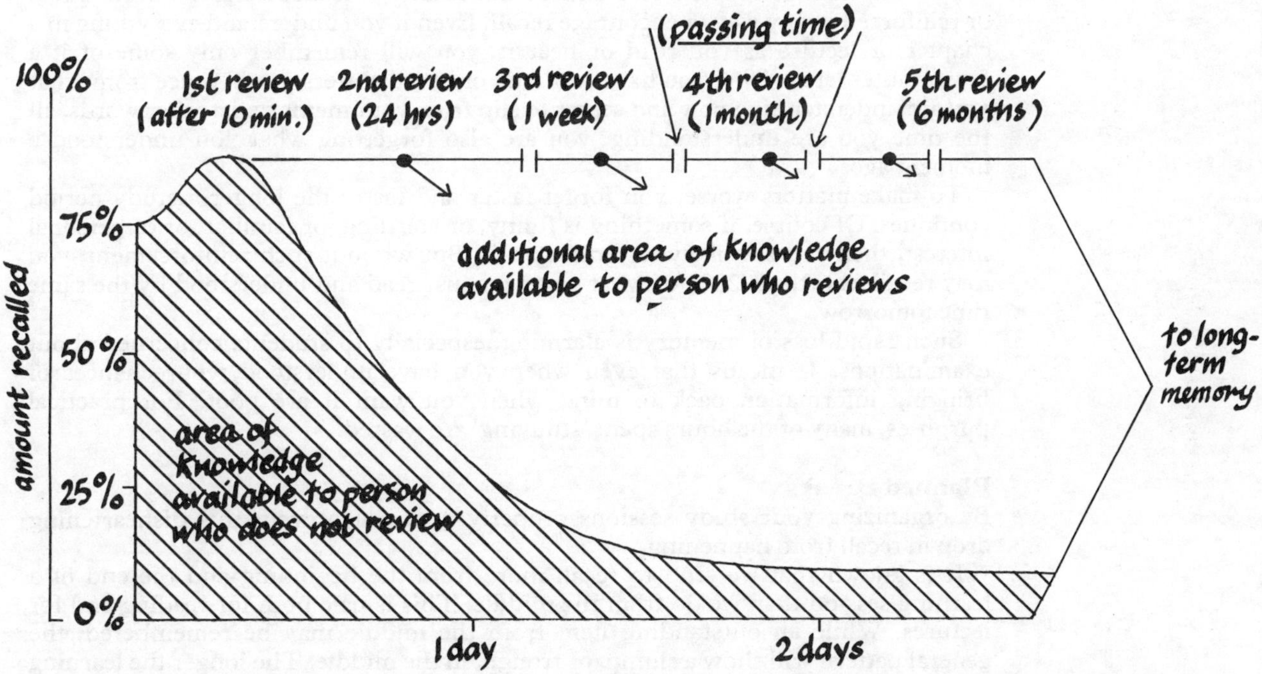

*Figure 11: EFFECT OF REVIEWS ON RECALL. Properly spaced review can keep recall constantly high. As with breaks during learning, there are intervals for reviewing which have been found to work best. The most important reviews are the first two because they prevent the steepest declines.**

* Figures 7–11 are taken from T. Buzan, *Use Your Head*, BBC, 1982.

4 At the signal, preview the entire passage (Parts A and B) by looking at the headings and the first sentences of paragraphs only. Recall, link information to what you understood from the diagrams, and anticipate.

5 At the next signal, read Part A as rapidly as you can. Follow the instructions at the end of Part A.

Remembering More: the Break-and-Review Routine

Part A: Recall During Learning

Planned breaks between the Recall and Review steps of SQ3R make it possible to learn and remember more. The Break-and-Review combination improves recall, prevents forgetting, aids further comprehension, strengthens the memory and saves time and effort to a greater extent than Review can do alone. Research into how recall works, during and after learning, has shown why this is so.

Recall is the ability to get out of your brain what you have stored there: to find a name, a fact, an idea or an impression and bring it back to the conscious mind. To be available for recall, an item has to be registered—mentally noted—in the first place. Then it must be linked with familiar items which will lead you to it when you visit that part of your memory store. The more connections there are with other items, the more likely it is that the new piece of information will be met again, and again, until it too becomes available whenever you want it.

New information is often 'lost' almost immediately because it has not been linked or reinforced in any way to encourage recall. Even if you understand everything in a chapter or lecture as you read or hear it, you will remember only some of it a few minutes later. What you have just read or heard suffers interference from what you are understanding now and seems to slip from your memory. In other words, all the time you are understanding, you are also forgetting what you understood a moment ago.

To make matters worse, you forget faster and faster the longer a study period continues. Of course, if something is funny, or startling, or familiar, or of personal interest, then you are likely to remember it. But without such reinforcement, you may recall as little as 20% of what you have just read and understood by the same time tomorrow.

Such rapid loss of memory is alarming, especially to students concerned about examinations. It means that even when you have understood, your chances of bringing information back to mind when you want it are poor. For practical purposes, many of the hours spent 'studying' are wasted.

Planned Breaks

By organizing your study sessions properly, you can prevent this disheartening drop in recall from happening.

It is known that we tend to recall more from the beginning and the end of a learning session than we do from the middle. This is true both for reading and for lectures. While an outstanding item from the middle may be remembered, the general pattern will show a slump, or trough, in the middle. The longer the learning goes on without a break, the deeper the trough will sink.

The way to stop the trough from slumping deeper, is to shorten the length of the learning period. Dividing a long study session into a number of shorter periods, separated by breaks, means more beginnings and ends of high recall with less slumping in between.

The best time span seems to be between 20 and 40 minutes. A shorter period may not give enough time to establish the train of thought. A longer one gives the mind too much information to hold: as a result, concentration, comprehension and recall all suffer. You can decide how to divide up a total study task during the survey stage of SQ3R.

Within the shorter learning periods, the SQ3R steps can be combined in various ways, but you should always end with Recall followed by a complete break and then, immediately, by Review. The length of the break will vary. After the first period, 3 minutes may be enough. After the third, you may need 10 minutes before making a final overall review.

(635 words)

Stop. Record your time for Part A. Recall what you have just read. Then rest your mind and eyes for a moment.

Before the signal to begin Part B: Recall. Anticipate. Get mentally set to find the key words and ideas as quickly as possible.

Part B: Recall After Learning

When you return from the break, you will be able to recall more information than you could before it. This slight rise in recall after learning is called the *reminiscence effect* and it can be used to great advantage.

By taking a break, you have given the material being learned a chance to 'soak in' without interference from further information. All the while you have been resting your conscious mind, your subconscious has continued to sort, organize and link up the various new facts and ideas, integrating them with what was already stored. This process of completing and interconnecting has increased both understanding and recall.

Unfortunately, the reminiscence effect does not last long. It is after this initial rise in recall that the steep downward plunge of forgetting will begin—unless everything recalled can be captured immediately. Although you have understood it, most of the new learning is not yet fixed strongly enough in the memory to stay there without further consolidation.

The way to prevent forgetting is to review what you have learned promptly. The object is to catch and secure what you have learned before it has had time to escape. When you catch it at the highest possible point of recall, the maximum amount of information is in the fore of your mind when you review. Simply re-viewing this body of information as a whole will establish more connections and fix it more firmly in mind. A quick and effective way to do this is to make a Key Word Pattern.

The Break-and-Review combination boosts concentration and recall levels, consolidates what has been learned so far and re-establishes a good mental set for the next task. You will therefore digest new information more easily and keep reinforcing recent learning. That is, you will learn and remember more.

The most remarkable evidence for this is a comparison between recall scores with and without immediate review. If you make a quick review after a break but before the reminiscence effect fades, you will be able to recall as much as 80% of what you have learned 24 hours later. If you fail to make this review, you may *lose* that much!

As with learning periods, certain time intervals for review have been found to work best. A second review, of perhaps 3 minutes, 24 hours after the original learning, will bring recall back to or beyond the required level and hold it for a week. Then a third review will hold it for a month, after which a fourth review of a few minutes will keep the recall level so high that your examination revision need take only minutes instead of hours, and much of the information will have become part of your Long Term Memory. The information that has been most used will need the least reviewing.

No study minutes are more valuable than those spent on the Recall-Break-and-Review routine. They improve learning and remembering to a degree out of all proportion to the time invested and ensure that study time has not, after all, been wasted.

(550 words)

Record your time for Part B. Then average your WPM for the two parts. Go on to the questions on Parts A and B.

1 The entire passage is mainly about
a recall during learning.
b recall after learning.
c the value of planned breaks and reviews.
d how we forget.

2 From the information in the passage we can conclude that 24 hours after reading a person normally
a remembers less than half of what he read.
b remembers what he understood during the reading.
c remembers only the end of what he read.
d remembers about 80% of what he read.

3 We can conclude from the passage that a student is *least* likely to remember
a points made at the beginning of a lecture.
b points made during the middle of a lecture.
c points made at the end of a lecture.
d an amusing anecdote told by the lecturer.

4 Normally, after learning,
a recall drops a little, then levels off.
b recall begins to decline steadily.
c recall stays high if you have understood.
d recall rises slightly, then drops steeply.

5 According to the passage, the best time span for a learning period is
a between 20 and 40 minutes.
b between 3 and 10 minutes.
c about one hour.
d as long as you think you can concentrate.

6 What has just been understood often seems to be displaced in the memory by what is being understood now. This phenomenon is referred to as
a interference.
b recall.
c reinforcement.
d integration.

7 The term 'reminiscence effect' refers to
a a boost of concentration.
b recollections of childhood.
c a slight rise in recall immediately after learning.
d the amount remembered 24 hours after learning.

8 The passage is concerned mostly with the remembering that results from
a understanding what has been read or heard.
b registering an item in the first place.
c linking ideas creatively.
d preventing forgetting.

9 The most important review is the one
a closest to the examination.
b a few minutes after the initial learning.
c 24 hours after the initial learning.
d a week after the initial learning.

10 Which of the following is *not* stated or implied in the passage?
a Reviewing establishes more and stronger links between new items and familiar ones.
b Reviewing pays off in the amounts of time saved and information remembered.
c The recommended system of reviewing, though useful, is quite time-consuming.
d Information that has been used and thought about needs less reviewing.

WORDS PER MINUTE CHART:
Timed Reading Passages 5A and 5B *(635 and 550 words)*

Time	WPM 5A	WPM 5B	Time	WPM 5A	WPM 5B	Time	WPM 5A	WPM 5B	Time	WPM 5A	WPM 5B
1.00	635	550	2.00	320	275	3.00	210	185	4.00	160	140
10	545	470	10	295	255	10	200	175	10	150	130
20	475	410	20	275	235	20	190	165	20	145	—
30	425	365	30	255	220	30	180	155	30	140	—
40	380	330	40	240	205	40	175	150	40	135	—
50	345	300	50	225	190	50	165	145	50	130	—

Follow-up

A. Influences on reading speed

1 Was there a difference between your WPM rate for Parts A and B? How would you explain the difference?

2 Passage 5 contained more words, longer words and sentences, and more information than previous passages. However, you were able to study the illustrations and to preview the passage before you started reading, and some of the points had already been mentioned in Unit 4. Discuss how these various factors may have influenced your speed and comprehension scores.

B. Recall and review

The following questions require deeper understanding and stronger recall than multiple choice questions. First try to answer them without referring back to the passage. Then check up on the completeness and accuracy of your recall and improve your answer accordingly. Be clear and concise.

1 The passage implies that much of the time students spend studying is wasted. Why is it wasted?

2 It is recommended that study time should be divided up into periods of 20–40 minutes, each ending with a break, followed by immediate review. Why is a longer period *not* a good idea, even if you seem to be working well?

3 What does the passage say about the length of a break between recalling and reviewing?

4 How does the passage explain the rise in recall just after learning?

5 The passage recommends reviews of perhaps 3 minutes each at certain intervals after the original learning. What are these intervals?

6 Using *key words only*, sum up the reasons for taking a short break after learning.

C. Take a break

One way to rest your eyes (and your mind) is to cup your hands in front of your eyes to form a dome over them. If you prefer to stretch your arms, look out the window and yawn, go ahead. Refresh yourself in whatever way suits you.

D. Pattern review

Review Passage 5 by making a Key Word Pattern of it.

1 Take a sheet of paper and write on it: your name, the course title, your lecturer's name, Unit 5 and today's date.

2 Decide on the key words for the centre of your pattern and how you will make them stand out. Put them on the sheet.

3 What subcentres (or branches) will radiate from your centre? Put them on, then start to develop one of them.

4 Working hints:

a Use key words only (mostly nouns and verbs, sometimes adjectives or adverbs) and print them on lines.

b Use arrows, lines, shapes, colour, different sizes of print, sketches of Passage 5 diagrams, drawings etc. Use them in order to save words, link ideas, show relationships and increase the visual impact.

c If one branch dries up, switch to another. Keep your pen moving and the ideas coming to mind.

d Run your eyes quickly over the passage again to see if you are missing anything important. Make additions if necessary.

e When you finish, add tomorrow's date under today's. This is to remind you that tomorrow you should review the pattern (i.e. the summary of Passage 5) again.

5 Test your memory again tomorrow. Can you recall everything indicated on your pattern?

Related Skills: Planning Study and Review Time

Study time can be usefully organized on several different levels: long range planning, weekly study timetables, daily job lists, goals for an evening's work, strategies for a single learning period, a system for regular review in each subject. . . . This section will give advice for organizing study at several of these levels.

Use SQ3R to study the five parts of this section. If this is your own book, underline, write key words in the margin, or otherwise mark the pages so that the words and ideas you think are most important stand out on the page. (How does this help?)

A. Making a study timetable

You have been asked in previous units to make weekly Reading/Study Plans and to think out for yourself what improvements to make each time. Judge your attempts thus far in the light of the detailed instructions below:

1 Set out a chart with the days of the week written along the top and each hour of your normal working day listed down the left hand side. Each square will thus represent a particular hour of a particular day of the week. Write the inclusive dates of the week as part of your heading at the very top.

2 In the appropriate spaces, indicate the lectures and labs for each of your courses. Use capital letters or a special colour to make them stand out from everything else.

3 Now, in a less bright colour or smaller lettering, put in your routine activities: meals, laundry, shopping, church, etc. Include regular recreational and social activities like football practice, or going out with friends on a Saturday evening.

4 Survey the hours which are still available. Your task is to select the best specific times for working on a particular subject. Use another (bold) colour or a different type of lettering to distinguish study periods from classes as well as from routine activities. The following considerations will help you decide what to study when. In the beginning, the selection process may take you an hour or more. Once you have worked out a good basic plan, however, a few minutes a week will be enough to reassess your timetable and make any needed adjustments.

a Lectures, practicals and private study time *together* should total at least 40 hours per week; up to 50 hours may sometimes be necessary. (Your reading speed is one factor affecting the amount of time you need.)

e.g. If you are an arts student attending 15 hours of lectures per week, you should plan a minimum of 25 hours of private study; if you are a science student attending 24 hours of lectures and labs per week, you should plan a minimum of 16 hours of private study.

b Try to leave weekends relatively free. Or, if you prefer, give yourself one full day and two half days off in a normal week. This will allow 'legitimate' time for recreation and socializing. It also means you will have time available if you need it for special projects, extra reading or 'emergencies' such as the loss of a planned study hour or unexpected difficulties with an assignment.

c When do you concentrate best? Mornings? Early evening? 3 a.m.? Use these times for work which needs great concentration. Guard against frittering them away on routine chores (e.g. laundry) or undemanding tasks (e.g. tidying a file).

d Consider the implications of where you might be at particular times which are available, e.g.
- —in a corridor during an hour between lectures.
- —in the library for two morning hours.
- —in your room, shared with five roommates, after dinner.

e Budget time for a subject as soon as possible after a lecture or lab in that subject. (What are some reasons for this advice?)

f Allocate plenty of time for your more difficult subjects. You will need to reassess the relative difficulty of your courses from time to time, as the situation may change during the semester.

g When reading and assignments are relatively heavy, or you find the subject difficult, distribute the work throughout the week. One hour a night for four nights will produce better results than four hours, even with proper breaks, on a single night.

h Besides planning study periods to follow lectures and labs, plan others to precede classes in the subject. Reading up on the topic to be covered, and a quick review of the last lecture, establish an excellent mental set for getting the most out of class.

i Plan for variety in your studying, in the types of subject matter studied each day and in the kinds of activity required, e.g.
- —Do not study French and German consecutively; they may interfere with one another.
- —Work on a subject which requires you to solve problems or to draw diagrams in between two subjects which involve much reading.

Using SQ3R ensures a variety of activities within a learning period.

> **Study hint:** In addition to the times you allocate to particular subjects, *set aside a total of 1 hour a day for quick reviews covering all your subjects.* This will keep the recall level high for everything you have learned so far in each course so that you never have to spend time relearning before examinations. An easy system for planning what to review when will be outlined below.

B. Using a study timetable

1 Keep your timetable with you so that you can refer to it at any time.

2 Each day, look at the plan to see what subjects you are to study when. Then make a list of the specific jobs to be done for each subject, e.g.
- —Check references for essay on Role of Chemistry in Medicine.
- —Revise Chemistry lecture notes.
- —Work through exercises on p. 56 of Physics text.
- —Learn rules for ---------- in Maths.
- —Read last section of Ch. 5 in Biology text and make pattern of entire chapter.

—Faster reading practice with novel.
—Quick reviews.

What are the advantages of such a list? Here are two:

a You will always know what books, notebooks and equipment to take with you—both for classes and for private study.

b You will never need to waste time deciding what to do when you sit down to study. You can get straight to work and use the available time effectively.

EXAMPLE

Name: Bassey Henshaw
Dept. English and Literary Studies
STUDY TIMETABLE Week of 23-30 November

TIME	MONDAY	TUESDAY	WEDNESDAY	THURSDAY	FRIDAY
6-7am	Faster reading practice 30 min. News				
7-8am	BREAKFAST				
8-9am	Review: GSS 111: NIGERIAN HERITAGE	GSS 101: (L) USE OF ENGLISH	Review: GSS 111	GSS 101 (L)	Review: GSS 111
9-10am	GSS 111 (L)	Essay planning & writing practice	GSS 111 (L)	SQ3R on text for REL 101	GSS 111 (L)
10-11am	Recall: GSS 111 lecture Review: ELS 121	Other GSS 101 review and assignments	Recall & KWP: GSS 111 lect. Review REL 101	Other study skills practice or assignments GSS 101	Recall & KWP: GSS 111 lect. + week's review
11-12 noon	Break	Review: Antigone ELS 121	Library	Reading & review: ELS 121	Library: sources for ELS
12-1	ELS 121: (L) INTRO TO DRAMA AND POETRY	ELS 121 (L)	Reading and review: REL 101	ELS 121 (L)	Break
1-2pm	LUNCH - SIESTA				
2-3pm	REL 101: (L) INTRO TO RELIGIOUS STUDIES	Review & note-making ELS 121	REL 101 (L)	Review & note-making ELS 121	REL 101 (L)
3-4pm	REVIEW & KWP REL 101 Phonetics Practice ELS 111	Othello: characterization ELS 121	Review & KWP REL 101 Phonetics practice ELS 111	The Rivals: ELS 121	Review & KWP REL 101 Phonetics Practice ELS 111
4-5pm	ELS 111 (L) LANGUAGE FOR STUDENTS OF LITERATURE	Library: ELS 121 research	ELS 111 (L)	Library: REL 101 Research	ELS 111 (L)

(L) = Lecture

5-6 pm	Phonetics practice	Break	Phonetics practice	Assignments	Games
6-7pm	SUPPER				
7-8pm	GS 101 Assignments	Poetry: sonnets for ELS 121	Poetry: lyrics for	Attempt questions on Othello	Discussion: sonnets & lyric poems
8-9m	African novel for GSS 101	Reading and review: ELS 111	African novel + GSS 101 assignments	Review/ assignments as needed	Review of week's KWPs
9-10pm	TV Room News				
10-11pm	Dailies Light reading Quick reviews				
weekends:	emergencies, special assignments, laundry, church, visiting, rest				

3 Try to stick to your timetable. If you can't, then rearrange the study sessions, divide your time differently, or otherwise revise the timetable so that you *can* use it. Planning your time sensibly makes self-discipline easier.

Before you continue, how many reasons can you think of for making and using a study timetable?

C. Getting down to work

1 Estimate as well as you can the time a task ought to take. This will help you decide how to break up a large task into smaller ones, and encourage you to concentrate.

2 Having made your estimate, however, you should think about the *task*, not the *time*, and be specific about what you hope to accomplish. Which of these three goals is likely to yield the best results, and why?
a Spend one hour on ENGLISH lll.
b Spend one hour on Ch. 6 of *Introduction to Language.*
c Read and make key word notes from memory on the first major section of Ch. 6 (estimated study time: 30 min.).

3 Ways to begin:
a Review what you last read/heard/studied in this subject, perhaps by making a quick pattern.
b Survey. Set goals and decide how to adapt SQ3R for this particular task. What should you accomplish by break-time?
c Do a High Speed Drill.

4 When it is time for a quick break, take it, even if work is going well. Then review, and get down to the next task.

D. Using a review system

The simplest system for reviewing is to add at the top of the page, each time you make a review, the date when the next review is due. Each day you review everything with that day's date at the top. This is how the system works:

1 At the end of a study session for a particular subject, take a break and then make an overall review of what you have learned. Different forms are possible for the written product of this review (i.e. the proof that you do, in fact, remember), e.g.
—A key word pattern.
—One or more pages of formulae, definitions, lists or other items less easy to pattern (but set these out clearly all the same).
—Labelled diagrams.
—Marked-up class notes: key points circled and connected in green ink, numbered points, key words written in the margin, etc.

2 Label the page clearly at the top so that you can always tell at a glance exactly what the page represents.

3 Write today's date (Review 1) in the upper right hand corner. Immediately underneath it write tomorrow's date (Review 2). Tomorrow, when you review, you will add the date in a week's time (Review 3). And so on.

4 Each day, check your notes and patterns for any paper bearing the day's date. When you come to one, do a quick review and add a new date.

5 By the end of the semester, the top right hand corner of a page might look like this:

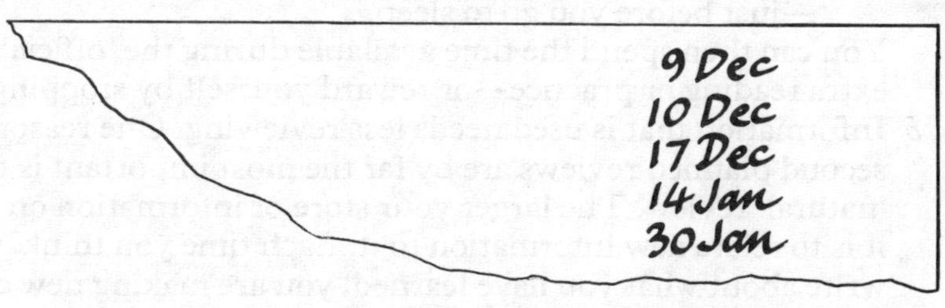

(The dates represent four 'normal' reviews plus a last reminder just before the examination in the subject.)

E. Using review times

1 *a* For most material, review times are best spent as follows:
Review 1: Make a key word pattern: sum up what you have learned in key words and visual form.
Review 2: Produce a quick sketch of the pattern from memory.
Review 3: Visualize the pattern and jot down the key words.
Review 4: Simply bring the key words back to mind again.

b Items which are less suitable for patterning, e.g. a poem to be learned, formulae, graphs, diagrams for an experiment, should also be reviewed by trying to reproduce them, orally or on paper, from memory.

c In all cases, check your recall against the original pattern, diagram, etc. and make any necessary additions, corrections or improvements to bring recall back to or beyond the required level.

2 Points to note on the role of key-words:

a If you learn well in the first place, key words will be sufficient to bring back the necessary information.

b A missed key word or one which fails to bring back the associated cluster of information probably needs to be replaced by a more effective word.

c It is the use of key words which makes possible a review of one hour's learning in as little as three minutes. They also improve comprehension and retention.

d If you do not use key words, review will take longer and will be less effective. (Why?)

3 Saving time and effort:

> Review in odd moments. Budget an hour a day for review; then see how much reviewing you can finish before the budgeted hour comes round.

a You can fit in reviews
—while waiting for a lecture to start
—while standing in a queue
—while walking from hostel to refectory
—just before you go to sleep.

You can then spend the time available during the 'official' review hour for extra reading or practice—or reward yourself by stopping work earlier.

b Information that is used needs less reviewing. One reason why the first and second planned reviews are by far the most important is that they encourage 'natural' review. The larger your store of information on a subject, the easier it is to relate new information to it. Each time you think, talk, hear, read or write about what you have learned, you are making new connections and also reviewing what is already stored.

Increasing familiarity and an expanding store of knowledge lead to greater interest in the subject, so you are more alert to new information, which can easily be attached to existing information—and so the process accelerates.

The more you use a review system, the more often you will discover that the material scheduled for review is already familiar and needs less than the allotted time for re-viewing. (What uses can you make of the saved time?)

MAKE TIME FOR REVIEWING

Students' say: 'It's difficult enough getting new work done each day. How can I afford to spend an hour each day just reviewing?'

Compare the following:

Student X works for one hour, without a break, on a topic which is inadequately covered in class. He doesn't use SQ3R and he 'doesn't have time' for review.

Two months later, as exams approach, he looks over the pages of notes he made during that hour. He realizes, in panic, that he remembers almost nothing on the topic. He worries: should he take the time to reread about the topic, or simply hope that there won't be a compulsory question on this topic in the exam?

Time spent: 1 hour   Amount recalled: 10% or less

And this is only *one* topic in *one* course.

Student Y also works for one hour on the same material. However, he applies SQ3R and reviews at planned intervals. When it is time for his pre-exam review, he finds that he can visualize everything on his original mind map, the key words bringing the entire topic back to mind. He checks on a detail or two to make recall complete, then moves on to other work.

Time spent: 1 hour, plus a maximum of 15 minutes review spaced over two months.

Amount recalled: 90% or more, much of which will be remembered permanently.

Suppose further that Student Y averages 5 hours a day, 5 days a week, on private study and uses one of the hours daily for review. By budgeting 20% of his total private study time for review, he can improve his long term memory from 10% of what he has learned to 90% of what he has learned.

This 80% gain works out to an overall gain in efficiency (time spent: amount recalled) of about 75%!

Question: Can you afford *not* to review?

Practice in Listening, Patterning and Reviewing

A. TL3R practice

1 Your lecturer will read a short passage about Key Word Patterns. TUNE IN by recalling what you already know about patterns and anticipating what your lecturer will say.

2 LISTEN. Concentrate on selecting the best possible words to use as key words and on associating each one mentally with the next idea(s). Most of the words you choose will be ones you hear, but occasionally you may have to think of some other word which sums up a group of words or a whole idea. The selection and associations combine the RECALL and REDUCE steps of TL3R.

3 REVIEW what you have heard by bringing back to mind the key words you selected, and by thinking out some of the ways you could link up the ideas or make them stand out in a pattern.

4 Look at the pattern on p. 86, which is one person's patterning of the passage you heard (plus an additional section you haven't heard on technique).
a What words match the ones you chose?

Figure 12: *Key Word Pattern of a passage on KEY WORD PATTERNS (slightly adapted from Mark E. Brown, 'Memory Matters', David and Charles, 1977.)*

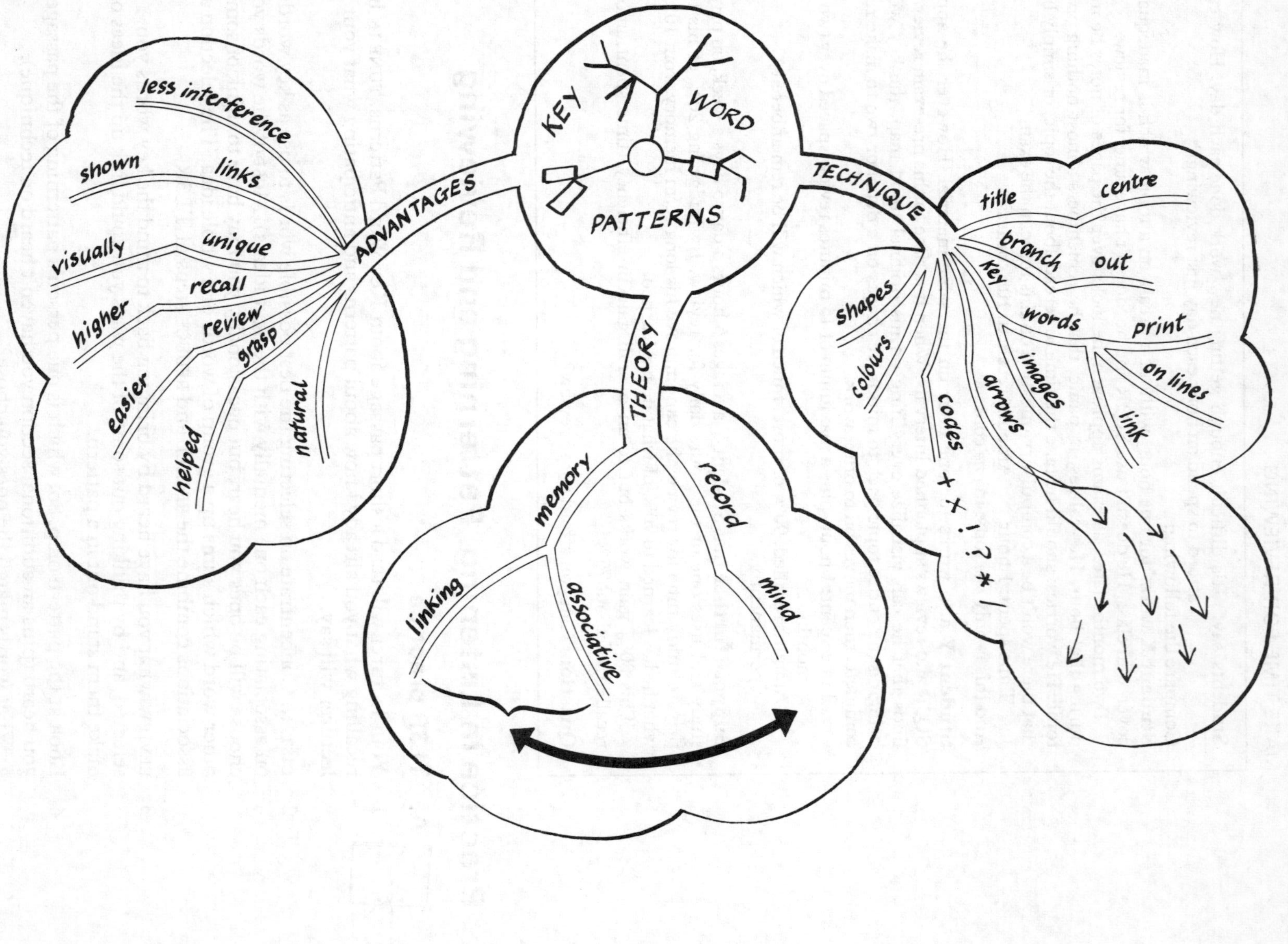

b Find examples of single words which sum up what you have taken several words to convey.
c How have the three topics in the passage been made visually clear, and distinct from one another?
d How has the maker of the pattern managed to use *only one word* per line?
e What non-verbal means have been used to record information?
f Can you learn anything from this example which will help you make more effective patterns?

B. Speaking or writing practice

Use the Technique branch of the pattern on page 86 to help you explain, orally or in a well-constructed paragraph, exactly how to make an effective pattern. Your linking up of the key words in consecutive prose should produce such a clear explanation that a listener or reader who has never seen a pattern could make one when you finish. Stay within the Present block of tenses.

C. Review of novel 1

1 By this time, you will have completed one novel and possibly read it a second time at a faster rate. If you have followed directions and practised daily, you will have read the last chapter at a WPM rate at least double the rate you began with, and you will have the characters and events quite clearly in mind as a result of reviewing.

2 (If you haven't doubled your rate, read the instructions in Unit 2 again, carefully, and carry them out this time. It is surprisingly easy to learn how to read and understand faster, and the benefits are too obvious and numerous to repeat.)

3 Later in this course your lecturer may ask you to look beyond the 'story line' in the novels you have read and to make some judgements about the books. Before you can do this, however, you must be clear about the story itself: what happens, to whom, in what circumstances, for what reasons, and with what results. The purpose of the present review is to complete your understanding at this fundamental level.

Instructions

Read and think about the five basic questions below and further questions which they generate for your particular book. (You will find that the questions interlink.)

Estimate how long you will spend on reviewing the book. Divide up the task accordingly. (If you have been testing your comprehension and reviewing as suggested, this review will take far less time than if you haven't!)

Skim, reread, recall and review as necessary until you feel you can answer the questions.

Take a break.

Present what you consider to be the most important information about the story in the form of one or more key word patterns. Your pattern(s) will serve as a summary of the book's contents.

REVIEW QUESTIONS

1 What is the *setting*, or background, of the story? Setting is more than the physical location (e.g. Lagos, rival Ibo villages). It includes the social environment and way of life of the characters as well, e.g.

—What are the rituals and customs which hold the community together?
—What are the values of the society in which the characters move?

2 Who is the *main character*? Who are the other important characters? What do you know about them? e.g.

—What are they like? How do you know?
—What do they want? Why do they do what they do?
—What incidents reveal their goals and motivations?
—Are the characters believable? Why or why not?
—How do the characters interact and affect one another?

3 What are the major *conflicts* in the story?

a Are there conflicts within the main character?
e.g. between what he wants to do and what he feels he should do?
b Are there conflicts between two or more characters?
e.g. between an individual and his community?
between the community and the world outside?
c How do these conflicts create tension and suspense?

4 What are the *key events* in the story? (or What are the stages in the development of the plot?)

a How are they related to one another?
b How do they reflect the conflicts and tensions in the story?
c How do they affect the main characters and vice versa?
d What would you say is the climax of the story, (i.e. What is the point of highest tension and excitement?)
e At what point did you realize how the story would end?
f What is the outcome of the story?

5 What would you say is the *theme* (the main idea) of the novel? State it in a sentence, or select the key sentence from the novel.

a Does the book's title give any clues? e.g. *Things Fall Apart.*
b Is the theme ever summed up by one of the characters? e.g.

> *He [the white man] has put a knife on the things that held us together and we have fallen apart.*

PLANNING THE PATTERN

You may decide that the central focus should be the main character, with the branches showing his major characteristics and also indicating how the reader knows what these are, e.g. through key events or relationships with certain other characters. Or you could show how a major idea is worked out, e.g. the stages by which 'things fall apart', in the book of that name, for Okonkwo and for his community. Whatever you select as your focal point and the key words leading from it, you will be trying to represent what you have perceived as the most important content of the book.

FURTHER QUESTIONS

The following questions help in judging a novel. They will be considered in Unit 8, but you may wish to think about them now.

1 Does the novel leave you with any dominant, overall impression or feeling?

2 Does the novel have a pattern/design/shape/structure?

3 Is the ending appropriate (even inevitable), considering what has gone before?

4 Have you noticed any special techniques of the author? e.g. flashbacks, or looking at the same event from the viewpoints of different characters?

5 Does the language contribute to the effectiveness of the book? e.g. Achebe's use of imagery which belongs to his characters' world:

Okonkwo's fame grew like a bush fire in the harmattan.

6 Are there ideas, types of event, feelings or images which recur through the book and help to give it unity?

Assignments

A. Continue or repeat previous assignments

1 Keep up your diary of reading and study practice: high speed drills, SQ3R, TL3R, reviewing. Add to your glossaries.

2 Work at improving your spelling and eliminating errors in punctuation, tenses and agreement.

3 Use SQ3R and TL3R whenever the opportunity arises, adding samples of your thinking and working processes to your file.

4 Work out memory aids for two more sequences of information you need to remember, stating what they are and how you will remember.

B. Make a study plan

Using the advice given in this unit, make a study timetable for the coming week to show to your lecturer. In Unit 6 you will be asked to say how well you were able to keep to the plan and what changes you should make in the next one to make it more workable.

C. Make a pattern summary

Review the novel you have read and summarize it in key word pattern form. See PLANNING THE PATTERN on page 88. Then begin the second novel. Be alert for similarities and differences between the two novels.

Unit Six Locating Information

Timed Reading Passage 6: Finding Something Quickly: Scanning and Search-reading

Instructions

1 Look at the title. Anticipate what the passage may say.

2 Preview for 30 seconds, using any method you choose (e.g. High Speed Drill, first sentences only etc.).

3 Recall, question and anticipate.

4 At the signal, begin to read for understanding at the fastest possible rate, aiming for 70% comprehension.

1 *Scanning* is a technique which efficient readers use frequently. It is so closely associated with *skimming* that the terms are sometimes confused. In this course, *skimming* means a way of rapid reading for understanding, when total comprehension is not necessary—at least for the moment. *Scanning*, however, is not really reading at all.

2 *Scanning* is the skill used for finding specific information quickly: a word in the dictionary, the answer to a particular question, facts about a certain person or topic, or a particular passage to reread. It involves running the eyes over material, without really reading it, until the wanted item or passage is recognized. Then scanning stops and some other appropriate technique takes over.

3 Everyone uses scanning in everyday life: to pick out a brother from among the passengers getting off a train, to find the yam stalls in a strange market, to locate a particular book on a bookshelf, to look up an address in a directory. We scan the crowd at the train station, the market, the bookshelf or the relevant page of the directory for the special person or item we wish to find.

4 In each case, we have a mental picture of what we are looking for. We know roughly where to look for it, and we are intent upon finding it. Thus we run our eyes over the faces or scene or books or names, without focusing or 'paying attention', until we recognize what we are seeking. It will seem to stand out from all the rest because it matches the image which has been brought to the front of our conscious minds.

5 Recognition is easy when the object of the search matches the picture in the mind and when the area to be scanned is limited. That is why anyone can learn to look up words in the dictionary very quickly once he is familiar with alphabetical order.

6 *Search-reading* is the name sometimes given to a more difficult form of scanning. In search-reading, the reader is looking for specific information, but he does not know what the exact wording or appearance will be and may not even know the general location. He must look without the benefit of a clear mental image of what he is to find. Yet there are three ways a reader can think ahead to ensure success in this kind of scanning too.

7 First, he must have the question he wants answered firmly in mind, e.g. 'Does the author discuss any of the crops grown in my area?' 'Will this book give me any new

information about 19th century patterns of social organization in what is now Nigeria?'

8 Next, he should think where the information he wants is most likely to be. A book's table of contents may lead him to the right chapter; the index may lead him to the right page. Within a chapter or article it is sometimes necessary to begin skim-reading in order to find the section for scanning or search-reading.

9 Third, the reader should have in mind the kinds of words likely to be used in giving the information. For a geography student seeking information about agricultural development in his part of the country, these would be phrases such as *land use*, *soil erosion*, *fertilizer trials* and *improved yields*. He would also be on the alert for the names of places and areas within his region, used in association with these phrases.

10 Search-reading and skimming are visually similar. The difference is that search-reading is concerned primarily with locating information; there is no attempt to understand or remember any other material the eyes pass over. In skimming, on the other hand, the reader seeks out the author's organization, and tries to understand some of the material for a particular purpose, e.g. to decide whether and how to read more thoroughly, to grasp the main points before rereading for detail, or to review what has already been learned.

11 The chief value of scanning and search-reading is that they are so much faster than skimming and can effect great savings of time. Further, a reader who learns to scan for specific information usually finds that he can recognize information related to his interests even when he is not especially looking for it. For example, a good reader scanning the newspaper for important world news is likely to notice an article on his home town as well. With practice, it becomes almost as easy to spot an article related to current classwork or some topic of campus debate as it is to recognize a friend in the refectory. Words or ideas with special meaning for us almost jump from the page to attract our attention.

12 Learning to scan and search-read makes it possible to use dictionaries, indexes, encyclopedias, atlases and other reference books more efficiently. These skills enable a reader to select what he wants to read from newspapers, magazines, reports and books without wasting time and effort. They are also very useful skills in reviewing. For example, a student who plans to write an essay on the development of a certain character in a novel can scan or search-read to find the references to that character.

13 By eliminating quickly what he doesn't need, a reader has more time to concentrate on what he does need.

(850 words)

Record your time and WPM. Go on to the questions.

1 The passage is mainly about
a the difference between skimming and scanning.
b recognizing words quickly in the dictionary.
c forming mental pictures.
d locating specific information.

2 Scanning is
a reading without understanding.
b a way of rapid reading for understanding.
c not really reading at all.
d a technique used mostly for reading the newspaper.

3 Scanning is appropriate for all of the following except
a locating a particular passage to reread.
b finding a friend in a crowded room.
c reading for the main ideas.
d using the index of a book.

4 Search-reading is
a a more difficult form of skimming.
b a more difficult form of scanning.
c a way of rapid reading for understanding.
d a way of finding out how the material is organized.

5 The passage lists ---------- ways a reader can think ahead while search reading.
a many *b* two *c* five *d* three

6 According to the passage, the first way a reader should think ahead is to have in mind
a a determination to concentrate. *b* the vocabulary of the subject.
c the author's organization. *d* the question he wants answered.

7 The passage implies that
a finding a word in the dictionary is easier than finding a friend in a crowd.
b scanning is more useful than skimming.
c practice in scanning increases a reader's general ability to recognize relevant information.
d scanning is not possible unless the exact wording is known.

8 It can reasonably be inferred from the passage that speed in scanning is affected most of all by
a how specific the question is and the form of the answer.
b what the reader already knows about the subject.
c the length of the passage.
d the extent of the reader's vocabulary in the subject.

9 Scanning and search-reading improve efficiency by helping to eliminate
a bad habits. *b* the need to skim.
c unnecessary material. *d* regression.

10 Scanning and search-reading are worth practising mainly because they
a improve concentration. *b* save time and effort.
c increase eye span. *d* develop reading speed.

K

WORDS PER MINUTE CHART: Timed Reading Passage 6 *(850 words)*									
Time	WPM	Time	WPM	Time	WPM	Time	WPM	Time	WPM
1.00	—	2.00	425	3.00	285	4.00	210	5.00	170
10	—	10	390	10	270	10	205	10	165
20	640	20	365	20	255	20	195	20	160
30	570	30	340	30	245	30	190	30	155
40	520	40	320	40	230	40	180	40	150
50	465	50	300	50	220	50	175	50	145

Follow-up

A. Scanning and search-reading practice

This exercise is like a race. The object is to see how quickly you can finish.

> The answers to the following questions are contained in Passage 6, but they are given in words different from those in the questions. At the signal, begin to search the passage for the answer to the first question. When you find it, note the number of the paragraph in which it occurs. You do not need to write the answer. Then look for the second answer, and so on. If you get stuck, go on to the others and go back later. When you finish, put up one hand and with the other jot down the time your lecturer is pointing to.

1 What is the author's definition of scanning?

2 What conditions sometimes make it hard to recognize the information we want?

3 How is search-reading different from ordinary scanning?

4 What are some uses of scanning?

5 Why is it easy to find a relative at the station?

6 How is skimming different from scanning and search-reading?

7 What can a reader do to reduce the amount of material he must scan or search-read?

K (Which answers were easiest and which most difficult to locate? Why?)

B. Recall practice

Now, without looking back, try to answer each of the questions in A above. Then check up on your recall by scanning again to locate the answer and compare your version with what the passage states.

C. More scanning and search-reading practice

1 Time yourself on this exercise, or compete with a friend to see who finishes first. Try to improve on your time when you look up other sets of five words.

> The following words from the passage all have more than one meaning. Look each one up in your dictionary, then select the definition closest to the meaning of the word as it is used in the passage. Jot down the page number and the appropriate meaning for each. Scan to locate the word, and search-read to determine which meaning is applicable.

a recognize *b* focus *c* alert *d* association *e* character

2 For many students, scanning is one of the most difficult of all reading skills. If this is true for you, do not be discouraged and give up. Just keep practising—when reading the newspapers, reviewing a textbook chapter, or rereading parts of a novel—and you will soon discover that this skill is saving you time and increasing your efficiency.

3 The following topics are referred to in more than one place in this book. Use the index to locate the various references; then search-read to find the information: *a* paragraphs *b* sentences *c* punctuation *d* revision *e* bibliographies

Related Skills: Using a Library

A. Know your library

Since a library is the independent learner's powerhouse, the hours you spend exploring your library's resources can be among the most profitable hours you ever invest as a student. The questions below will show you what you most need to find out. First see how many of the questions you can answer now; then search out what you don't know.

How will you do that? Most colleges and universities issue a Guide to the Library. Get a copy and study it, along with the information given later in this unit. If the librarian or your lecturer organizes a guided tour, be sure to attend. You will also learn a great deal from doing the exercises in this Unit because they require you to go to the library and *use* it. Finally, if you need information and advice which is not covered in the Guide, in class or in this unit, ask for it. Advanced students and lecturers can help, as well as library staff.

HOW WELL DO YOU KNOW THE LIBRARY?

1 Where, exactly, are each of the following located in your library?
a subject card catalogue
b information desk (or readers' services desk)
c general encyclopedias
d English dictionaries
e books in the lending section related to your major subjects
f current periodicals related to your major subjects
g reference books related to your major subjects
h books you can borrow on a specific topic you are interested in
i fiction by local authors
j index to books currently on reserve
k periodicals catalogue (serials catalogue)
l this week's newspapers
m books on the history of your country
n government publications
o atlases
p photocopy machine

2 What are the opening and closing times for the library
a during the week?
b at the weekend?

3 Explain how to
a borrow a book.
b return a book.
c renew a book.

4 How many books may you have out at a time and for how long?
5 *a* If a book is *on reserve*, what does this mean?
b What are the rules for using books on reserve?
c How can you find out if a particular book is on reserve?
6 What are the penalties for
a overdue books?
b damaged or lost books?
c unauthorized removal of books from the library?
7 *a* What is the name of the classification system your library uses for organizing and arranging its materials?
b How many main classes are there and how are they denoted?
8 List the subjects you are studying. Then, depending on the classification system used by your library, give the numbers *or* the letters which represent these subjects.
9 For each of these terms, say what is meant and give an example:
a class mark
b call number
c location mark
10 Describe the process of locating a book on the shelves if you know that its call number is 916.69 *or* if its call number is PR 9387.9
.A28
11 If a book you want is not on the shelves, what further steps can you take to try and locate it?
12 What types of card catalogue does your library provide for readers?
13 Explain clearly how you would find out whether your library has
a any books written by local writers.
b a book for which you know only the title: *Scientists Must Write*.
c books about libraries and how to use them.
14 Rearrange these headings in the order they would appear in an author/title catalogue:

African Women	African Political Parties
Agriculture in Nigeria	The African Awakening
Africanus	Afikpo, A.E.
African Food Production Systems	Africa Yearbook and Who's Who
Agricultural Development in Nigeria	African Cultural Development

15 For each of these terms, say what is meant and give a specific example:
a reference book *d* periodicals index
b subject encyclopedia *e* abstracts
c bibliography *f* microform
16 For each of the following, name one specific example and tell how you would go about finding the required information in it:
a general encyclopedia *d* handbook
b subject dictionary *e* yearbook
c atlas
17 Choose a specific example of each of the following. Then name any appropriate reference source for the kind of information asked for in parentheses:
a one of your main subjects (basic reference books and recommended reading)
Sample answer:

chemistry — Guide to the Literature of Chemistry

b any topic you need to know more about (general background)
c an important term or concept in one of your major subjects (explanation)
d any scientific or technical field (recent advances)

e any specific country (key facts)
f any sport (world records)
g a famous historical figure (biographical data)
h any topic related to your studies (where to find recent journal articles on the topic)

18 Name any three journals relevant to your studies which your library subscribes to.

19 *a* For any book you choose, record the information you would need if you were going to include this book in a bibliography. Pay attention to the arrangement and to the punctuation.
b Do the same for an article in a journal.

20 *a* What is the name of your college or university librarian?
b Find out the names and posts of any other two members of library staff who might be helpful to you.

Go on to the rest of this unit. When you finish, return to the quiz and fill in the gaps.

B. Locating books in a library

To locate the books you need in the library, you must know how they are arranged on the shelves—the classification system—and how to use the card catalogues. The information summarized here on these aspects of library use will prepare you for the practical exercises in the next session. Use SQ3R to understand it.

LIBRARY CLASSIFICATION AND SHELF ARRANGEMENT

1 Libraries are arranged according to a recognized *classification system* which puts books on the same subject together on the shelves and near to books on related subjects. Each book or journal is classified according to its subject and labelled with an identifying code, or *call number*, which serves as its address in the library. The classification also appears on all catalogue cards for the book. So, whether you look up an author or a title to find out if the library has a certain book, or you look up a subject to find out what books are available, you will always be given the call number you need to locate a specific book. Since the arrangement of the shelves is in classified order, the book should be easy to find (if it is there) and easy to reshelve in its proper place if you decide not to use it.

2 *The Dewey Decimal System* of classification is used by many state, school and college libraries. Devised by an American librarian named Melvil Dewey, it uses numbers decimally and is very easy to understand. As you can see from Table 3, it divides all knowledge into ten main classes (e.g. 500s for Sciences) and each of these into ten smaller classes (e.g. 530s Physics, 540s Chemistry). Any of the resulting 100 groups can in turn be divided, and subdivided, as far as is necessary, e.g. 916 Geography in Africa, 916.9 Geography of Nigeria, 916.695 Geography of Northern Nigeria. The principle is to work from the general to the particular, with each move to the right indicating a more specific aspect of the general subject. Large libraries which have many books on the same subject achieve more precision by completing the call number with the first three letters of the author's surname. A book with the call number 916.9 OLA would then be shelved before one with the call number 916.9 UDO.

3 University libraries often favour the more detailed *Library of Congress System* because it provides an exact place for the smallest possible sub-topic; it takes its name from the United States Library of Congress in Washington, D.C., where it was developed. This system, outlined in Table 4, divides knowledge into twenty-one main classes, each represented by a single letter of the alphabet, e.g. Q for Sciences. A second capital letter is added to denote divisions of these classes, e.g. QC Physics, QD Chemistry. Further divisions and specific aspects of a subject are indicated by a number, which may range from 1 to 9999, to give a *class mark* such as GF 721. Usually this is enough identification for you to locate the book, but the complete call number always includes also a letter/number combination indicating the author, e.g. F55, and sometimes an additional combination is inserted to represent some further subdivision, e.g.

GF 721 (class mark)
.N6 F55 (subdivision by country – Nigeria, plus author number).

Although all material on the same subject will have the same class mark, some items, such as reference books and periodicals, will be shelved in separate sequences. For any item kept elsewhere than in the Lending Section, you will find a *location mark* either before or after the call number, to tell you in which room it belongs.

Stop to recall. Note the numbers/letters in the two systems which represent the subjects you are studying. Check your Guide for the location marks used in your library and for any other information on classification and shelf arrangement.

Table 3

The Dewey Decimal Classification System

Main classes

000–099 General works, e.g. libraries, general encyclopedias, journalism
100–199 Philosophy and Psychology
200–299 Religion
300–399 Social Sciences, including Law and Education
400–499 Languages
500–599 Science
600–699 Applied Sciences
700–799 Arts and Recreation
800–899 Literature and Rhetoric
900–999 Geography, Biography and History

Examples of sub classes

500 Sciences
- 510 Mathematics
- 520 Astronomy
- 530 Physics
- 540 Chemistry
- 550 Geology
- 560 Fossils
- 570 Life Sciences
- 580 Botany
- 590 Zoology

Examples of further subdivisions

570 Life Sciences
- 574 Biology
  - 574.1 Physiology
  - 574.2 Pathology
  - 574.3 Development and maturation
  - 574.4 Anatomy
  - 574.5 Ecology
  - 574.6 Economic biology
  - 574.8 Tissues, cellular biology
  - 574.9 Geographical treatment

575 Organic Evolution and Genetics
576 Microbes
578 Microscopy in Biology
590 Zoology
- 591.1–591.9 (same as for 574)
- 592 Invertebrates (animals without backbones)
- 593 Protozoa, Metazoa, e.g. sponges, corals, jellyfish
- 594 Molluscs, e.g. slugs, snails, sea shells
- 595 Other Invertebrates, e.g. worms, spiders, insects
  - 595.7 Insects
    - 595.71–595.79 Specified orders of insects
- 596 Vertebrates
- 597 Fishes
- 598 Reptiles and Birds
- 599 Mammals
  - 599.1–599.9 Specific orders of mammals

960 History of Africa
- 961 North Africa
- 962 Countries of the Nile
- 966 West Africa
  - 966.4 Sierra Leone
  - 966.7 Ghana
  - 966.9 Nigeria
    - 966.91 Lagos
    - 966.92 Western Nigeria
    - 966.94 Eastern Nigeria
      - 966.941 East Central State 1967–76
        - 966.9411 Anambra State 1976–
      - 966.942 South Eastern State 1967–76
        - 966.9421 Cross River State 1976–
    - 966.95 Northern Nigeria
      - 966.951 Kano State 1967–76
        - 966.9511 Kano State 1976–

Table 4

The Library of Congress Classification Scheme

Main classes, with examples of subdivisions

A General Works, e.g. encyclopedias, directories

B Philosophy, Psychology and Religion
- B-BD Logic and Philosophy
- BF Psychology
- BL Religion, Mythology
- BP Islam
- BR-BX Christianity and the Bible

C General History
- CB History of Civilization
- CC Archaeology
- CT General Biography

D History (except Americas)
- DA Great Britain
- DE Classical Antiquity
- DS Asia, Islam
- DT Africa

E History of North America

F Local American History, the West Indies, Latin America

G Geography, Anthropology, Folklore, Recreation
- GB Physical Geography
- GC Oceanography
- GF Human Geography, Regional Geography
- GH Economic, Political and Historical Geography
- GL Town Planning
- GN Anthropology, Ethnology
- GR Folklore
- GV Recreation, Sports and Games

H Social Sciences
- HA Statistics
- HB-HF Economics
- HG-HJ Finance and Accounting
- HM-HV Sociology

J Political Science
JF Public Administration
JQ Politics: Asia, Africa
JX International Relations

K Law

L Education
LA History of Education
LB Theory of Education
LF Education in particular countries

M Music

N Fine Arts

P Language and Literature
PB General Literature, Theatre, Film, Journalism
PE English Language
PN Literary History and Criticism
PR Literature in English (including African authors)
PS American Literature

Q Sciences
Q General Science, History and Philosophy of Science
QA Mathematics and Computing
QC Physics
QD Chemistry
QE Geology
QH General Biology and Microscopy
QK Botany
QL Zoology
QM Human Anatomy
QP Physiology and Biochemistry
QR Bacteriology and Microbiology

R Medicine
RA Public Health
RC Internal Medicine, Tropical Medicine, Psychiatry
RD Surgery
RG Gynaecology and Obstetrics
RM Pharmacology
RT Nursing

S Agriculture
SB Plant Culture and Horticulture
SD Forestry
SF Animal Culture and Veterinary Medicine
SH Fish Culture

T Technology
TA Civil Engineering
TH Building Construction
TJ Electrical Engineering
TK Mechanical Engineering
TN Mining and Metallurgy
TP Chemical Technology
TR Photography
TX Home Economics

U Military Science

V Naval Science

Z Bibliography and Library Science

Examples of further subdivisions

DT History of Africa
DT 364–469 History of East Africa
DT 471–720 History of West Africa
DT 515 History of Nigeria

QM Human Anatomy
QM 1–511 General
QM 531–549 Regional
QM 550–575 Human Histology
QM 601–679 Human Embryology

CARD CATALOGUES

The card catalogues are the index to the entire library, telling you what it has and where each item is located, and often leading you to shelves where you would never have thought of looking for information on a particular topic.

For each book in the library, at least three cards are made, for filing alphabetically by *author*, by *title* and by *subject*. As Figure 13 shows, the cards are alike except for the headings at the top. Many libraries file the author and title cards in one alphabetical sequence called the *author/title catalogue*, with subject cards forming a separate *subject catalogue*. Instead of a subject catalogue, some libraries using the Dewey Decimal system have a *classified catalogue* in which the cards are arranged in call number order; readers then have to consult a *subject index* nearby to find out what numbers to look under for the topics they want.

Besides the call number, a catalogue gives these facts, which you must record for any book you intend to use for a written assignment, e.g. a research paper:

—author/editor/compiler (last name first)
—full title (and edition, if relevant)
—place, publisher and date.

To save time, library typists capitalize only the first word and proper nouns in a title and do not underline the title, but you should capitalize all the important words and underline the title when you record it, because these are the conventions for a bibliography.

Author card

```
CHANDLER, George                                  011.02
                                                  CHA

How to find out: printed and on-line sources.
5th ed.  Oxford: Pergamon Press, 1982.

xviii, 250p.
```

Title card

```
How to find out                                   011.02
                                                  CHA

CHANDLER, George

How to find out: printed and on-line sources.
5th ed.  Oxford: Pergamon Press, 1982.

xviii, 250p.
```

Subject card

```
REFERENCE BOOKS - Bibliography                    011.02
                                                  CHA

CHANDLER, George

How to find out: printed and on-line sources.
5th ed.  Oxford: Pergamon Press, 1982.

xviii, 250p.
```

Figure 13: Author, title and subject card for the same book (Dewey Decimal classification).

A title card

```
Africa remembered                           DT
                                            471
CURTIN, Philip D.  ed.                      .C8

Africa remembered: narratives by West Africans
from the era of the slave trade, edited by
Philip D. Curtin.  With introductions and
annotations by Philip D. Curtin (and others).
Madison, Wisconsin: University of Wisconsin
Press, 1967.

x, 363p.  illus, facsims, geneol tables, maps,
ports.

Bibliographical footnote
```

A subject card

```
AFRICA, WEST - Hist.                              DT
                                                  471
Ajayi, J.F. Ade,     ed.                          .A4

A thousand years of West African history;
a handbook for teachers and students, edited
by J. F. Ade Ajayi and Ian Espie; with a
forward by K. O. Dike.  Ibadan: Ibadan
University Press, 1965.

xii, 549p.  maps, diagrs.

Bibliography: pp. 501-511
```

Figure 14: Catalogue cards which include descriptive notes (Library of Congress classification).

Practice in Using the Library

Set aside as much time as you can for getting to know the library. You will probably discover that using a library is both less difficult and far more rewarding than you now imagine.

A. Get to know the shelf arrangement

Tour the shelves in the lending section, beginning at the 000's or A's and ending with the 990's or Z's. Note especially the location of shelves containing books on the subjects you are studying. Stop occasionally to 'read' a shelf: look at the call numbers of the books as they stand on the shelves to note their order and see how the classification system works in practice. (This will also help you appreciate the importance of never replacing a book you have been looking at 'just anywhere' on the shelves.)

Make a sketch plan of the shelf arrangement in the lending section. Then, in the appropriate spaces of your plan, write in the numbers, e.g. 330s, 370s, 916s or the letters, e.g. DT, LA, PE, representing the subjects you are studying.

B. Use the card catalogues

Go to the card catalogues. Note the types, look at any instructions or labelled examples provided, and look at the guide letters on the drawer fronts, e.g. AAR-ADA, to discover the general sequence. Do some of the exercises below, then make up similar ones of your own, jotting down author, title and call number for any book you wish to try finding on the shelf. Experimenting and practising will develop speed in using alphabetical order, a knowledge of filing rules and the ability to choose the 'right' key words in looking up a subject.

1 Go to the author/title catalogue and try to find the title card for a book you expect the library to own, e.g. a recommended text. Study the information given. You might also try to find the author card for the same book.

2 Look up any writer in the author/title catalogue, e.g. Achebe, Soyinka. If there are several cards, note how these are arranged, and compare the call numbers. Is the same author also listed in the subject catalogue? i.e. Does the library have books *about* as well as *by* him or her?

3 Scan through the cards in any drawer of the author/title catalogue to find an example of any three of the following:
a A book written or edited by two or more persons (a *joint author* or *joint editor* entry).
b A book whose 'author' is a government body, an institution, a society or association (a *corporate entry*).
c A book kept in the reference room.
d A journal or other periodical (serial) publication.
e An item kept in some other collection, e.g. Africana, government publications.

4 In the subject catalogue (or list of subject headings), look up two countries or geographical regions, e.g. Africa, Nigeria, your state, Ghana, Great Britain, India. Note how much drawer space is taken up by cards with your chosen headings, how the major heading is subdivided, e.g. AFRICA – WEST and how cards with the same heading/subheading (or the same call number in a classified catalogue) are arranged.

5 Look up any two subjects you study, e.g. BIOLOGY, EDUCATION, noting how much drawer space is taken up, how the subject is divided and how the cards are arranged. Look at the cards before and after to find headings with related words, e.g. BIOLOGICAL . . . EDUCATIONAL . . .

6 Think of headings under which you might find information on some aspect of the subject and look them up, e.g. ANIMAL BEHAVIOUR, ECOLOGY, BOTANY. If there are many cards, try a more specific topic, e.g. MAMMALS instead of ZOOLOGY. If there are no cards, try a more general heading, e.g. INSECTS instead of COCKROACHES.

> List briefly any three discoveries you have made about the way a card catalogue is organized and arranged or how to use it.

7 Select from the catalogue two or three books you think would be worth finding and try to locate them on the shelves. (Even if you do not find them, your use

of the catalogue will have led you to shelves with other books on the same or similar topics.) Preview the selected titles, if found, and also some of the surrounding books, for the purpose of choosing the most useful ones. Make bibliography slips for any you might use again.

Bibliography slips
Divide a sheet of paper into six or eight equal parts. Use two of them to make bibliography slips for two of the books you have previewed:

1 Record the call number in the upper right hand corner of the slip.

2 Turn to the title page and record from it
—the author(s) or editor(s)
—the full title (and edition, if relevant)
—the place of publication and name of publisher

3 Turn over the title page to find the latest copyright or revision date and record that. (Ignore the dates of mere reprints.)

4 At the bottom add a brief note as to what you might use the book for, or give the title of a chapter you would read.

Bibliography slips are essential for term papers and useful in general because you can add to, discard and rearrange them as needed. They can be kept together in an envelope or with a rubber band.

C. Get to know reference books

To give yourself some idea of the tremendous range and variety of reference books available for all fields, make a tour of the reference room, following classified order and scanning the shelves for titles which might be of interest to you. Then try the exercises below which will help you to get acquainted with general reference works and introduce you to those dealing with your major subjects. A book which might assist in building up your own personal list of potentially useful reference works is the one used for Figure 13, here given as it would appear in a bibliography:
Chandler, George. *How to Find Out: Printed and On-Line Sources*, 5th ed. Oxford: Oxford University Press, 1982.

1 Go to the 030 or the A section of the reference room and find out what general encyclopedias your library has and which is most recent. Do some sampling, i.e. locate and skim the advice on using the encyclopedia, note whether there are any special volumes (e.g. Index), use the guide letters of the spine to find articles on particular topics. Compare the treatment of the same topic in different encyclopedias as to length, reading difficulty, illustrations, questions at the end, etc.

Also look up the same topic in the indexes, noting how much information on a subject is offered in articles other than the main entry. (If you are using a recent edition of the *Encyclopaedia Britannica*, begin with an article in the *Micropaedia*, which will lead you to further information in the *Macropaedia*.)

For any topic you choose, say which of two encyclopedias would be more useful if you were researching the topic, and briefly give reasons for your choice. Record the title of each encyclopedia, the number and/or date of the editions you are using, and the volume number, e.g.

Encylopaedia Britannica, 15th ed. (1974), *Micropaedia 14*

2 Go to the 420 or the PE section of the reference room and browse among the general dictionaries there, noting the general features of each. Look also at some of the dictionaries devoted to special aspects of English, e.g. slang, idioms.

Give the full titles and dates of any two general dictionaries and then say which one has the clearer instructions on how to use it and which, in your opinion, treats the words you look up more satisfactorily. If there are any outstanding features, mention them.

Give the full titles and dates of any two dictionaries which deal with some aspect of English; one of these can be a translation dictionary (e.g. English–Hausa) if you wish.

3 Many students do not realize that atlases are useful in nearly every field (e.g. *Atlas of the Earth* has 'something for everyone') and that there are specialized as well as general ones: historical, economic, political, scientific and medical. Because of their size, atlases are usually kept on a special stand. Examine some of them.

Give the titles and dates for two atlases in your library, at least one of which contains information of special relevance to your own studies. Say what you looked up or found in each one.

4 Experienced scholars and advanced students often begin library research by consulting a bibliography such as *African Research and Documentation* or *Current Geographical Publications*, or a list of sources on a particular topic. At this stage, you may find a guide to the literature of your subject more useful. (Chandler's *How to Find Out* is an example of a general guide.)

Use the card catalogue or consult an advanced student, lecturer or librarian to find out about at least one guide to the literature or important bibliography in one of your subject areas. Make out a bibliography slip for it.

5 The number of reference books for specific subjects is enormous and they are of many different types, e.g. *Dictionary of the Earth Sciences*, *Shorter Encyclopedia of Islam*, *The Writer's Handbook*, *Who's Who in Nigeria*, *Industrial Directory of Nigeria*. Use a guide to the literature and the card catalogue, browse on the appropriate shelves and preview to find subject reference books likely to be of use to you in future. Note how each is arranged and look for instructions on how to use the book.

Make out bibliography slips for at least five subject reference works you might need to consult for your studies. At the bottom say how each is arranged (e.g. alphabetically, by region, by categories).

You can add other slips from time to time. They might usefully be kept in call number order.

D. Get to know periodicals

Journals and magazines (i.e. periodicals) are so vital a source of up-to-date information that some researchers, e.g. in science and medicine, use them much more than they do books. Get acquainted with the journals in your fields of study, beginning with the current issues of the most general and readable ones, e.g. *New Scientist*. First tour the room where current journals are kept, following classified order. Stop to look in the periodicals (serials) catalogue to see how it works. Browse among the journals with class marks representing your subjects and interests. Scan the tables of contents for articles which look readable and relevant.

Choose one article each from any two journals and record this information on a bibliography slip, arranged as in the example below: author of article, title of article, title of periodical, volume and/or number (and/or date), inclusive page numbers of article. Note the punctuation.

Achebe, Chinua PR
'An Image of Africa.' Research in African Literature, 9 (Spring 1978), 1-15. .R

Periodical indexes are systematically arranged lists of articles in journals, giving enough information about each one to enable it to be identified and traced. It would be impossible to keep track of periodical literature without them as there are over 10,000 current journals in the sciences alone, and separate articles number in the millions! Examples are *The Reader's Guide to Periodical Literature*, *Biological and Agricultural Index*, *Education Index*, *Applied Science and Technology Index*.

Abstracts go a step further than indexes, not only listing articles or doctoral dissertations but also summarizing their contents. Examples are *African Abstracts, Biological Abstracts, Science Abstracts, Education Abstracts.*

> Find out what are considered the most important indexes and abstracts for your disciplines. List them and, if possible, have a look at them.

Your first priority should be to learn your way around in the more general reference works. Then you will find the more specialized ones, such as indexes and abstracts, less formidable when the time comes to use them.

E. Find out about special collections

Books recommended by lecturers are often withdrawn from the open shelves and put 'on reserve', where they are available for controlled use within the library, giving more people the chance to use them. You should find out how the index to this collection works, and it is a good idea to check the index from time to time to see if books you should read have been placed on reserve.

It is also worth finding out what is in the library's special collections, e.g. Africana, government publications, etc. and asking who can use them. This may lead you to useful material you would otherwise miss. It may also spare you the frustration of choosing a topic to write on for which essential material is 'out of bounds' to first and second year students.

Assignments

A. Continue or repeat previous assignments

Continue

—reading and patterning of second novel
—adding to glossaries
—adding to your diary of reading and study practice
—reviewing and reducing notes
—correcting language errors in your written work.

B. Improve your study plan

Evaluate your use of the study plan you made last week. How well did it work? Decide what changes need to be made and draw up a plan for the week ahead.

C. Get well acquainted with the library

Become familiar with its various resources and services. Apply to this task as many as possible of the skills introduced so far in this course. Complete the quiz 'How Well Do You Know the Library?' and the practical boxed-off exercises in the Practice section if you have not already done so.

Unit Seven Organizing Information

Timed Reading Passage 7: Noting Relationships: Structuring Information

Instructions

1 Think about the title of the passage.

2 Preview the passage for 30 seconds, using any method you choose.

3 Question and anticipate.

4 At the signal, begin to read for understanding as rapidly as you possibly can.

1 Reading, listening, note taking, studying and writing all involve paying attention to the way material is organized—its structure or pattern of relationships. It is by noting the relationships among ideas, facts, details, words and things that we understand, remember and make ourselves clear to others.

2 A reader or listener comprehends a new fact or idea when he can link it with something he already knows. The more he already knows about the subject, the faster he will understand, because he can attach the new items to 'hooks' available on an existing framework. In previewing, the reader looks for the overall arrangement. In skimming as a way of rapid reading, he looks more closely at arrangement within individual paragraphs to determine what is essential and what is not. In making notes and also in reviewing, a student calls back to mind the basic structure in the form of key words which, in turn, should remind him of any associated ideas he wants to remember. In studying, he will need to read some material several times, each time reinforcing the existing structure while adding more details to it.

3 A good lecturer or writer—including the student writer—first plans what he wants to get across, in what order, and then considers how he can best express the relationships among his thoughts so that others will grasp exactly what he wants to convey. By organizing first, he clarifies his own thinking and improves his presentation.

4 Organizing information is a basic human instinct, on which depends our ability to find things, whether they are tangible objects, ideas on a page or items stored in the memory. Books in a library, words in a dictionary, topics in a textbook, students in a university, courses in a faculty, kinds of plants and animals, members of a clan, functions of government, goods in a shop: any object, person, fact or idea can be classified and assigned a place within particular systems or structures.

5 The process of forming patterns of relationship—either mentally or on paper—is sometimes called *structuring*. Making a key word pattern is a fast and effective way of structuring, whether the purpose is to note the essentials of a chapter or a lecture, to test immediate recall, to review, to think out a course of action, or to plan a talk or an essay.

6 A more formal way to summarize content and organization is the outline. It also expresses structure in a visual way. The relative importance and the interrelationships of facts and ideas are shown by indenting items of equal importance

the same distance from the left-hand margin and assigning the same kind of symbol to them, e.g. A, B, C or 1, 2, 3 or a, b, c. Since each level of subdivision is further toward the centre and has its own type of symbol, the completed outline tells at a glance how important any item is and how it fits into the total pattern.

7 Outlining forces the reader to notice how the items in each new subdivision are related to their more general idea. Are they parts of it? Or do they prove it? Explain it? Illustrate it? Understanding the purpose of details makes them easier to recall and gives the general idea more meaning too.

8 An important aspect of a reader's or listener's skill is his ability to find and use the organizational clues provided by the writer or lecturer. The quality of his notes, key word patterns, outlines, summaries and essays depends on this ability to determine essentials and perceive different types of relationship. The major clues are provided by the order in which facts and ideas are given and by the words and phrases linking them.

9 The most likely place to find essentials is at the beginning. In news reports, for example, the first or 'lead' paragraph gives the most important or newsworthy information. In textbooks, the most common paragraph arrangement is to present a general statement, called the *topic sentence*, and then explain or illustrate it with details. The reader in a hurry can often grasp the gist of an article simply by reading the first sentences of paragraphs.

10 The second most likely place to find essentials is at the end; details accumulate until they lead to a generalization or conclusion. There are variations on these patterns. Sometimes, the topic idea occurs at both beginning and end but in different words. Sometimes there are only details, and the reader must infer the topic idea. If the purpose is to compare or contrast or qualify, there are two or more parts to develop and the reader must be alert for clue words marking the transition between them.

11 If the purpose is to list the steps in a process, the arrangement will be chronological. If it is to describe a scene, movement will follow the writer's eyes in some logical sequence. Other patterns are: question-answer, fact-implications, problem-solution, effect-cause, and cause-effect. In these cases, there may be no expressed topic sentence, but there is always an order, dictated by the purpose. In all cases, the faster the reader can answer the question 'What is the author's purpose here?' the faster he can decide what to read more closely, or what to select as key words.

12 Certain words and phrases also act as clues to purpose and arrangement. Some announce what the reader should look for: 'There are three reasons why . . .' or 'The four steps are . . .'. Other 'signal' words and phrases reveal how the writer's points are related to one another: *Second, another example is, a final reason is,* indicate that the writer is adding more support for a major point. *But, however, yet, in contrast to, nevertheless,* warn that he is changing the direction of the discussion.

13 A paragraph beginning 'This explains . . .' or 'That is why . . .' tells the reader to note the end of the previous paragraph. *For instance, a good example is* or *thus,* announce further elaboration of a point already made. *Consequently, as a result, therefore* or *the outcome is,* signal a conclusion.

14 Picking out essentials and understanding relationships accurately require hard thinking. A good pattern or outline can prove that this thinking has been done.

(1050 words)

Record your time and WPM. Go on to the questions.

1 According to the passage, structuring is
a listing all the members of your clan.
b making a formal outline.
c organizing material according to its relationships.
d a way of classifying information.

2 The passage implies that
a organization is more important for readers than for writers.
b organization is more important for writers than for readers.
c organized information is better understood and remembered.
d an outline is the best means of showing structure.

3 The passage states that details are easier to remember when
a they explain the general idea.
b they illustrate a main point.
c they prove a main point.
d their purpose is understood.

4 A good outline of material you have read should always
a show the relative importance of ideas.
b be brief.
c list points chronologically.
d attach most of the details.

5 The passage implies that the way a writer puts together his facts and ideas is determined primarily by
a their value.
b the details at his command.
c the vocabulary at his command.
d his purpose.

6 Essential ideas are found most often ---------- of a newspaper article.
a at the beginning
b in the last paragraph
c in the middle
d in the longest paragraph

7 The passage states that the topic sentence in a paragraph
a is usually very simple.
b is often followed by details.
c often contains the most difficult words.
d can always be found.

8 The passage mentions ---------- of arranging ideas in a paragraph.
a various ways
b about a dozen logical ways
c the three best ways
d the six most common ways

9 Words such as *finally*, *however*, *therefore* and *also*
a should be ignored in skimming.
b distinguish main ideas from details.
c serve as clues to organization.
d should be included in a pattern or outline.

10 Adding information in the passage to information in previous units, one might conclude that the chief difference between outlines and key word patterns is that
a outlines always give sentences while patterns give key words only.
b patterns show structure visually while outlines do not.
c outlines are more concerned with relationships than patterns are.
d outlines use a conventional form while patterns allow more freedom and creativity.

K

WORDS PER MINUTE CHART: Timed Reading Passage 6 *(1050 words)*													
Time	WPM	Time	WPM	Time	WPM	Time	WPM	Time	WPM	Time	WPM	Time	WPM
1.00	—	2.00	525	3.00	350	4.00	260	5.00	210	6.00	175	7.00	150
10	—	10	485	10	330	10	250	10	205	10	170	10	145
20	—	20	450	20	315	20	245	20	200	20	165	20	145
30	700	30	420	30	300	30	235	30	190	30	160	30	140
40	630	40	395	40	290	40	225	40	185	40	160	40	135
50	575	50	365	50	275	50	220	50	180	50	155	50	135

Follow-up

A. Noting the structure

1 Speed exercise: Beginning on the signal, go through the passage as quickly as possible, reading just enough of the first sentence of each paragraph to determine whether or not it is a topic sentence. If it is, jot down the paragraph number quickly. If it is not, write nothing. In either case, move directly to the beginning of the next paragraph. Ignore all sentences in between. Put up your hand or note the time when you finish. Seconds: ________

2 Return to paragraphs whose numbers you omitted. Can you locate the key sentence, or do you have to supply the topic idea? Can any paragraphs be grouped together because they share the same topic idea?

3 Test your recall of Passage 7 by making a quick pattern, showing the structure. When you have gone as far as you can, finish your review by looking at the pattern on page 123. It was made by a student as part of his review. Would you add anything? Omit anything? Change anything?

B. Achieving coherence

Coherence in a piece of writing is achieved through a variety of linking and transition devices. Paragraphs 12 and 13 give some examples of words and phrases which help a reader to grasp relationships quickly and tell him what to expect next, but such connecting words and phrases are not the only means to coherence. Study the list of devices below and note the examples indicated. Then search out further examples in the passage for yourself.

MEANS OF ACHIEVING COHERENCE

1 **Parallelism** or **parallel structure** means expressing similar ideas, or sentence

elements which are similar in function, in the same grammatical form, as in this example from Passage 9:

> While everyone knows that we learn to speak the kind of language that we hear, not everyone realizes that we tend to write the kind of language that we read.

In the timed passage you have just read, the last four sentences of paragraph 2 begin with *in*+a kind of reading (e.g. *previewing*, *skimming*), making it clear that they are parallel ideas. The first words of paragraphs 9 and 10 provide another example. Look for others.

2 **Repetition** of a key term, for emphasis or deliberate reference (in the same or different words) to an idea already discussed, ties ideas together and helps a reader to follow the thread of thought. Two examples are the word *organizing* at the end of paragraph 3 and beginning of paragraph 4 and the words *outline* and *outlining* in paragraphs 6 and 7.

3 **Transition paragraphs** connect sections of a paper, while *transition sentences* link paragraphs. They remind the reader of what has just been said and form a bridge to the next idea. In paragraph 4, the writer leads in to a discussion of organization as a study skill by establishing that organizing is a normal human activity. The first sentence of paragraph 5 refers to the previous paragraph's idea, then introduces the concept of structuring to be discussed next.

4 **Referring words** are substitutes for other words which have already been mentioned or, less often, are about to be mentioned. They are usually pronouns or relative adjectives, e.g. *he/she, him/her, his/hers, it, its*; *they, them, their*; *who, whom, whose*; *what, which, that*; *this, these*; *that, those*; *there, then*; *one, some*. Another kind of example is *a more formal way* (paragraph 6), which raises the question 'more formal than what?' and thus refers the reader to the way discussed in the previous paragraph.

5 **Subordination** announces the relative importance of ideas within a sentence by putting main ideas in main clauses and less important ideas in subordinate clauses, phrases or single words. In the first sentence of paragraph 4, for example, the main idea is that 'organizing information is a basic human instinct'. The other ideas are subordinate to it.

C. Inferring the topic idea

The authors of the following paragraph wanted to convince readers of a certain point. State as clearly as possible in your own words what the point is; then say what method is used to get it across:

> A group of readers, while being tested on a long passage containing a lot of unnecessary detail, received a signal every five seconds, and the moment they heard it, they automatically marked the place that they had reached. By comparing the number of words that were read during these five second periods, we found that some of the fast readers had read certain significant parts of the text almost as slowly as the slow readers; but they had made up for it elsewhere and there was clear evidence of skimming. The slow readers seemed to take everything as it came, with little variation in speed, except that some of the irrelevant detail was read particularly slowly, instead of being skimmed. The fastest readers had the best comprehension.
>
> (Manya and Eric deLeeuw, *Read Better, Read Faster*, Penguin, 1965)

Having grasped the main point of the passage, pair off with another student and try to give one another a clear account of the experiment, using your own words. What helps you—in the absence of a topic sentence—to infer the topic idea?

D. Memory tests

1 Look at this list of numbers for one minute. Then, without looking, write down as many as you can remember, in the correct order.

4 5 4 7 5 0 5 4 5 9 6 5 7 2 8 0 8 9

If you have not already done so, figure out how the list was constructed. When you discover the principle, try again to list all the numbers in the correct order.

2 Look at this list of words for two minutes, then see how many you can write down without looking again.

yam	comb	knife	pawpaw	shampoo
pen	glass	towel	pencil	cassava
fork	mango	maize	banana	notebook
soap	paper	plate	potato	pineapple
rice	spoon	ruler	orange	toothpaste

If you remembered all, or nearly all, how did you do it? If you couldn't remember many, look now for a way to organize the 25 words for easier recall.

3 Read these nonsense syllables three times, with the intention of reproducing them in order. Then put the page aside and see how many you can write down:

cax	tuj	mib	sef	biw	rof
juk	nuz	fap	goc	mev	laq

Next, read these twelve words three times, trying to memorize them. Test your memory.

hostel	field	shoes	ditch	oranges	newspaper
bridge	road	watch	chair	pen	notes

You will have been more successful with the words than with the nonsense syllables, but you can remember the entire word list, in order, more easily if you link the words in a story which you can visualize, e.g.

> I left the *hostel* and went across the *field*, getting my *shoes* muddy. When I got to the *ditch* I bought *oranges* and a *newspaper* from the sellers there and then crossed the *bridge* onto the *road*. My *watch* told me I was still early so I found a *chair*, took out my *pen* and revised my *notes*.

If you can see yourself doing these things, in order, you will have no difficulty remembering the list, because you have created a *chain of associations*, with each item linked firmly to the next. (When items in a list are less easy to relate to one another than these are, your story will be less sensible, but absurd images are often more easily remembered.) This method of remembering is known as the *Chain Method*.

As these exercises have illustrated, things are easier to remember when they are understood and when they are organized. When you organize (structure) what you have understood, so that the items are part of a system, you are cutting down on the number of separate items you have to hold in mind at once, because one thing leads to others logically associated with it. A single cue, e.g. a key word, can trigger off your memory of the entire structure.

E. Chunking and ordering

Few people can hold more than seven items of information at one time in the memory. However, the seven items do not need to be isolated facts. They can be key words or ideas, or memory aids, which in turn will lead to related items attached to them. The efficient grouping of items to be remembered is known as *chunking*.

When *chunking* is combined with efficient *ordering*—within and between the chunks—the amount of available information is multiplied many times over. Improving your efficiency in chunking and ordering will improve your memory quite remarkably.

1 Look again at the outline of the Dewey Decimal System (pp. 96–98) paying attention to the principles of organization. You have already noted, for example, that the scheme works always from the general to the more particular and the more particular still. What other observations can you make? And can you suggest why school, college and public libraries usually prefer this system?

2 Practice in Chunking: Look at the following list and decide what categories of things are represented. Make each category the heading of a column and under each heading list the items that belong to it.

encyclopedia	reference room	scanning
search reading	previewing	lending section
serials collection	reading room	publisher
place	yearbook	date
appendix	glossary	skimming
handbook	title	title page
card catalogue	subject dictionary	author
reviewing	index	almanac
table of contents		

3 Practice in Ordering

a For each of the following tasks, try to state clearly and in an appropriate order the stages and thought processes involved and then say how you think the information could best be presented on paper:

—Locating the word *structure* in a dictionary

—Naming all the states or provinces of your country

—Listing all the relatives of your own and your parents' generations

—Giving directions from the campus to your house

b Choose at least one of the four tasks and present the information asked for in whatever form you think most effective.

Related Skills

A. Improving sentence clarity

1 Faults which destroy sentence clarity and therefore the coherence of a paragraph include these:

Faulty parallelism: using a mixture of constructions for parallel ideas

Faulty pronoun references: using a pronoun when there is no noun or noun equivalent for it to refer to

Improper subordination of one idea to another: e.g. emphasizing the less important idea

Dangling modifiers: failing to name the subject which a modifier is intended to describe

Misplaced modifier: putting a modifier too far away from the word it is supposed to explain

Most of these faults can be detected if you keep asking these questions:

Does the sentence make good sense?
Is the meaning of every word clear?

2 Identify the faults in these sentences and then write versions which are clear and grammatically correct.

a The book was about a young girl who fell in love and then lost him.
b When reading the book, the character reminded me of you.
c I almost answered every question.
d My dream is to have a good job, a happy family and building a house in my village.
e Stopping all growth, the insects eat the plant off just below the soil.
f The teacher's remarks about bad behaviour referred to Inyang, but Bassey assumed they referred to him. This is often true.
g Calling on one of my classmates, he pronounced 'etiquette' with the *qu* as in *quiet* and even the teacher laughed.
h The professor made it clear during the lecture why plagiarism is wrong on Monday.
i Each of my courses has contributed to my being more intelligent to talk with and to help me learn more efficiently.
j Our new English master knew his subject so well and the learning of English in our lessons was soon made more lively for us by him.

K

B. Notemaking

Start by listing, in key word form, as many reasons as you can think of for making notes from books and lectures. Why has *making* been used instead of *taking*?

NOTEMAKING SHORTCUTS

Selecting key words and omitting unnecessary ones is the first way to streamline notemaking. The second is to arrange the key words to show relationships, by making either a pattern or an outline. A further way to save time is by using symbols and abbreviations.

1 Symbols not only reduce the amount of writing; they also clarify the type of relationship. Note that a particular symbol can be used for a number of different words or phrases which express a similar kind of relationship. Some examples:

Symbol	Meaning	Symbol	Meaning
∴	therefore, thus, then, this being so, with the result that, so that, it implies that	//	is parallel to, alongside
∵	because, since, as a consequence of, resulting from	↑	grows, rises, improves, climbs, helps, increases; growth, rising, improving/improvement, increasing
→	leads to, causes, results in, passes into, becomes, makes	↓	shrinks, declines, falls, gets worse, hinders
←	comes from, leads from, results from, refers back to	>	more than, greater than, more important than, better than
=	is equal to, is the same as, is made up of, represents, is called, is like, may be regarded as	<	less than, smaller than, less important than, worse than
≠	is not equal to, is different from	/	per (e.g. 100 m/hr), or (e.g. he/she)
		&/+	and, also, in addition to, plus the fact that

Symbols should be used not only to record what the writer or speaker has said, but also to indicate what is especially important, what you question, further relationships between one point and another, etc. Some examples:

underline, CAPS, circle box * X .!??

→ Mark it! ←

2 Abbreviations are great time-savers providing you will know what each one means when you return to the notes for revision. There are three kinds of abbreviation:

Standard abbreviations, such as *e.g.*, *cf.*, *i.e.*, *N.B.*, *p.*, *wpm.*, *hr*. Check the abbreviations given in the appendix of your dictionary and learn the ones likely to be of most use to you.

Subject abbreviations, understood by specialists in a certain field, e.g. *Ca* for Calcium or *H* for Hydrogen in chemistry; *L1* and *L2*, for Language 1 and Language 2, in Linguistics.

Personal abbreviations, made up or adopted by you for words used often or in a context where there is no risk of confusion, e.g. *S* for Shakespeare when he is the subject of the lecture. Writing only the first part of a word, or omitting vowels, are two other methods of reducing word length, e.g. *amt*, *b/4*, *cld*, *wld*, *shld*, *expt*, *poss*, *usu*, *w/o* (amount, before, could, would, should, experiment, possible/possibility, usually, without).

NOTEREADING EXERCISE

Try to express the content of the following notes in normal speech. The original paragraphs for the points marked with an asterisk (*) are given on page 117 so that you can see just how they have been reduced in the notes.

Notes

A. <u>Content</u>

- *1. Gd notes <u>product</u> of underst (not substit for) Rephrase, don't copy. <u>Prove</u> underst. Fix in memory
- *2. Bks: Read – pen down. (Mark text?) Write: bk closed. Lectures: Listen to all. Write key pts.
- 3 Like telegram. Symb. Abbrev.
- 4 Label clearly: course, topic, source, date, rev. dates...

B. Form: Should show rel impt and rltnships

- 1. Patterns — Branch — sub-branch
- 2. <u>Outlines</u>:
  - I.
    - A.
      - 1.
        - a.
        - b.
      - 2.
    - B.
      - 1.
      - 2.
  - II. etc.
- *3. <u>Two pg. combination</u>: Pattern || Diagrams, Formulae, Definitions, Quotes
- *4. <u>5R Method</u>:
  - Record – Lv space on L. Write on R.
  - Reduce – Key words on L.
  - Recall – Use key words.
  - Reflect – Complete? Correct? Difficulties?
  - Revise – As needed

C. <u>Layout</u>: v. impt ⟶ Visual IMPACT

- 1. Space: plenty 2. Colour 3. Links
- 4. Dramatize: <u>underline</u>, CAPS, (circle) [box]

** [Mark it.] ! ? ⟶

D. Uses:

- 1. Test recall
- 2. Quick ref. main pts
- 3. Memory aid
- 4. Review: reg.

Sample Original Paragraphs from which Notes were made:

A1 Good notes are the produce of understanding, never a substitute for it. Rephrasing what the author or lecturer has said more briefly and in your own words both demands and proves understanding. It also fixes material in the memory.

A2 It follows that in taking notes from books you should read with pen down. If the book is your own, you may wish to go back to mark and underline important points, or write key words in the margin, but the actual writing of notes should be done with the book closed, or aside. Only thus do you really test your recall. In taking notes from lectures, listen to everything, but write down only the key points, rephrased for brevity.

B3 Different forms of notemaking can sometimes be combined with good effect. One highly recommended form for taking notes, especially from lectures, is to use two pages concurrently, one for key word pattern notes and the other for more linear and graphic information, such as formulas, special lists, definitions, graphs, diagrams and quotations.

B4 Another combination system is the 5R method of notemaking. It involves these steps: **R**ecord, **R**educe, **R**ecite, **R**eflect and **R**eview. In this method, the student leaves the left-hand third of the page blank and *records* notes on the right-hand two thirds. As soon as possible, he *reduces* the fuller notes by writing headings and key words in the left-hand column. Using these key words, he then tries to *recall* the content of the fuller notes. He then *reflects* on his recall: Is it complete? Are there difficulties to clear up? He then *revises* accordingly, making additions and corrections both to the notes and to the information stored in his mind.

NOTEMAKING EXERCISE

If possible, this should be a listening rather than a reading exercise, with your lecturer or a coursemate reading aloud the passage below. You should not look at the paragraph until after you have finished making your notes. Using only your notes, try to give the gist of the paragraph orally, then judge your accuracy by referring to the written version.

Most of the words in standard 'linear' notes are unnecessary for recall purposes. The wastage may be as high as 90% of the words recorded. This becomes more alarming when a closer look is taken at what happens with standard sentence notes. First, time is wasted recording words which have no bearing on memory. More time is wasted later re-reading the same unnecessary words. (In both cases, waste may be as high as 90%.) Further, time is wasted searching for the words which *are* key words because they are usually not distinguished by any marks and thus blend in with the other non-recall words. A fourth problem is that the connections between the key words are interrupted by words which separate them. We know that memory works by association and any interference by non-recall words will make the connections less strong. The key words are separated in time by intervening words and in space by their distance from each other on the page. The longer the time and the greater the distance between connections, the less chance there will be of proper connection being made.

(Adapted from Tony Buzan, *Use Your Head*, BBC.)

C. Outlining

The advice on How to Deal with Examinations which appears on the next pages (Part I: Preparation) and in Unit 12 (Part II: Techniques) might have been written in normal paragraphs. Instead, it has been set out in *sentence outline* form for greater clarity. Most of the outlines you will need to make (e.g. for a research paper) will be *topic outlines* made up of key words, and much less detailed, but the basic system remains the same. Learn the standard system.

1 Symbols are used in this order of priority: **I, A, 1, a, i.** That is, **I** or **II** is always more important than **A** or **B**, and **A** or **B** is always more important than **1** or **2**. You can enter the system where you wish (**A** or **1**) but from then on you can only use symbols to the right in the priority list.

You can have		but not	
	1.		**A.**
	a)		**I.**
	b)		**II.**

2 Symbols of the same type represent items of the same level of importance and of less importance than items to the left. For example, **a, b** and **c** will be parts of, examples of or reasons for the **1** above them and to the left.

3 Symbols of the same type are always placed directly under one another. Use a ruler to line them up if necessary. If an entry takes more than one line, begin the successive lines directly under the first word of the first line, never to the left of it. The outline loses some of its point if you spoil its visual clarity by violating left-hand margins.

4 There must be at least two items at each level, e.g. if there is a **1**, then there must also be a **2**. If you divide anything, you get at least two parts! Reference to the next pages should make these points clear.

Study and Notemaking Practice: How to Deal with Examinations: Part 1

Reduce the following information on preparing for examinations to one page of notes. You may use key words, symbols, abbreviations, sketches, patterns, outlining or any combination of these. The result should be visually clear, show relationships accurately, and enable you to bring back to mind the points you have represented in reduced form.

Sound preparation + effective technique = success in examinations

I. PREPARATION FOR EXAMINATIONS

A. **Start early** (i.e. on the first day of the course)

1. Find out about the course:
   a) What will it cover?
   b) What will you be expected to know at the end of it?
   c) How will your knowledge be tested?
2. Prevent forgetting by revising regularly
   as preventing forgetting is much easier than relearning;
   takes far less time than relearning;
   is more effective than relearning.
   a) Without revision, we forget about 80% of what we have read or heard within the next 24 hours.

b) With a few minutes' immediate revision, we can recall most of the material after 24 hours.
c) With a few minutes' revision
  i) the same day
  ii) the next day
  iii) a week later
  iv) a month later
forgetting is prevented, and the information goes into your 'long term memory' store.
d) Besides, there is never enough time to relearn everything.
e) Also, regular revision helps you learn new material faster:
the more you already know,
the more 'hooks' you have available for attaching new information.
f) If you keep the memory level high, then
  i) you will not have to cram, stay up all night, and enter the exam room in a state of panic;
  ii) you can get a good night's sleep before the exam and enter the room feeling calm, confident and clear-headed.

3. If you have not revised systematically thus far, then at least:
a) Start now.
b) Revise and use the information already presented in Units 4 and 5 on how to review.
c) Determine to start earlier and do better next semester.

B. Find out about each examination

The more you know about what to expect,
the better you can plan what and how to study and
the less anxious you will be.

1. When is the examination, and where?
2. What time does it start and how long does it last?
3. What topics will it cover? Will any topics in the syllabus be omitted? Will any topics studied independently be included?
4. What form will the questions take: objective testing, short answer, essays, problems, or a combination of these?
5. Will the questions be based on lectures, textbook, other assigned reading, lab work or some combination of these?
6. How many questions will you need to complete?
Are any questions compulsory?
Is there choice within questions?
7. What percentage of the total marks will be assigned to the different kinds of questions?
8. Are any past papers available?

C. Make a revision timetable for the last weeks

1. Write in the examinations you will take: date, time, place, length. The examination dates are your deadlines.
2. Write in the lectures you will attend during the revision period. The last lectures before an examination may be the most useful ones to attend. It is a mistake to miss them.
3. For each subject, make a list of the topics to be revised.
a) Decide on the order of importance of the topics and the relative amounts of time needed for revising them.
b) Put your lists up on the wall and/or carry them about with you and tick off the items as you revise them so you can see how you are progressing.

4. Write in your revision sessions: what you will revise when.
   a) Be specific. Write in the topic, not the larger subject, e.g. Fungi/forces/gases NOT Biol/Physics/Chem.
   b) Allow for emergencies, e.g. It sometimes happens, unfortunately, that an examination date is brought forward for some reason, with little advance notice. Arrange to complete your fundamental revision *before* the scheduled date so you are not caught unprepared. If all goes as originally planned, you will have extra time for still further revision.
   c) Limit each session to an hour or less.
   d) Allow for planned breaks:
      i) Within a session, take a three minute break each half hour: stand up and stretch, touch your toes, take deep breaths, look into the distance . . .
      ii) Between sessions, take 5 to 10 minutes: get a drink, go to the toilet, juggle oranges, do some calisthenics, run on the spot . . .
      iii) Before a break, stop to recall what you have just learned.
      iv) After a break, recall what you already know on the topic and set your goals for the coming study session. Aim to achieve your goals.
   e) Allow for repeats of the same topic, or for combining related topics.
   f) Plan to revise several topics a day, for the sake of variety and interest.
5. Plan some time for socializing, for physical activity or for getting away from the tense revision atmosphere.
6. During the revision period, limit your working hours (including lecture time) to 50 hours a week.

D. Revise by doing what the examination will require you to do

1. Examinations require you to recall information (not merely recognize it) and to use it in new ways.
   Therefore, revision time should be spent:
   a) proving that you can recall the facts and ideas;
   b) re-organizing, re-combining and applying what you have learnt.
2. Do not waste time merely rereading the text or your notes. Instead:
   a) Try to frame questions which you would ask if you were the lecturer. In forming the questions, make use of
      i) headings and subheadings in the text (or your notes);
      ii) key words in the margins of your notes or text.
   b) Make sure you can answer the questions adequately.
      Prove that you can, by:
      i) saying the answer to yourself or to someone else;
      ii) jotting down the main points, then checking them against the original.
3. Make your review as much as possible a *new view* of the topic.
   a) Revise at the same time all the material you have on the topic: from text, lectures, supplementary reading, lab work, tests, returned essays . . .
   b) Concentrate first on the most important ideas. Then learn as many relevant supporting details as you have time for. As with your initial study reading, it is best to work from the general to the particular.
   c) Revise two or three related topics at the same time, noting how they are linked together. This will:
      i) give you more associations for each fact or idea;
      ii) increase your chances of remembering—by association—what the examination asks for.
   d) If the topic can be approached from several points of view, force yourself to think out arguments supporting different opinions or to plan two or three different approaches to the topic.
   e) Be critical, particularly of your own notes.

i) Read the notes as if they belonged to someone else, looking for omissions and weaknesses.
ii) If the notes seem unclear, one-sided, incomplete or in any way inaccurate, make necessary changes or even re-do them (briefly).
iii) To recopy notes is of little use, but to improve on them or to rework the information, e.g. into pattern form, gives excellent practice. Revising or patterning requires rethinking
what points the notes should make,
how they should be organized,
how they can be conveyed most clearly.*

4. In preparing for essay type questions, spend most of your revision time making essay plans. Many students find that key word patterns are the fastest and easiest way to make plans.
   a) Planning is the most crucial step of all in answering essay questions.
   b) You can prepare three plans in the time it would take to write out one full answer.
   c) By setting out all the basic information on a topic in pattern form, on one sheet of paper, you provide a visual image of the topic and the relationships of its parts. Visualization aids the memory.
   d) The more plans you can do, the better.
   e) Keep the plans and use them for your last-minute revision before the examination.
5. Give yourself an occasional 'mock' examination. For example:
   a) Make yourself plan, write and check over an essay within a time limit of, say, 45 minutes.
   b) Try an entire past paper under examination conditions (i.e. with a time limit and without reference to books or notes).

   Such practice can increase your ability to concentrate and build up your confidence that you can cope in the actual examination.
6. Form a syndicate with congenial colleagues.
   a) First, learn all you can on your own. The object of the syndicate is to share knowledge, not ignorance.
   b) Then test yourself by comparing your revision notes and practice plans with those of your colleagues.
   c) It is likely that different interests and abilities will lead to each member of the group 'teaching' the others about a particular topic.
      Having to teach someone else about anything is perhaps the best way to learn about it for oneself!
   d) Working within a group, you are more likely to see the syllabus as a whole and less likely to overlook some important part of it.
   e) Discussion reinforces learning by presenting the topic in yet another form.
      Reading, taking notes, listening, discussion, writing, doing—the more ways of dealing with information, the better it is remembered.
   f) You can cover more ground when you work with others, and find out more surely what you really know and what needs more revision.
      i) Each member can prepare an answer plan for a different aspect of a common topic and present it to the group for comment and criticism.
      ii) Each member can prepare a plan on the same topic, to compare with the others.
      iii) Members can ask one another questions.

---

* See Fig. 16 for an example of a pattern useful for revising a topic or planning an essay.

g) Sharing revision with others helps you to keep a sense of proportion about examinations.
   i) Realizing that you are not the only one afflicted with examinations reduces anxiety.
   ii) Proving to others as well as to yourself that you know something about the required topics increases confidence.

E. Use the last day sensibly
On the day before the examination:
1. Check again the time and place, and your examination number.
2. Make sure you have all the necessary materials:
pen*s* (note the plural: one may run out of ink),
pencil(s), rubber, ruler, maths instruments . . .
3. Revise the top priority items once more.
4. Do not do any new learning. This would simply block out things you have already studied.
5. Break off before bedtime and relax so that you do not stay awake all night with an overactive mind.
6. Arrange to be wakened in good time so that you can wash, dress and eat breakfast without rushing, and get to the examination room early.

(Part II of the outline, EXAMINATION TECHNIQUES, will be presented in Unit 12.)

Assignments

A. Continue or repeat previous assignments

Continue
—reading of second (or third) novel
—adding to glossaries
—using SQ3R and TL3R
—getting to know the library
—improving the weekly study plan, or making a revision timetable (see Preparation for Examinations, section C.)

B. Note signal words and phrases

Note signal words and phrases in lectures and assigned reading. You could do this by recording the title of a lecture, deliberately listening for the clue words and phrases, and jotting down a few of them in addition to the main points they introduce. Here are some examples of the kinds of signal you might hear:

I want to start by trying to explain . . .
There are at least three ways of looking at this problem.
The point I am making is . . .
This is very significant because . . .
Now, if these facts are true, then . . .
Some experts argue that . . . but . . .
So what one must conclude from all this is . . .

C. Reduce 'Preparation for Examinations'

Reduce the outline to one page and submit the result to your lecturer. (Note the hints on pp. 114–15).

Figure 15: Key Word Pattern
Review of ORGANIZING INFORMATION.

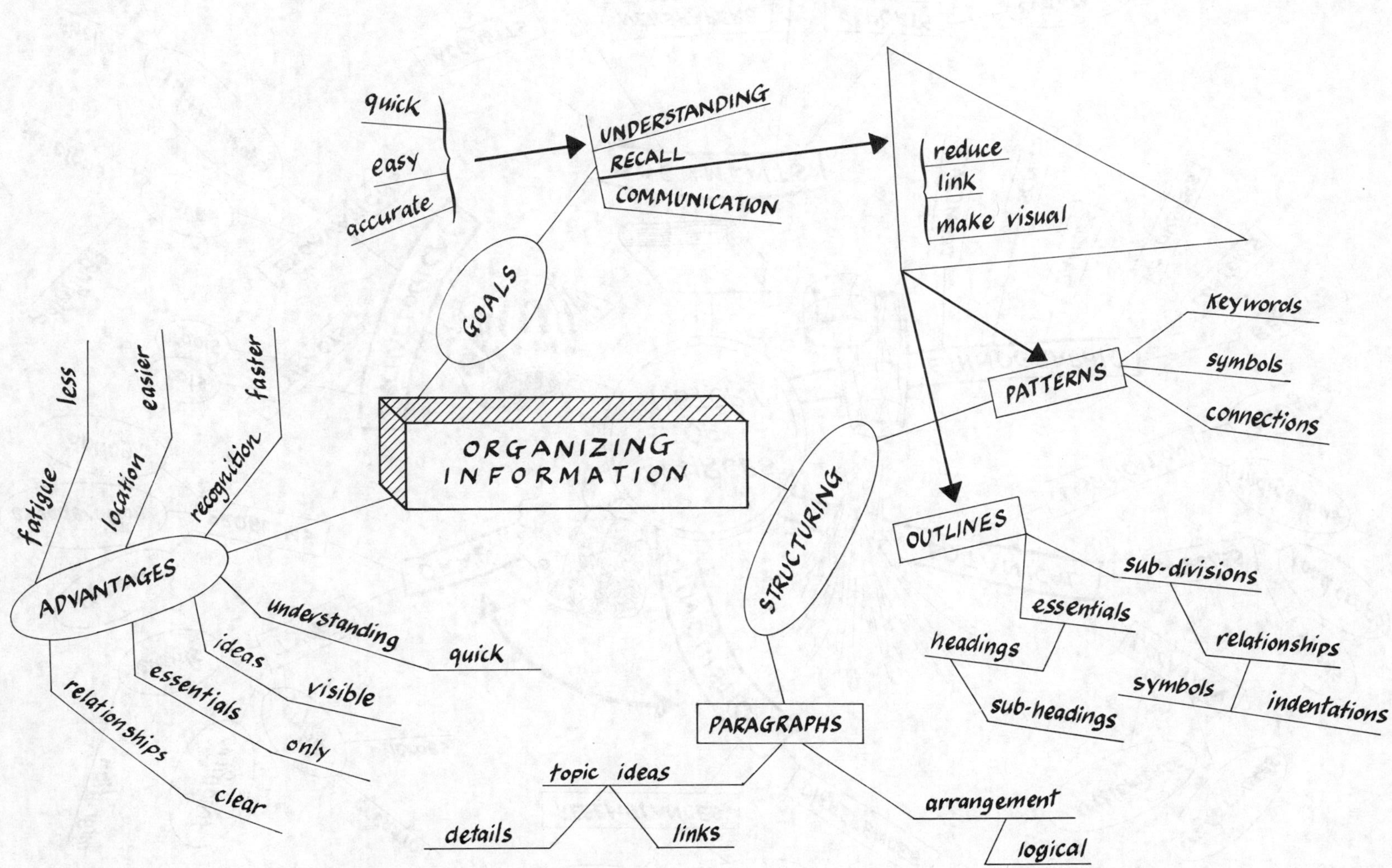

Figure 16: Key Word Pattern
PATTERN OF A HISTORY LECTURE (an example).

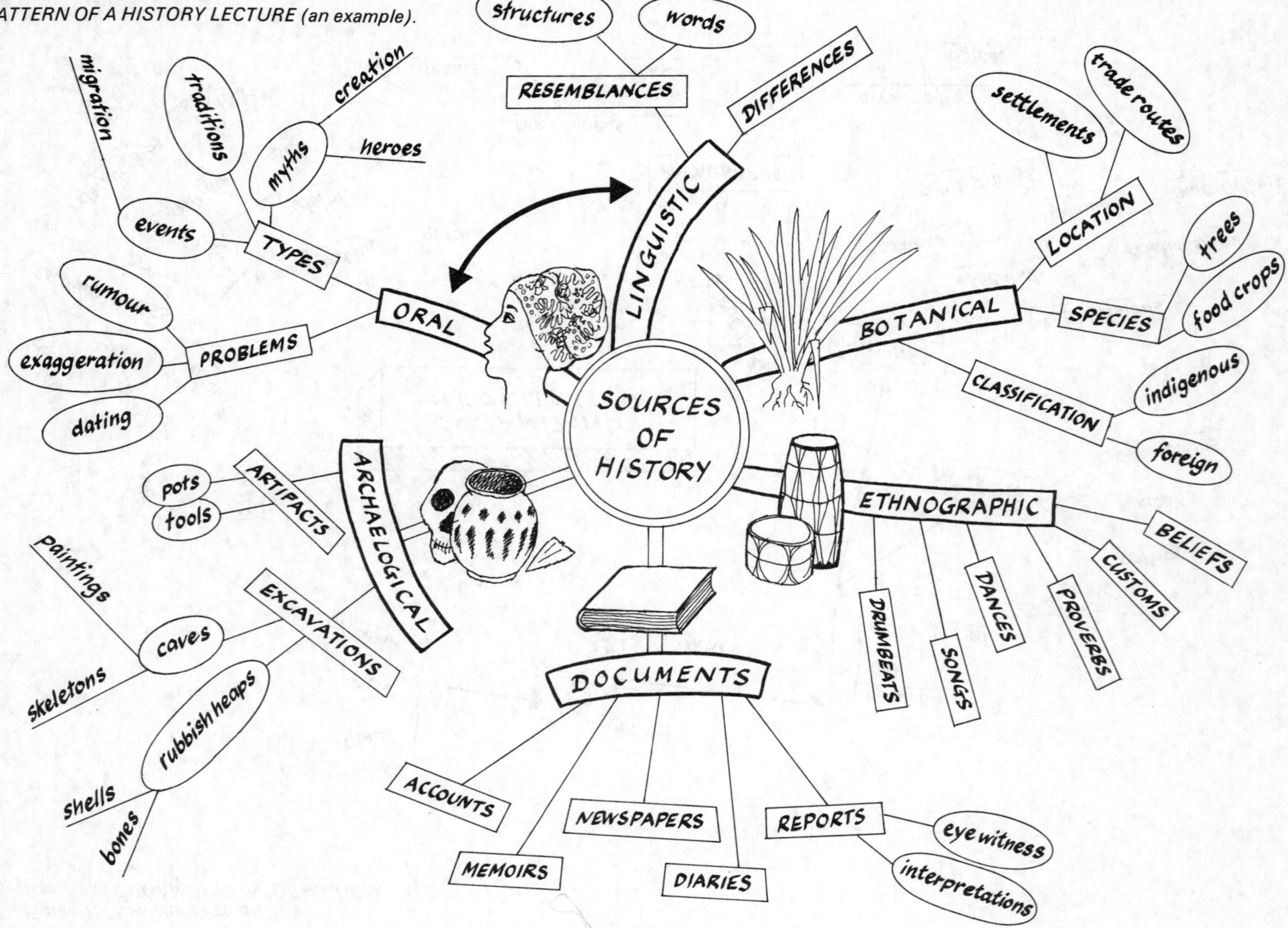

D. Practise writing clear instructions

1 Using one side of one page only (two or three paragraphs), write clear instructions for one of the tasks below. If necessary, do some investigation first. Be sure to decide on the order of points before you begin writing:

How to locate library sources on improving one's written English
How to set out a business letter
How to use a piece of apparatus or equipment (e.g. microscope, calculator, photocopy machine)

2 Revise what you have written, then exchange papers with a classmate. Use the following questions to help you judge one another's papers:
a Is the order logical?
b Is any essential information missing?
c Is all the information accurate?
d Is every point unmistakably clear?
e Is every word necessary?
Assign grades if you wish. Discuss ways of increasing the *clarity* and *economy* of the essays.

E. Criticize your notes

Criticize your notes for at least one other course. Compare them with those of two or three other students.

1 Here, in note form, are some faults to watch for:

<u>General</u>: ntbk too small
notes unorg e.g. topics mixed
wrong order
pgs crowded
handwr illeg

<u>Layout</u>: labels at top inadeq
poor vis impact: solid prose
relat unclear

<u>Content and Wording</u>: impt pts, diagr omitted
unnec detail, words
too much copied
meaning nt clear

2 Here, by way of example, are some possible decisions:

General: Use files .... more flex arrang
Use wider margins
Lv more space

Layout: ALWAYS label: name, course, topic, source, date
MK notes

V I S U A L keywds / outline
abbr
symbols

Content and Wording Pick key ideas / wds
Relate details
Use own wds
Omit unnec wds
Check notes & diagr -- accurate?

Unit Eight Giving Information

Input and *Output* are terms borrowed from computer science to refer to the taking in and giving out of information and ideas. The emphasis so far in this course has been on increasing your information *Input*: how you can understand, absorb, organize and store information so as to have the maximum amount available when the time comes for *Output*: telling someone else what you know or think.

In the rest of this book, more attention will be paid to skills essential for successful Output, especially in written coursework and examinations. The first requirement is an ability to sum up what you have read or learned accurately, clearly and economically. This unit therefore gives practice in writing summaries and making every word 'tell'.

Timed Reading Passage 8: Conveying Essentials: Summarizing

Instructions: Use the two paragraphs above to help you anticipate what the passage may say. Preview. Set your mind to read this passage at a rate 100 WPM faster than you have read any previous timed passage and still achieve a comprehension score of 70%. Make this your best score yet.

Summarizing is the basic Output skill for university and college work because all the 'higher' forms of speech and writing depend on it. To summarize effectively, you must pick out the key words and ideas—of a passage, a chapter, a story, a lecture, a discussion, a syllabus topic—and then link them up in continuous speech or writing for smooth transmission to someone else's mind. The aim is to be brief and to the point.

The skill has many applications and can be developed in many ways. For example, trying to sum up what you have read or heard accurately, briefly and in your own words, is an excellent way to test (and increase) your comprehension in study sessions, while conversations and letter writing provide countless everyday opportunities for practice. Essay or examination instructions to *define*, *describe*, *list* or *explain* are really asking you to sum up what you know on some aspect of the course. More searching questions which ask you to *discuss*, *comment on*, *compare*, *assess*, *criticize* or *justify* require you first to sum up the relevant facts and ideas, in order to interpret, judge or apply them in some way. To make responsible judgements based on facts, to discuss ideas intelligently or to persuade other people to your point of view, you must be able to state what the key facts are and express clearly the ideas you are discussing.

One of the most important uses of summary in higher education is in making notes on library research. Facts and ideas in written assignments may be drawn from various sources (which you must acknowledge) but they must be blended skilfully to form a unified whole and there should be only one style—your own. By taking most of your notes in summary form you eliminate the risk of plagiarism or a clash of styles and you also make your writing task much easier.

Plagiarism, as most students know, means stealing someone else's words or ideas and presenting them as if they were your own. It is a serious offence with severe penalties such as a failing grade for the course or dismissal from the university. What many students do not realize is that poor notemaking techniques—such as copying instead of summarizing—can lead to plagiarism even when there is no conscious intent to deceive. Other students mistakenly think that acknowledging the sources and putting quotation marks around all the copied bits will be enough to make their papers acceptable. They do not realize that stringing together chunks of other people's writing can never produce an original or forceful argument or a smooth and pleasing style.

The surest way to avoid these pitfalls is to digest, select and summarize information at the reading and notemaking stage. Put the different points on separate noteslips so that you can arrange them in the order you want. When it is time to write, you can simply put your organized pile of slips in front of you and work steadily through. With decisions about what to include already made, you can concentrate on blending, relating and expressing the ideas to maximum effect. (The copier, meanwhile, may be struggling desperately to make some sense out of his undigested mass of material, much of it irrelevant or even incomprehensible.)

How, then, do you make a good summary?

The aim of a summary is precision, which means you must convey exactly what the author wanted to get across, but in fewer words. Students are sometimes surprised to learn that it is easier to be both accurate and brief if the main ideas are entirely rephrased, except for any irreplaceable key words or technical terms necessary for precision. Trying to patch together pieces of the original is difficult and rarely results in a clear summary. To do the job effectively, you will need to substitute words for phrases, phrases for sentences and general statements for lists of details.

Such rephrasing demands a wide vocabulary and the ability to choose the most appropriate words for conveying what the author intended. This is one reason why it is so important to read widely and become acquainted with words as they are actually used. Learning words in context not only adds to the number of words known. It is also the best way to become aware of subtle differences in near- synonyms. The search for appropriate language develops an appreciation of shades of meaning. By demanding a precise use of words, therefore, the habit of summarizing encourages further vocabulary growth.

A good summary never misrepresents an author by making him say something he did not intend to say, connecting his ideas inaccurately or changing his emphasis. Neither does it add information or conclusions not in the original. In making research notes it is very important to distinguish clearly between your summary of the author's ideas and your personal comments on the ideas; the difference must be clear in the talk or essay based on these notes too.

For most summaries, it is best to begin with the usual previewing and a rapid reading for general comprehension. The close reading which follows can be broken into manageable parts by pausing after each paragraph or group of related paragraphs to phrase the main idea mentally. At the end of a section, the ideas can often be unified in a more general statement. One advantage of these pauses is that you are continually testing and improving your comprehension. For research notes, pausing also encourages you to check the relevance of the information for your purposes before you go to the trouble of recording it.

Having already established what the main ideas are and how they can be condensed, you can concentrate at the writing stage on choosing accurate words to link the ideas together. Transition words such as *because*, *however*, *although* and *also* indicate how ideas are related and contribute to a smooth style.

The length of a good summary depends on how much information you need; how much detail, repetition and illustration the passage contains; and how concisely the author has expressed his or her thoughts. If you have understood a passage and thought carefully about how best to express the main ideas, you are likely to achieve a satisfactory style and length without undue worry about either.

The major cause of bad writing—including bad summaries—is not 'poor expression' but failure to think carefully enough about what has to be said. If your vocabulary is reasonable, then good comprehension and clear thinking will lead quite naturally to good summaries.

(1020 words)

Record your time and WPM. Go on to the questions.

1 The main emphasis in the passage is on the relationships between summarizing and
a reading. *b* research papers. *c* understanding. *d* vocabulary.

2 The passage discusses the advantages of summary notes over
a copying from source books. *b* chapter outlines.
c pattern notes. *d* writing essays.

3 According to the passage, using other people's ideas in written assignments
a is a punishable offence.
b is acceptable so long as you quote their words.
c requires skill in summarizing.
d leads to a clash of styles.

4 The passage implies that plagiarism
a should be punished less severely.
b is less serious if it stems from poor notemaking techniques.
c is often the fault of the unconscious mind.
d is prevented by good notemaking habits.

5 Which of the following do *not* belong in a summary?
a related facts known to the reader
b general statements derived from details or illustrations
c linking words
d essential ideas in briefer form

6 According to the passage, the ability to summarize ---------- greater vocabulary development.
a determines *b* is determined by
c must be preceded by *d* goes hand in hand with

7 Words in the original passage should be retained in a summary
a as often as possible. *b* when precision demands it.
c when they are difficult. *d* whenever they are technical.

8 The best way to write a summary, according to the passage, is to
a pick out important phrases. *b* alternate reading and writing.
c rephrase essentials. *d* reduce sentences to phrases.

9 The main cause of bad summaries is insufficient attention to
a the content. *b* transitions. *c* vocabulary. *d* expression.

K 10 The most important quality of a good summary is
a brevity. *b* precision. *c* style. *d* good expression.

WORDS PER MINUTE CHART: Timed Reading Passage 8 *(1020 words)*											
Time	WPM	Time	WPM	Time	WPM	Time	WPM	Time	WPM	Time	WPM
—	—	2.00	510	3.00	340	4.00	255	5.00	205	6.00	170
—	—	10	470	10	320	10	245	10	200	10	165
—	—	20	435	20	305	20	235	20	190	20	160
1.30	680	30	410	30	290	30	225	30	185	30	155
40	610	40	380	40	280	40	220	40	180	40	155
50	560	50	360	50	265	50	210	50	175	50	150

Follow-up

A. Input and output

Nearly all learning, talking and writing involves both Input and Output, with emphasis shifting from one to the other. Discuss the shifts called for in using the SQ3R study method.

B. Oral or written summary work

1 State the topic idea of the first five paragraphs of the passage in one sentence.

2 Sum up the advantages of summary notes in collecting information for written assignments such as term papers.

3 Sum up the advice on making a good summary, using no more than five sentences.

C. Understanding paragraphs

1 Examine some of the paragraphs in the passage to see how they are developed and how the ideas are linked together. How often can you tell from the first sentence what the rest of the paragraph is likely to do? Discuss your observations.

2 The following paragraph begins, 'In terms of complexity and versatility, the human brain far surpasses any computer on earth.' Write two additional sentences which summarize the author's support for this statement.

> In terms of its complexity and versatility, the human brain far surpasses any computer on earth. Computers, it is true, are very fast at mathematical calculations and step-by-step logical processes, but these represent only a small part of the brain's many abilities. Not only can the brain work in a linear step-by-step fashion, it can also process, integrate and synthesize information simultaneously, and abstract generalities from it. Whereas the human brain can recognize a face in less than a second, there is no computer in the world that could do the same. Computers have been developed which can recognize a simple object, but they will take several minutes to do this. Moreover, they cannot recognize individual objects—only general classes of objects.
>
> (Adapted from Peter Russell, *The Brain Book*, Routledge and Kegan Paul, 1979, p. 7).

Compare your summary with your classmates'. Can you make your two sentences more accurate? more concise?

Related Skills

A. Generalizing and drawing conclusions

Summarizing often involves seeing and expressing a generalization which can be derived from a series of details or examples. Each of the following is an account of an experiment to do with learning. After reading each account, decide what principle is being illustrated, or what conclusion you are meant to draw, and write or complete the statement at the end as clearly as you can.

1 In one experiment, 118 university students were divided into two equated groups. One group was shown how to preview a chapter by skimming for such things as the central idea, major supporting points, topic sentences and the summary or conclusion; the other group was not. When the two groups were given a selection to read, the trained group read 24 per cent faster and just as accurately as the students who read in the usual way.

The implication of this experiment is that ....

2 There is considerable evidence that retention is not the same for all types of learning. For example, Frutchey found that for a chemistry course the retention after a year varied from 66 per cent for terminology, 70 per cent for symbols and formulas, 84 per cent for facts, and 92 per cent for the application of principles. And Tyler reports that fifteen months after they had finished a course in zoology, college students had lost 77 per cent of what they had learned about the names of animal structures, 25 per cent of their ability to interpret new experiments, but less than one per cent of their ability to apply principles to new situations.

These findings encourage us to ....

3 That practice or repetition alone is not enough has been shown by numerous studies. In one study, 134 educational psychology students were divided into five groups. Group I heard a passage just once; group II heard it twice; group III heard it three times; group IV heard it four times; and group V heard it five times. Testing ten minutes after completion of the experiment revealed a small gain from the second exposure but no advantages from additional repetitions. Generally similar results have been obtained when students have been asked to re-read the same material several times without intervening questions or re-direction of any kind. (Write a concluding statement.)..

....

4 The value of asking and attempting to answer questions has been established by research. Holmes, equating two groups of college students, presented one group with questions based on the material to be read. Both groups read the same English literature and science materials. Not only did the group with the list of questions learn better, but a re-test two weeks later indicated that they retained better. As early as 1922 Judd and Buswell referred to the value of questions. They suggested that waiting for the teacher to raise questions at examination time frequently does not lead to any well-ordered plan of attack on the content of the passage read.

Students should be encouraged to..

5 Gates found that learning is improved when a part of study time is devoted to recall or recitation rather than when all the available time is given to reading. Generally, he obtained best results when about forty per cent of the time was devoted to reading and the remainder to recitation. We cannot of course conclude from his observations that a specific percentage of study time should be spent on recall because the percentage will depend on the type of material to be learned. Perhaps Gates's most important observation is that recall not only speeds learning; it enhances the permanency of learning.

Gates's findings suggest that a student should ....
because ....

6 A reading film was shown at a fairly fast rate to two groups of students. Group I was asked to go ever the material mentally before resuming regular class work. Group II resumed immediately. After a week, both groups were asked to answer 10 questions on the material. The average score for Group I was 85%, for Group II, 45%. (Write a conclusion.) ....
....

7 A simple way to demonstrate the importance of knowledge of results is to get two subjects to draw straight lines freehand, with instructions to make them three inches long. Each line should be covered up as it is drawn so that it cannot serve as a copy for the next. Give one subject no information about the accuracy of his performance, and he will not improve. Give the other subject exact information about each line that he draws, telling him by how much it is too short or too long. After a few tries he will be able to draw a three-inch line very accurately. Many other experiments yield essentially similar results. In order to improve, the learner needs to know whether his responses are correct or not.

One of the implications for a student working on his own is that ....
K ....

(from Henry P. Smith and E. V. Dechant, *Psychology in Teaching Reading*, Prentice Hall, 1961 and Harry Maddox, *How to Study*, Pan.)

B. Avoiding wordiness

An effective piece of writing has a clear purpose, which every sentence helps to achieve. Every word is necessary, either for the meaning or for grammatical correctness.

Superfluous words are enemies of effective communication because they obscure meaning, confuse and distract the reader, and waste time and space which might have been used for more facts and ideas. It is worth remembering that written work is marked not on the number of words, but on the quantity of information, the quality of the ideas and the way you relate and apply what you have understood.

Writing hint: You can stop many useless words from getting on your pages in the first place, but some will always slip through. Train yourself *always* to read through your written work asking over and over:

—What does this contribute?

—Can I say it more concisely?

Then revise and rewrite. Remember:
—If a word contributes nothing, cut it out.
—If the expression is roundabout, make it direct.
—If the meaning is not clear, make it clear.

At this stage of your education, the habit of always trying to say more in fewer words is likely to do far more to 'improve your English' than any number of additional grammar exercises; the best time to learn more about an aspect of grammar is when doing so will help you to say something in particular more effectively. The exercises below will show you some of the ways you can get rid of excess verbiage in your own writing.

1 You have probably been cautioned against at least some of the following:
verbosity, waffling, padding, longwindedness, pomposity, bombastic language, circumlocution, jargon, gobbledegook, tautology, clichés.

What do you understand by each term? Can you give examples? Think, discuss and (where necessary) consult your dictionary.

2 Some words and phrases should not be used at all because they add no meaning or have lost all their force through overuse, e.g.

in actual fact, so far as X is concerned, from this it can be seen that, cannot be overemphasized;
from time immemorial, march of progress, boon to mankind, explore every avenue

Suggest some further expressions to avoid.

3 Why use several words when only one is necessary? Replace each circumlocution below with one word only:

a greater in number
b a greater length of time
c a sufficient number of
d if it is assumed that
e due to the fact that
f on a regular ongoing basis
g the question as to whether
h in a large number of instances
i am not able to see my way clear to
j carry out some experiments
k which goes under the name of
K *l* in view of the points I have mentioned above

4 You can train yourself to eliminate repetitious expressions from your writing simply by making a habit of looking for them. Get rid of any unnecessary words in the following, e.g.

the resultant effect: *the result*

a This course teaches very essential basic skills such as reading, studying, using the library, etc.
b We could visibly see that we were surrounded on all sides.

c Although summarizing can be hard work but it can be useful.
d This solution apparently seems reasonable.
e History is always repeating itself over again.
f Personally, I have never happened to cheat in exams.
g The subject of the paper will be about the growth of Yoruba towns or urban centres.
h I know many lecturers who always try to give you every possible assistance that they can.
i Obviously the vast majority seemed to think he was the more preferable candidate.
j The teacher said or conveyed that the students had been guilty of a high degree of great carelessness.
k In many books I read the setting is very often in some foreign country.
l According to medical specialists who are experts in this field, it is now possible for mammals, including human beings, to be developed in the laboratory and outside the body.

K

5 For each of the following, first decide what the writer wanted to say, then say it in the fewest possible words, e.g.

The answer was given in the negative: *He said no.*

a The standard of English among the various candidates who took the examination was considered to be fairly high in the majority of cases.
b On the title, this humble reviewer sees it as being unable to explain the theme of the novel at first sight.
c The way we speak at any given time depends on what speech community we happen to be operating in at that particular time.
d It cannot be disputed that through their coming to live together in one place at a university, students get to mix with others from ethnic groups other than their own and in this way they are able to get to know each other and learn the language and customs of other people and also more about their different ideas.

K

6 The unnecessary use of 'big' words and specialized terms in a show-off attempt to sound important and knowledgeable is a common cause of bad writing. It usually attracts other forms of wordiness which make matters worse. The writer George Orwell illustrated this by writing a longwinded version of Jesus's injunction to 'Render unto Caesar the things that are Caesar's:

> In the case of Caesar, it might well be considered appropriate from a moral and ethical point of view to render to that potentate all of those goods and materials of whatever character or quality which can be shown to have had their original source in any portion of the domain of the latter.

What sense can you make of this description of a patient?

> This elderly geriatric female has multiple joint problems which limit perambulation. Absence of verbal intercourse aggravates her detachment from reality and reinforces isolationism. She is unable to relate to events at this point in time. Psychogeriatric consideration in the context of conceptual distortion and paranoia is also a parameter in the total dimensions of her problems.

If you have not given up altogether, you will have spent some time trying to puzzle out the meaning, and still be uncertain that you have understood properly.

Long, inflated and unfamiliar words take more time to decode than short, plain familiar ones, especially in large doses, and they are more likely to be misinterpreted. Abstract and general words can have a confusing range of possible meanings, but specific, concrete ones help the reader understand precisely what is in your mind. Thus, 'in the classroom' is understood more quickly than 'in the context of the teaching situation'. And you will probably have no difficulty in understanding this translation of the passage you just struggled through:

> This old lady has arthritis, cannot get about and is lonely, confused and frightened.
>
> (Example from a letter in the U.K. *Guardian* of 18 January, 1978, criticizing 'psychobabble'.)

7 Most of the writing you do as a student is *expository*: it requires you to expose what you know on a topic by presenting, explaining or interpreting facts and ideas. If your reader cannot make out your meaning, or suspects there *is* no meaning, then you have failed to communicate. The reader whose time you have wasted will be bored and irritated, not impressed, by your piling up of useless words. A reader/examiner looking for points will only reward you for the information you provide.

Look for some examples of verbosity and unnecessary jargon in reading, listening and writing. Strip away the excess verbiage, then translate the essentials into plain English.

C. Organizing paragraphs

If you start paying more attention to paragraphs in different sources, you will discover a variety of common patterns. Many begin with a generalization and then give illustrations and examples, or supporting facts and details. Others define, classify, describe, explain, analyze, compare or contrast. Points may be made in time order, spatial order, order of importance or step-by-step. Movement may be from challenge to response, question to answer, problem to solution, cause to effects or effect to causes.

Out of this bewildering array of possibilities, how can you choose the best methods for the paragraphs you write? Here is a hint for improving your paragraphs without agonizing over pattern choices:

Writing hint: Write topic sentences that are also 'commitment' sentences. That is, use the first sentences to make a promise not only about the subject matter, but also about the 'shape' of the discussion. If you write 'Learning and remembering are not the same thing', you are committed to using the paragraph to explain the difference between them. The means of development is dictated by the statement. The skill is in making a statement general enough to allow development but specific enough to deal with adequately.

1 Examine each of the following commitment sentences to see what promise has been made. State the question you would expect the rest of the paragraph to answer. What does this imply about the method of development?

a Scientific knowledge increases our ability to control events.
b A paragraph is an essay in miniature.
c Every minute of our lives, sleeping or waking, we burn up energy.
d Nationalism is a word which has both positive and negative connotations.
e Without oxygen the world would die.
f A communication process has three elements: a source, a signal and a destination.
g Motor vehicles are a major source of air pollution.
h From the moment a baby first opens his eyes, he is learning.
i Early Nigerian newspapers paved the way for the formation of political parties.

2 Now think of any topic you have been studying on which you might have to write an examination essay. What are the essential points to be made? Write three commitment sentences, each of which could be developed into a paragraph.

Summary and Notemaking Practice

A. Types of research notes

One of the skills in notemaking for research purposes is judging how much information you need and what form to put it in. These are the possibilities, among them the summary note discussed in the passage:

NOTES RECORDING FACTS OR DETAILS

Sometimes you only need specific items of information: names or dates, biographical facts, selected examples, stages in a process. Since you will be weaving these details with other material at writing time, you need not put them in sentence form now.

SUMMARY

The summary note is the one called for most often. It is used when you want the main idea or the gist of a paragraph, a passage or even a chapter. Summarizing, in sentences, forces you to digest, select and re-express information and eliminates the risk of plagiarism. The main concern is to record the information and relationships accurately; you can improve the expression at writing time when you link up the ideas on your various note slips.

PARAPHRASE

While a summary condenses information, the paraphrase may have almost the same number of words as the original—but they will be your own words. Paraphrasing proves you have understood, and leads to consistency of style. To make a paraphrase, first read and understand, then put the book aside and express the idea in your own words, then check back to see that *your* version conveys the author's meaning fairly. If you find you have used more than five consecutive words of the author's, enclose them in quotation marks or paraphrase them too.

QUOTATION

A quotation reproduces *exactly* what the author said, exactly the way he wrote it in every detail. Put quotation marks around the author's words on your note slip and check the accuracy of your copying. Since your paper should represent your selection and reworking of thoroughly understood material, you should use quotations very sparingly and always for a good reason, as, for example, when the author expresses an idea with special force or originality, or you want to discuss the quotation itself.

COMBINATIONS

Sometimes within a summary or paraphrase you want to keep a particular expression or a sentence of the author's. Remember to enclose the original words in quotation marks.

PERSONAL COMMENT

If a thought or question or relationship occurs to you as you write a note, by all means add it to the bottom of the note slip before you forget it—but put it in square brackets [ ] so you will remember later that it is *your* comment, not the author's.

Write a one paragraph summary on 'Types of Research Notes'.

B. Techniques of notemaking

The method of notemaking outlined below enables you to add and discard, shuffle and rearrange your notes at any stage of the work, and to avoid any confusion over what information has come from where. Like countless other researchers, you will find that the method makes the tasks of outlining and writing a paper much easier.

Practise the method by making a note slip for the ten points below, reducing each one to key words. Be sure to cite the source (i.e. this book) and to give the slip a heading.

Note slips

1 Use cards or slips of uniform size, kept together with paper clips or in envelopes. You may wish to use a larger size or a different colour to distinguish these from bibliography slips.

2 Use ink. Pencilled notes become blurred with repeated rearrangement of the slips.

3 Write only one idea, from one source, on each card. If you are likely to use two or three ideas from the same page in different parts of your paper, put them on separate slips. Never put ideas from two different sources on the same slip.

4 Before you make any notes from a book, check the bibliography slip to be sure the information is complete and accurate. Make any necessary additions or corrections now, while you have the book in your hand.

5 Before you write the note, identify the source by writing the author's surname, or a key word of the title, at the top of the card, on the right. You do not need the full information here because this is already on the bibliography slip which you have just confirmed is accurate.

6 After the identification of the source, write the page number(s) on which the information you are noting appears. You will need the page references later for your footnotes. Record them now.

7 At the top left goes a short heading to indicate the kind of information the note contains. This heading, called a *slug*, will help you to arrange your notes; you can write it in pencil because you may change it as you work. You may not be able to label each slip at the beginning, but you will soon realize that certain slips belong together and eventually, the slugs should all match parts of your outline.

8 Decide what kind of note is most suitable: extraction of facts, summary, paraphrase, quotation or a combination of these.

9 Write the note. Except in the case of quotations, use any abbreviations and symbols you find convenient. Just make sure that you will be able to understand the notes when you come to use them. For quotations, it is important to copy everything exactly, including punctuation.

10 Check the note for accuracy.

Assignments

A. Complete or repeat previous assignments

Continue work on

—patterning of second or third novel
—glossaries
—revision timetable
—essay plans in pattern or brief outline form
—thinking out your response to the novels you have read.

B. Explain a key concept

Choose a key concept in any of your major subjects, e.g. *locational analysis* in geography, *cell theory* in biology, and consult any three library sources which discuss the concept. Following the directions in Techniques of Notemaking, record the significant points on note slips. Then draw on the selected information to write one concise paragraph explaining what the concept means. Hand in your note slips as well as the paragraph.

C. Write a synopsis

Attempt a one page synopsis (summary) of one of the novels you have read. Think carefully about the essentials before you begin and revise carefully afterwards so that you give maximum information in the space allowed.

D. Improve an essay

Go through any essay you have written looking for words which could be eliminated and ideas which should be stated more clearly. Make improvements.

E. Develop paragraphs

Develop any of the paragraphs for which you earlier wrote a commitment sentence. Put it aside for a day, then revise it.

Unit Nine Seeing Connections and Making Judgements

Timed Reading Passage 9: Creative and Critical Response to Fiction

Instructions

1 Take two minutes to preview the entire unit. (There will be another chance to preview the passage itself.)

2 See how many uses of the creative imagination in different fields you can think of in two minutes, e.g. being a character in a play, making models for physics teaching, mock interviewing in management training, making up a tune.

3 Name as many products of creativity in your own fields of study as you can in one minute: great discoveries, inventions or ideas.

4 In what sense do you expect the word *criticism* to be used in the passage?

5 Anticipate how the subject matter of the passage might be relevant to you, whatever your major subject.

6 Preview the entire passage, using any method you choose. Recall, question and anticipate some more. At the signal, begin to read Part A at the fastest possible rate.

Part A: Using the Creative Imagination

Man is distinguished from other animals by his imaginative gifts—his ability to relate what he sees to what he cannot see, to move through time and space simply by projecting and moving images within his mind, to visualize the past, to anticipate coming events, and to plan the future. The most highly prized of these gifts is his creative imagination: his ability to fuse two or more previously unconnected ideas to create something quite new.

Think of the wheel, the alphabet, the law of gravity, the principle of natural selection, antibiotics, space travel, systems analysis, biofeedback, an apt metaphor, a Benin bronze, the xylophone, *Macbeth*, a well-written term paper, Soyinka's poetry or the novels you have read for this course. Curiosity, sound preparation, hard work, experimentation, critical evaluation, perseverance and patient revision have made their vital contributions to the end product, but each one owes its very existence to a key idea sparked in the creative imagination of a human being.

That is why both art and science are unique to humans and why creative thinking is needed in every field of human endeavour.

One of the most enjoyable and useful ways to develop your imagination is through the reading of creative fiction. A story which is well-told both invites and demands creative reading. After all, the characters and events imagined by the author are no more than words on paper unless you, the reader, can use your imagination and your own experience of living to 'bring them to life' again.

Inevitably, your own real-world experiences will influence your reaction to the book characters. For example, you may identify with one character because he is what you wish you were, or because his problems resemble yours—or because you know from experience just what he feels like or why he behaves in a certain way. You therefore feel emotionally involved in his sufferings and in the choices he has to make. At the end, you may feel that you understand yourself better for having shared vicariously in his life.

More rewarding still may be the novel which asks you to project yourself 'into the shoes' of someone very different from yourself and to understand, through imagination, what it would feel like to be blind, to be a slave, to feel alienated from your own society, to experience to the extreme some great human emotion such as joy, hate, grief, despair, love—or explore what you might be like if you had a different family background, or different beliefs, goals, talents or problems from those you do have.

The responsive reading of good fiction thus enables you to try out various roles, in different times, places and societies, to test yourself in a wide range of human situations and to experiment with the consequences of various choices—all without suffering the disasters which such trial-and-error approaches might bring in real life. Cumulative experience with this kind of reading can lead to a 'reciprocity of viewpoint' which helps one to understand and cope better with the complexities of human existence: a sensitivity to other people, an awareness of alternatives and their implications, the ability to make sound choices, the flexibility to modify an opinion, the confidence to take a stand on an issue.

What are the roles of writer and reader in creating meaning? Two roles which they share are to select and to associate. An author spins a story around an idea, a theme. The choices of characters, events, details, images and words and the way they are woven into the overall pattern suggest all kinds of further associations and insights.

The reader, in his turn, perceives selectively, according to his experience, needs, interests and values. No good book can ever mean exactly the same thing to any two readers. Yet a really good book leaves any creative reader with the feeling that he will never look at the world in quite the same way again. In connecting characters, events and suggestions in the book with people, happenings and feelings in the real world, he discovers the author's deeper meanings and at the same time creates layers of personal meaning which enlarge his understanding of both life and literature.

Not surprisingly, the novels known to make the greatest impact on readers are those in which the writer allows the reader to experience the chief character's thoughts and conflicting emotions by re-creating them from the inside. Okonkwo in *Things Fall Apart* is a good example; the imaginative experience of getting inside Okonkwo's mind enables a reader to understand him better than any of the characters around him can do.

(800 words)

Stop. Record your time for Part A. Recall what you have just read. Watch for a convenient time to start Part B. Intend to improve on your time for Part A. Note your start time and begin Part B.

Part B: Does It Matter What You Read?

Obviously, neither a shallow book nor shallow reading can provide the kind of reading experience we have been discussing. Creative reading of fiction demands a book which offers experiences worth re-creating and a reader willing to engage his mind and emotions in extracting the experience. Every step—from choosing a book to read, through making sense of it, to judging it when you have finished—is a chance to use and develop your critical powers.

To begin with the matter of choice: A great many books might at best be called 'subliterature'. They are cheap, accessible, and easy-to-read because the characters are either Good or Bad and the reader knows who will win in the end. It may be argued that such books help a learner of English develop reading fluency, and it is certainly true that most people want escapist reading sometimes, but there is evidence that a steady or exclusive diet of shallow, undemanding reading can impair reading stamina, blunt the imagination and retard linguistic growth.

In the formula romances, for example, love is an instantaneous happening somehow related to lots of money; fun means fast cars and dancing at nightclubs; success means marrying the Handsome Boss who at last realizes he doesn't want Fickle Type after all, and the predictable ending assumes that hero and heroine will be married as soon as the book is finished and live 'happily ever after'. The world is often populated only by white people and free of the problems real-life people of any colour or country have to face. There may be plenty of action (a punch to the jaw of Predatory Male, an auto crash) punctuated by romantic sighs, but the motives and implications of actions are ignored and any exploration of personal values or the possible meanings of 'love', 'happiness' or 'success' is carefully avoided. The characters, with their trite emotions, are more like cardboard cut-outs than flesh and blood individuals and are often interchangeable from book to book.

While such stories may function as temporary wish-fulfilment, they fail to satisfy deeper needs because neither the characters nor the reader are any different when the book ends; nothing has been honestly felt or newly understood. Anyone concerned with African culture, black dignity or women's lib can easily think of further objections.

Why then do some people go on reading such novels to the point of addiction? Part of the answer seems to be that when all is familiar stereotype, calling for stock response, there is no need to exercise the mind. The range of associations is limited and there are no layers of meaning to be probed. Everything comes out right in the end with minimal effort by either heroine or reader. This simplistic representation of life, however false, is far easier to cope with than the many complications of life in the real world. For the same reason, full length books and quality writing may also seem like 'too much work'.

Full living and quality writing require—and encourage—an openness to new experience, use of the imagination and a willingness to struggle with the complexities of both life and language. The more often lazy readers retreat into a world of no demands and simple solutions, the lazier they are likely to become. The passivity encouraged by so much narcotic reading makes them less and less willing to use language as a tool for probing feelings and making sense of an uncertain world. In an important sense, they become emotionally, imaginatively and linguistically disabled.

It must be said, of course, that love has been the subject not only of the most banal pulp fiction but also of the greatest world literature. Some detective fiction is extremely well-written, though much of it is not. Many books which might seem to be unrelated to the real world—science fiction, for example—can be extraordinarily illuminating and mind-stretching. Differences in quality stem not from the subject matter but from what the author does with it, which is one of the main reasons why a reader needs to develop the ability to discriminate.

There is a further reason. While everyone knows that we learn to speak the kind of language that we hear, not everyone realizes that we tend to write the kind of language that we read. In fact, the quality and quantity of the reading you have done probably has far more to do with the quality of your writing than the number of English language exercises you have completed. Cliché-ridden language, muddled thinking, inappropriate slang, second-hand opinions, insincerity: all too often these are symptoms of an impoverished reading diet. Reading which draws on the creative imagination and invites genuine response encourages writing of a different kind: more direct and honest, reflecting independence of judgement and the willingness to grapple with words until they say just what you want them to say.

(850 words)

Stop. Record your time for Part B. Recall what you have just read. Watch for a convenient time to start part C. Intend to read and understand at your fastest rate yet. Note your start time and begin Part C.

Part C: Judging What You Read

Assuming that you have chosen a book worth reading, and tried to involve all your creative and critical powers in the reading of it, how can you make the experience more memorable and valuable?

As you will realize, the first task is to recall the content of the book: its theme, important characters, events, relationships and ideas. The patterns you have made for your African novels show how well you have understood them on this fundamental level.

What really matters about a novel, however, is your own personal response to it. What did the book make you think and feel—and why? What made it worth reading? To answer these questions implies judging the book. In particular, once you have seen the author's overall purpose—to present a certain way of life or to show some truth about human nature—it is important to note how he has gone about achieving this purpose and to judge from your response how well he has succeeded.

Questions like these can help you begin: What is the significance of the title? Do you think your response to the book or to certain characters is what the author intended? How do particular incidents and details contribute to the total pattern or dominant impression? How do the language and imagery reinforce the meaning? Of what value to the story is the point of view from which the author tells it? How effective are any special techniques, such as flashbacks? Is the dialogue realistic? How reliable do you consider the view of the world represented in the book? If the book has made you think or feel or understand anything new, how did the author lead you to make the connections and achieve the insights? Do you wish he had done something more?

Some of these aspects can be appreciated during a reading of the novel when you are understanding and responding emotionally. Others are better appreciated upon reflection and review afterwards. You will discover, however, that asking questions like these will help you to see more and increase your pleasure in reading fiction. With practice, you will come to appreciate the overall design of a novel and the way all its parts are woven together; you will see the significance of an episode or a conversation; you will discover that a symbol can spray out myriad associations; you will feel a conscious delight when you find that words are exactly right for their ideas, and you will realize that the content of a story is really inseparable from its form and style. This kind of conscious appreciation of the aesthetic as well as the human and social aspects of a novel is considered the highest stage of development for a reader.

Finally, make sure you put your judgement and your reasons for it into words. At the very least tell yourself, clearly, what you think and why. Better yet, discuss the book with a friend. State your views and be willing to defend them. For books that really make an impact, clarify and develop your thoughts by putting them on paper in some form.

For anyone who has learned how to read efficiently, the reading of good fiction is an enjoyable activity but, happily, it offers more than pleasure. Creative and critical reading, followed by verbal expression of your responses, gives practice in nearly all the thinking and verbal skills discussed in this course. More important, in the end, this kind of reading and response increases your awareness of all it can mean to be human.

(580 words)

Record your time for Part C. Average your time for the three parts. Go on to the questions.

1 According to the passage, creative imagination is
a the ability to form mental images.
b the ability to write imaginative literature.
c the ability to get inside another person's mind.
d the ability to link ideas in new ways.

2 Your response to a book is likely to be influenced by
a your experience of life.
b your previous reading experience.
c your attitude to new experience.
d *a* and *b*
e *a*, *b* and *c*.

3 In the context of the passage, 'reciprocity of viewpoint' refers to
a coping with life's complexities.
b being able to imagine yourself in someone else's position or someone else in yours.
c experimenting with choices without suffering the consequences.
d understanding the author's point of view on an issue.

4 The passage implies that creative reading is
a the opposite of critical reading.
b appropriate only for fiction.
c grasping the author's intended meaning and extending it according to your own experience.
d selecting ideas and experiences in a book to create your own meaning.

5 As used in the passage, 'subliterature' refers to
a books written for children and teenagers.
b detective and love stories.
c books which take one out of the world one lives in.
d books which make few demands on the reader's imagination or language skills.

6 According to the passage, the best readers of good literature are able to
a take pleasure in the relationships between ideas and their expression.
b solve their real-life problems as a result.
c identify with characters unlike themselves.
d appreciate all the human and social aspects of a novel.

7 Judging from the passage, the author is convinced that
a the best reason for reading novels is to improve one's English.
b a student should never read easy or escapist fiction.
c a student should write a critical review of any novel he reads.
d a teacher can often guess from a student's writing what kind of reading he or she has done.

8 Which of the following is *not* mentioned as a reason for reading creative fiction?
a It provides experiences the reader might not otherwise have.

b It offers hope that dreams will come true.
c It can help you understand yourself and other people better.
d It can develop the capacity to make sound choices.

9 Critical reading means
a reacting to the book and making judgements about it.
b reading that is urgent or important.
c the reading done by a literary critic.
d searching for a book's faults.

10 According to the author, the most important thing about a book you read is
a whether the characters can be brought to life again.
b the values portrayed in it.
c your response to it.
K *d* the quality of its language.

WORDS PER MINUTE CHART: Timed Reading Passage 9 *(800, 850 and 580 words)*

Time	WPM 9A	WPM 9B	WPM 9C	Time	WPM 9A	WPM 9B	WPM 9C	Time	WPM 9A	WPM 9B	WPM 9C
0.50	—	—	695	—	—	—	—	—	—	—	—
1.00	—	—	580	2.00	400	425	290	3.00	265	285	195
10	685	—	500	10	370	390	270	10	255	270	185
20	600	640	425	20	340	365	250	20	240	255	175
30	535	570	385	30	320	340	230	30	230	245	165
40	480	515	350	40	300	320	220	40	220	230	160
50	435	465	315	50	280	300	205	50	210	220	150

Time	WPM 9A	WPM 9B	WPM 9C	Time	WPM 9B
4.00	170	200	145	5.00	160
10	165	190	140	10	155
20	160	185	135	20	150
30	155	180	—	30	145
40	150	170	—	40	140
50	145	165	—		

Follow-up

A. Assessing your progress

A comparison of Passage 9 as a whole with Passage 1 would show not only that Passage 9 is much longer but that its ideas, vocabulary and sentence structure make it more complex and demanding for the reader. Even if you averaged the same speed on both, you could claim to have improved as a reader, but you have almost certainly achieved a better speed on Passage 9. *Your improvement may be greater than you think!* Are you aware of some of the techniques you used in reading parts of Passage 9 efficiently, e.g. speeding up when you came to a list of examples?

B. Noting relationships

1 Look at the first sentence of each successive paragraph in Part A to establish its connection with the paragraph before. Pick out the clues which help you to see the relationships.

2 Explain how the first paragraphs of Parts B and C function as transition paragraphs.

3 Scan for further examples of transition and linking devices not covered in 1 and 2 above, e.g. signal words, repetition of a key word or idea, parallel structure, referring words.

C. Making inferences

In the third paragraph of Part B, capital letters are used for Handsome Boss, Fickle Type and Predatory Male. Why? What is the tone of the same paragraph? What does it tell you about the purpose and attitude of the author?

D. Recall and summary

1 Make a quick pattern or a sketch outline of the main points in Part A.

2 In Part B, the author gives an opinion on the question 'Does it matter what you read?' Give the gist of the author's supporting argument in three sentences.

3 Sum up the main point of Part C in one sentence.

E. Making judgements

1 To what extent do you agree with the opinion expressed in Part B, and why? Suggest an experiment, or further types of evidence, which might help in determining the validity of the opinion.

2 Consider the fiction that you and your friends have read recently. Rank some of the books according to the demands they made on you. Then rank them according to the pleasure or value you think you got from them. Is there any relationship between the two lists?

F. Giving reasons for judgements

Much written work at college or university requires you to go beyond mere summary or exposition and demonstrate your skill in argument. This is the ability to think your way to some point of view on a subject, then convince others that this point of view is the logical result of examining the facts fairly. Imagining what people with different views might say is often a useful technique in planning convincing arguments. See how much you can learn about the process through trying these practice exercises:

1 Imagine that you are science student A, who feels that the time spent on reading and discussing fiction in this course could be better spent on something else. List the points you would use in arguing your case.

2 Imagine that you are science student B, who happens to enjoy literature and thinks any educated person should appreciate it. List the points you would use in arguing that any student of higher education should be given some experience in reading and evaluating fiction.

3 Imagine that student C, majoring in English literature, has just complained to you about having to take a General Studies course on science and technology. List the points you would use in trying to persuade C that such a course could be interesting and useful.

4 You might find it interesting to return to this section when you have completed the rest of the unit. Look for ways to strengthen, add to or refute the different arguments. Try out your reasoning for one of the cases on other students to gauge its effectiveness. Remember to begin with a commitment statement.

G. Imagining a character

This exercise should give you new insights into a fictional character. Think for a minute about a major character in one of the novels you have read for this course. Then imagine this character (person) entering the room where you are now. Use what you know of the character to imagine how he would react to finding himself in the room and how you and other people there would react to his arrival. Analyze (or discuss) the result, e.g. what makes you think that your scenario is plausible? You could go on to imagine what would happen if you put this character in your second novel, e.g. would he dominate or be dominated by the main character in the 'host' book?

Related Skills

A. Using information

1 Identify some of the creative and critical elements in reading and responding to *non-fiction*, e.g. library books consulted for written assignments.

2 Study the outline notes on The Creative Process (p. 148). Use the notes to help you compile a list of points you would include under the heading 'How to Be More Creative' for people in your field of study. Put the points in the same grammatical form, e.g. all as 'commands'. Be concise.

Outline Notes

THE CREATIVE PROCESS
Stages and Their Characteristics

Stage I: Preparation: conscious, wilful, vigorous effort

A. Initial stimulus, e.g.
1. A problem, assignment, challenge
2. Dissatisfaction with existing answers, method, situation
3. An observation or a feeling
4. A shadowy idea, e.g. for a poem

B. Motivation: A desire to solve the problem, meet the challenge, find a better answer, express the feeling

C. Immersion: active involvement by:
1. Defining the problem, identifying the key questions
2. Building up background: facts, ideas, previous research, methods, related issues
3. Playing around with ideas and arrangements: exploring possibilities, looking for connections; sorting; rejecting some ideas, thinking about others

D. Struggle:
1. A sense of wrestling to impose order on chaos
2. A strong desire to win through the difficulties

E. Tension:
1. Discomfort, even frustration; a sense of being blocked
2. (sometimes) Exhaustion from the intense effort to reach an elusive goal
3. A need for relief

Stage II: Incubation: subconscious mental activity

A. Turning aside from conscious effort by
1. Giving attention to some other task
2. Sleeping or taking a break
3. Leaving the ideas to 'soak'

B. Letting the unconscious take over:
1. To uncover, select, reject, combine, reshuffle the 'chaos' of accumulated facts, ideas and images
2. To remove the constraints of left-brain thinking and allow the right brain a chance to 'see things whole'
3. To make connections, integrate, form a pattern, achieve a synthesis

Stage III: Illumination: the spontaneous emergence of insight

A. Sometimes a flash of intuition, an inspired moment, the 'Eureka' phenomenon, often appearing
1. In the form of a visual image or analogy
2. In unexpected or apparently unrelated circumstances
3. While dozing or in a reverie, e.g. before or after sleeping (when ideas can collide more freely)

B. Sometimes simply a realization of what to do next or another approach to try

Stage IV: Verification and Revision: conscious, patient, critical effort

A. Checking, experimenting, testing, evaluating to make sure the intuition is valid

B. Clarifying the thoughts, ordering the steps, marshalling the details in verbal, logical terms

C. Translating the discovery for communication to others
  1. Writing and revising so that others can understand, replicate experiments, experience similar feelings—and judge the value of the work
  2. Polishing the style, checking documentation and presenting the work in suitable form

D. Seeking ways to use the knowledge and experience gained during the process.

B. Cultivating the imagination

STARTING POINT

On pages 155–164 are a sample outline and a sample *term paper* (or *library research paper*) which will be used for several purposes in this and the remaining units. Read the paper *now*.

LOCAL CONNECTIONS

The examples of creativity in the paper are drawn from 'Western' science. These exercises ask you to think of examples from other cultures, drawn from any field.

1 *Things Fall Apart* by Chinua Achebe, a Nigerian, is read by students of English literature throughout the world. It is a good example of 'creative synthesis'. If you are familiar with the book, try to say why it is a good example. Think of other examples from the literature, art, architecture or festivals of your country.

2 Find out about eminent persons from your country who have achieved prominence in a field other than the one they were trained in. (Examples: a doctor turned politician, a physicist turned novelist.)

3 What discoveries, inventions or improved systems would better the quality of life on your campus, in your community or in a workplace you know? Some starter ideas: cheaper and more efficient ways to collect waste and convert it to something useful (e.g. recycled paper, fertilizer); lowcost 'instant' student housing units; vaccines against malaria, sleeping sickness, leprosy; ways of reducing the number of road accidents; wider use of solar energy.

SUBJECT CONNECTIONS

Your mind should be incessantly busy making connections among all the things you take into it if you wish to improve your ability to learn, remember and communicate. (Are the reasons behind this statement running through your mind now? They should be.) Here are some examples of ways to get your mind working on the interconnections among college and university subjects. Go on to devise some exercises of your own.

1 Think, fast, of some specific connection between *religion* and each of the following: art, music, science, medicine, agriculture, economics, sociology, history, politics, architecture, engineering, business, languages, geography. Use your own major subject as the key word and go through the same process with it.

2 The sample paper refers to disciplines created when a significant connection was discovered between two existing disciplines, e.g. biochemistry. Three more examples would be bioengineering, geophysics and educational psychology. How many more can you think of?

3 Practise multiplying word associations by taking key words or concepts and linking them with as many other subjects and contexts as possible. Try to produce streams of associations at high speed. When you can't think of any more, look the word up in your dictionary to increase your understanding of its many facets. For example, after a lecture on *wave theory* (physics), you might think of these other contexts for *wave*:

light wave, wave good-bye, flag waving, ocean waves, waves of migration, heat wave, wavy pattern, wave length, wave band, wave mechanics

4 Other examples for multiple word associations:

a You have learned about library classification systems. How is the word *system* used in:

education, physics, biology, medicine, astronomy, economics, mathematics, geology, geography, engineering, office practice, accounting, traffic control

b What does the word *environment* mean to:

an engineer, a teacher, a homemaker, an ecologist, a town planner, a psychologist, a social worker

c Now try any of these:

adaptation, cell, chain, circulation, communication, core, culture, cycle, law, power, reproduction, space, structure

5 Practise looking for analogies between concepts encountered in different subjects.

Example: *How the mind works*
Analogy from this course: key word patterns
Other analogies: spider's web, lightning, tree roots and branches, a river delta, chemical bonds, nerve cells, water spraying, an explosion.

PROBLEM SOLVING THROUGH VISUALIZING

Visualization can help you observe more accurately, recall during exams, solve problems, write more vividly and practise a skill mentally. Can you solve these by visualizing?

1 A woman went to the stream to get 4 litres of water. She had two containers: one 5-litre tin and one 3-litre tin. Neither of the tins was marked for smaller measures. Figure out and then explain clearly how the woman obtained exactly 4 litres.

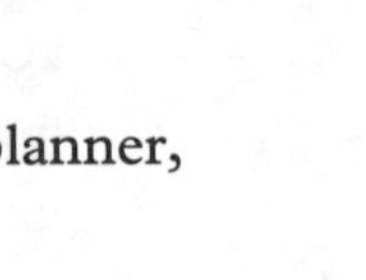

2 Draw four straight lines which join all nine dots—without lifting your pencil from the paper.

VISUALIZING A LECTURE

This sample exercise in visualizing has obvious uses and is suitable for oral work in pairs. Tell one another what you are 'seeing' and 'hearing'.

1 Choose a lecture you have attended on a topic you need to understand or revise.

2 See yourself arrive and find a seat. Watch the lecturer arrive. Visualize him (or her) clearly. What is he wearing? Get ready to listen by thinking about what you already know on the topic and what you hope to find out.

3 Pay attention to the opening words. Hear the lecturer's voice, his accent. Watch his movements. What does he do with his hands? His eyes? Does he pace back and forth? Gesticulate wildly? Scrawl on the blackboard? Point at diagrams? Does he get excited? Does his voice rise or his speech get faster and faster? (Or does he read in a monotone from prepared notes with nary an upward glance?)

4 What has he been saying? Pick out the key ideas. Attach some details. Hear how he pronounces the most important words. Listen to the most interesting part of the lecture. Struggle with a concept that doesn't seem clear. Watch yourself as you decide what to record in your notes. Criticize the notes. How does the lecturer end? Do you want to ask the lecturer a question?

5 Run over the lecture in your mind before leaving the room. Do you feel satisfied? Confused? Inspired? What are your classmates saying about the lecture?

Now make a pattern summary of the information you remember from that lecture. (Can you infer from this exercise why children tend to do better on examinations when they take them in the same room where the subject is taught—and better still when the teacher invigilating is the same?)

C. Using critical judgement

1 Comprehension, invention, oral communication and every kind of writing all depend on the ability to *judge what is significant*. Summarizing tests and develops this skill. For each of the following paragraphs, sum up the general idea in 12 words or less and then suggest a title. Compare your summaries and titles with those of other students. Decide which is best and why.

Title...

The novelist has tremendous power over time and place: he can compress a day into a sentence, or he can allow several pages to tell what happened in a single minute; he can use as many places as he likes, change them as often as he likes, furnish them as he likes, move them as he likes. He also has great power over character and plot; he can tell us in his own subtle words what goes on in the thoughts of his characters, and can weave the most varied incidents, characters and places into his plot. (Adapted from Phyllis Bentley, *Enjoy Books*, Gollanz, 1964).

Title...

We are all of us, since we are human beings, interested, absorbed in human nature; but in the ordinary traffic of living we can know few other human beings with anything like intimacy. Still less can we fully understand them or their behaviour. Indeed, it is rare that we really understand ourselves. Fiction offers us the opportunity of knowing representations of human beings with a far greater intimacy than we can ever know actual human beings, and so much is this true that there are many characters in the world's fiction which are in a sense more 'real' to us, more comprehensible, than all but one or two of all the living people we know personally. So the novel ministers to our passion to understand our fellows; indeed in this age this is the novel's principal expression. (Walter Allen, *Reading a Novel*, Phoenix, 1963).

2 Put the following passage aside when you have read it and give its gist in no more than three sentences. What title would you give the passage?

Title..

Fiction comes from the Latin word meaning 'to form, invent, feign or imagine' and is most often associated with the novel. People often think of fiction as opposed to fact, but the matter of historical truth or falsity is not the real basis for the distinction between real life and literature. The real distinction is that the novel has form or structure. A good novel takes the chaotic experience of life and gives it order. Thus while a 'real' day may include hundreds of small events, many of them insignificant, in fiction each detail narrated should make some contribution to the overall theme, even if we do not see the connection immediately.

Fiction is primarily concerned with the truth about human nature. In a good novel, the characters are plausible human beings within the particular physical and social world which they inhabit. Action and suspense are created as tensions build up to crises and then a climax through the dramatic interplay of characters and events. At the end, a permanent change in the relationships of the conflicting forces has occurred, but a successful novel leaves us with a feeling of inevitability: 'things had to be like that'.

3 Connect, in as many ways as possible, the passage you just summarized and
a the sample term paper on 'The Creative Imagination in Science'.
b the novels you have read for this course and the questions you considered at the end of Unit 5.

4 Compare the outline for the term paper with the paper itself.
a Locate the thesis (topic idea) in the paper. It often appears in this location.
b This outline combines sentence and topic outline forms, using sentences for the main points and subpoints, but only topic headings for the examples. Note other details of the form such as the lay-out, symbols and use of parallel structure. It is not always appropriate to use parallel structure for the major sections as is done in this sample outline, but the relevance of these headings to the thesis must always be clear.
c Locate in the term paper points given in the outline. The paper must develop in their order each heading in the outline, but there are no rules about the number of paragraphs to be used in covering a heading, or the number of headings that may be covered in a paragraph. Your own papers will usually deal with a more limited topic, in more depth, than the sample does and therefore require more detailed treatment of points and examples. Broad topics require much more reading and are more difficult to organize for a balanced treatment.

Essay Practice: Critical Evaluation

A critical evaluation of the novels you have read

1 Think out carefully your reactions to the novels you have read for this course. What are the likenesses and differences? Which author do you think has written the more satisfying book? Why? (Refer to Unit 5 if necessary.) Jot down your thoughts in pattern, outline or brief note form.

2 Read carefully the following instructions for an essay. The question appeared on an examination for a course similar to this one.

Which of the two novels you have read for this course did you enjoy more—and why?

Instructions

1 Be sure to plan your essay before you write it. Include the plan.

2 The introduction should mention the title and author of each book, give the gist (only) of each, and indicate which one you preferred.

3 The body of your essay must offer reasons for your choice and give enough specific details and examples to support each point. Refer to the second book by way of comparison.

4 Your conclusion should round off the essay and leave the reader with the conviction that you have made a sensible choice.

5 Make sure that everything you write helps to answer the question asked. What you must *not* do is simply retell the story. You have already done that in pattern form.

6 Read over the entire paper for the purpose of making improvements and corrections. Eliminate all unnecessary words and all careless errors. Pay special attention to tenses, agreement and sentence clarity.

3 Since you are using the questions and instructions for essay *practice*, this further advice is offered:

a Get mentally prepared. Think about the essay for several days before you sit down to write it. Preview the rest of this book to see if there are any sections it might be worth reading as part of your preparation.

b If you are writing the essay in your own time, rather than in class, set yourself a firm time limit. Produce the plan, write the essay and revise it within a *maximum* of one hour.

c Make sure you follow the instructions exactly. Ignoring directions is a major cause of lost marks on exams. Make every word count.

Assignments

A. Continue or repeat previous assignments

Make a revision timetable.

B. Exercise your imagination

1 It would be impossible to count the number of scientific discoveries, inventions, theories of human behaviour and works of art and literature which began with a 'What if . . . ?' or a 'Suppose . . .' See where any one of the following leads your imagination and write up the result:

Suppose: you could design your own curriculum
you could create your ideal lecturer
you could say how ₦1million was to be spent on your campus
you could decide now what your situation in 10 years' time will be
you could choose something to invent, discover or create.

2 Visualize any of the following clearly:
—the refectory at the busiest time of day
—your hostel room at 7 a.m.
—the largest lecture hall during the changeover between two mass lectures.

Decide on the dominant impression you wish to convey (e.g. confusion), select and arrange details accordingly, and write a description which will effectively convey the scene or impression to a reader. Make every word contribute to the intended effect.

Exchange efforts with a classmate and make improvements.

C. Begin a library investigation

Use any topic, person or idea mentioned in the sample essay (or determine your own, related, investigation). Whereas the sample essay gives a broad survey of a large topic, your aim is to investigate some particular aspect in more depth.

1 Use your library skills to locate information on possible topics. Do some exploratory reading for general background. Do not waste time making notes until you know exactly what your topic will be—but do make bibliography slips for books you expect to use. Use your findings to direct your next reading and help you narrow the topic.

2 Combine with two or three classmates and share what you have found out. Look for connections. Is there an overall idea (thesis) to which all your investigations might contribute? (e.g. 'For success in scientific research, tenacity of purpose is as important as inspiration'—illustrated by reference to the work of Pasteur, Darwin and Edison.) Attempt to state the idea in one sentence.

3 Make notes which will help you develop your part of the overall theme (i.e. a major section of the outline). Frame a commitment sentence for your section.

D. Improve your practice essay

Write and put aside temporarily the practice essay on your African novels. Later, reread it critically and make improvements.

E. Make essay plans

Make essay plans in pattern form for topics you think might be covered in examinations. Include *any three* in your file for this course.

Outline for a term paper based on library sources

<u>The Creative Imagination in Science</u>

Thesis statement: From productive scientists, no less than creative writers and artists, we can learn how to make better use of our creative imaginations.

I. Productive scientists, like creative writers, stress the value of intuition, imagery and 'seeing things whole'.

   A. They often write of their creativity in poetic terms.

   B. They often regard visual imagery and sensory awareness as essential to their creativity:

      1. The example of Einstein

      2. Faraday, Kekule and other examples

   C. They use analogies and metaphors both to make their discoveries and to describe them.

      1. The analogies of Newton and Bohr

      2. Archimedes' flash of insight

      3. Franklin and other examples

   D. They try to form patterns and complete them.

II. **Productive scientists, like creative writers, encourage ideas to fuse in new ways.**

A. They use 'lateral thinking' and cross-fertilize ideas.

1. Pythagoras and musical pitch

2. Gutenberg and the printing press

3. Darwin and the idea of survival of the fittest

B. They are observant and curious by habit, which gives them wide knowledge and broad interests.

C. They turn accidents into experiments by asking 'Why?' and 'Why not?'

1. Pasteur and Fleming: 'prepared minds' favoured by chance

2. Haüy and other examples

III. **Productive scientists, like good writers, strive for a creative synthesis of multiple interconnections.**

A. They recognize that the whole is more than the sum of its parts.

1. Einstein's success in linking physical sciences

2. Fused subjects, e.g. biochemistry

3. The interdependence of science and technology

4. Teamwork and interdisciplinary approaches

(a) Treating infectious diseases

(b) Implementing universal immunization in West Africa

B. They produce ideas and associations in quantity from which come some of quality.

1. Bionics: studying biology to get ideas for inventions

2. Synectics: a technique for generating ideas

C. Their ultimate goal is to find unity in diversity.

An example of a term paper using library sources

THE CREATIVE IMAGINATION IN SCIENCE

by

Ngozi E. Onwuka

Department of Biology

GS 101: Use of English

Section 23

Dr. C. Ajayi

9th March, 1985

THE CREATIVE IMAGINATION IN SCIENCE

We have all known moments when an idea strikes, understanding dawns or a solution springs to mind in a flash. This is the experience of intuition: the sudden emergence in the conscious mind of a clarifying idea or pattern synthesized in the subconscious from previously unrelated or muddled ideas. Studies by and about creative people have tried to analyze the process of achieving insight and to suggest ways of stimulating the subconscious mental processes which give birth to intuitions. It is clear from these studies that creative scientists, no less than creative writers and artists, can show us how to make better use of our imaginations.[1]

Some of the most illuminating accounts of the creative process have come from mathematicians and physicists, those by Henri Poincaré and Albert Einstein being well-known examples.[2] A point often made about such accounts is that a reader might guess the authors to be poets or musicians, so strong is the emphasis on intuition--Einstein calls it 'the really valuable thing'--and on the aesthetic desire to achieve beauty, order and harmony. This seems less strange when one considers that physical scientists are often working with things which cannot be seen with the eye and therefore need to rely, as poets do, on analogy, metaphor and a vivid imagination.

Outstanding scientists, no less than artists, tend to use intense visual imagery and often report a heightened awareness of auditory or kinesthetic senses too. Einstein, for example, considered 'combinatory play' with images an essential feature of his productive thought and always saw his discoveries in mental pictures and felt them in his muscles first. Putting them into words or mathematical symbols came later. When he was sixteen he was lying on his back in the sun one day and wondered what the world would look like if he were able to ride on a beam of light. After ten years of contemplation, the answer came to him as he got out of bed one morning; the end result of the 'imagining' was published as the Theory of Relativity.[3]

Years earlier, Michael Faraday had seen stresses surrounding magnets and electric currents as curves in space; his vision led first to the dynamo and then to the electric motor.[4] Frederich von Kekulé produced what has been called 'the most brilliant piece of prediction in the whole range of organic chemistry' as a result of a vision in which atoms behaved like snakes. He saw one snake swallow its own tail and realized that some molecules, such as benzine, must be rings rather than open structures.[5] More recently, James Watson and Francis Crick discovered the double helix structure of a DNA molecule ahead of rival searchers through the use of visualization. Louis Pasteur, Max Planck, Clerk Maxwell and Paul Ehrlich are other important scientists who claimed that the pictorial representation of ideas was essential to their creative thinking.

The analogy is a close relative of the mental picture and another form of 'connecting' used as much by the scientist as the poet. Newton connected the behaviour of the moon with a falling apple and formulated the law of gravity.[6] Neils Bohr saw the atom as a miniature solar system with the proton in the centre and electrons in orbit, and went on to liken the spectrum of the atom to a window for looking into it. It was he who said 'When it comes to atoms, language can be used only as in poetry.'[7]

One of the most famous 'flash of insight' stories is that of Archimedes, in ancient Greece, who realized how to find out whether a gold crown was really all gold when he got into the bath and watched the water rise. He is supposed to have streaked down the street shouting 'Eureka! Eureka!' ('I have found it'), an expression which has come to symbolize intuitive discovery.[8] Other examples of discovery by analogy are Benjamin Franklin's invention of the lightning conductor,[9] Alexander Graham Bell's invention of the telephone (which resembles the human ear), Elie Mechnikoff's discovery of defensive phagocytes ('cell-eaters')[10] and Otto Loewi's discovery of the chemical transmission of nerve impulses.[11]

Sometimes seeing similarities leads to the construction of a whole pattern or system which, to be complete, should include things not yet discovered. Mendeleev's prediction of undiscovered elements,[12] Harvey's prediction of capillaries in the blood system, and the idea of 'black holes' in space all resulted from a desire to complete a design, forming a unified whole.

Productive scientists make their discoveries and inventions, as authors write novels and poems, by encouraging ideas to fuse in new combinations. For example, when the usual approaches to a problem do not lead to a solution, they may look for a completely new way of thinking about the problem. Searching for a way around a blocked path is sometimes called 'lateral thinking' because it involves stepping aside from well-worn paths of thought and a willingness to allow completely unrelated ideas to bump into each other.[13] There are many examples of intuitive flashes which came in this way.

Pythagoras understood the connection between musical pitch and mathematical physics when he noted the sounds made by iron rods of different lengths being hit in a blacksmith's shop.[14] Johannes Gutenberg put the idea of an engraved coin or seal together with the way a winepress works and invented printing with movable type.[15] Charles Darwin (as well as Alfred Wallace, independently) read an essay by Malthus on population and connected it with his work on evolution to produce the idea of the survival of the fittest. Darwin's career is considered an outstanding illustration of the thesis that creative originality is mostly a matter of cross-fertilizing ideas from different sources.[16]

Obviously, people with a lively curiosity, a venturesome attitude and a diversity of experiences, memories and interests to draw on are far more likely to make unusual connections than those who put knowledge into tight compartments, confine themselves to a narrow specialism and reject the unusual.[17] There are dozens of examples of eminent scientists and inventors whose greatest fame is in a field other than the one they were trained for, and many whose accomplishments span several fields. The life and work of Leonardo da Vinci, Franklin, Pasteur, Einstein, Ronald Ross (who discovered how malaria is transmitted), William Thomson (Lord Kelvin), Mechnikoff, Luigi Galvini, Marie Curie and, more recently, Carl Sagan and Jacob Bronowski, all illustrate one or both of these truths.

'Lucky accidents' happen to people with appropriate knowledge and experience and a habit of finding interconnections, who ask 'Why?' and 'Why not?' when something unusual happens in their presence. Pasteur's outpourings of discovery and invention illustrate his own belief that 'chance favours the prepared mind'. The experiments which led to his successive discoveries that fermentation, putrefaction and contagious diseases are all caused by living things (micro-organisms)[18] began with a 'spoiled' mould in much the same way that Alexander Fleming discovered penicillin because, instead of throwing a 'spoiled' culture away he was curious to find out why it had spoiled.[19] Abbé Haüy became a pioneer of crystallography because he accidentally dropped some beautiful crystals one day and noticed the fractured faces.[20] Galvani discovered current electricity, Hans Oestered discovered electro-magnetic induction,[21] Thomas Edison invented the phonograph, Wilhelm Röntgen discovered X-rays, Henri Bequerel discovered that uranium was the source of the rays,[22] Charles Goodyear found out how to vulcanize rubber and John Dunlop invented the pneumatic tyre because they turned 'accidents' into 'experiments'.

A discovery or invention, like a good novel, is worth far more than the sum of its parts. Combining copper and tin created not just bronze, but the Bronze Age. As ideas are cross-fertilized and interconnections proliferate, the rate of further discovery speeds up and 'separate' subjects are found to be close relatives. Bronowski remarks that in his lifetime, 'Einstein joined light to time, and time to space; energy to matter, matter to space and space to gravitation', each advance opening up new worlds of discovery.[23]

Consider the sciences born of new connections: biochemistry, electromagnetism, molecular physics, microtechnology, agricultural economics--the list is almost endless. And consider also the interdependence of science and technology, advances in the one stimulating further progress in the other. Improvements in telescopes and microscopes, for example, lead to further advances in astronomy and microbiology, which in turn demand more refined instruments and techniques.

Awareness of this interdependence is also reflected in the teamwork and interdisciplinary approaches so common in science and technology today. Discussing ideas with others can clarify one's thoughts and stimulate new ones, while the world's major problems--e.g. feeding a growing population; child health; pollution, waste, the destruction of rainforests and other problems of the environment; the threat of nuclear war--are so interlinked and multi-faceted that only a multi-disciplinary approach to them is appropriate. Tremendous advances in treating infectious diseases have been possible because techniques developed for other purposes have been applied: filtering processes, microscopic techniques, tissue culture and genetic statistics, to name but four.

Advances in vaccinology have made it possible to control, if not eliminate, the childhood diseases of measles, diphtheria, tetanus, whooping cough, tuberculosis, polio and yellow fever, but devising a way to carry out universal immunization calls for the skills and dedication of people in many different fields: technicians, rural health workers, sociologists, medical geographers, administrators and even journalists. Successful two-injection-only programmes in Upper Volta and Senegal show that it can be done.[24] There may be another 'connection' in the fact that Dr. Jones Salk, who spearheaded the campaign, is the same man who once said he had discovered a vaccine for polio <u>because</u> he was determined to do so.

People who produce useful ideas are usually people who produce ideas in quantity--including many useless ones. This observation has led to new sciences and to new techniques for generating ideas. The science of <u>bionics</u> studies biological functions such as birds' navigation systems, the way dolphins dive, and how beetle's eyes work to get ideas for engineering inventions and improvements. Engineers and industrial product designers, among others, use synectics as a technique, deliberately joining completely unconnected words or concepts in 'combinatory play' to see if this will stimulate any new and usable ideas.[25]

The lives and thoughts of creative scientists show that they, like creative artists, religious mystics or humanists, have a deep sense of wonder and a strong urge to find unity in diversity.[26] They too develop skills, techniques and attitudes appropriate to their search--including ways of harnessing the imagination. Perhaps the seemingly different goals of creative people in all fields are but different forms of the same thing.

Notes

1 A book recommended in its entirety for students of science is W. B. Beveridge, The Art of Scientific Investigation (London: Heinemann, 1961). It has chapters on all aspects of scientific discovery including imagination, intuition and chance as well as preparation, observation, experimentation and reason. Arthur Koestler, The Act of Creation (London: Pan, 1970) is considered the classic study of creativity; it is very readable. A beautifully written and illustrated history of science in its broadest sense is Jacob Bronowski, The Ascent of Man (London: BBC, 1973).

2 Koestler, pp. 145-47 and 171. For Poincare's essay, 'Mathematical Creation', see P. Vernon, ed. Creativity: Selected Readings (Harmondsworth, Middlesex: Penguin, 1970), pp. 77-78.

3 Bronowski, pp. 244-57 gives a clear account of how the theory developed and what it means.

4 Koestler, pp. 170-71.

5 Koestler, pp. 118 and 169-70.

6 Bronowski, pp. 221-224; also Silvano Arieti, Creativity: The Magic Synthesis (New York: Basic Books, 1980), pp. 271-72.

7 Bronowski, pp. 334-40.
8 Koestler, pp. 105-8.
9 Koestler, pp. 202-4 and Bronowski, pp. 268-74.
10 Beveridge, p. 70 and Koestler, p. 199.
11 Koestler, pp. 204-7.
12 Bronowski, pp. 322-30.
13 Edward de Bono, Lateral Thinking (Harmondsworth, Middlesex: Penguin, 1970).
14 Koestler, p. 111.
15 Koestler, pp. 121-24.
16 Arieti, p. 273 and Koestler, pp. 131-44. Bronowski, pp. 291-94 and 301-9 gives a full account of Darwin's working processes.
17 George W. Ladd, 'Artistic Research Tools for Scientific Minds', American Journal of Agricultural Economics, 61, No. 1 (February 1979), pp. 3-7.
18 Koestler, pp. 193 and 446-52.
19 Beveridge, pp. 152 and 162; Koestler, p. 194.
20 Koestler, pp. 192-93.
21 Beveridge, pp. 160-61.
22 Koestler, pp. 195-96.
23 Bronowski, p. 256.
24 Michael Davie, 'Notebook: How to Save the Lives of 10 Million Children a Year', The Observer (London), 16 February 1983, p. 16.
25 Two examples of books which describe techniques are Barry F. Anderson, The Complete Thinker: A Handbook of Techniques for Creative and Critical Problem Solving (Englewood Cliffs, New Jersey: Prentice Hall, 1980) and Karl Albrecht, Brain Power: Learn to Improve Your Thinking Skills (Englewood Cliffs, New Jersey: Prentice Hall, 1980).
26 Two relevant essays are E. W. Sinott, 'The Creativeness of Life' and C. R. Rogers, 'Towards a Theory of Creativity' in the collection edited by Vernon.

List of References

Albrecht, Karl. Brain Power: Learn to Improve Your Thinking Skills. Englewood Cliffs, New Jersey: Prentice Hall, 1980.

Anderson, Barry F. The Complete Thinker: A Handbook of Techniques for Creative and Critical Problem Solving. Englewood Cliffs, New Jersey: Prentice Hall, 1980.

Arieti, Silvano. Creativity: The Magic Synthesis. New York: Basic Books, 1980.

Beveridge, W. I. B. The Art of Scientific Investigation. London: Heinemann, 1961.

Bronowski, Jacob. The Ascent of Man. London: British Broadcasting Corporation, 1973.

Davie, Michael. 'Notebook: How to Save the Lives of 10 Million Children a Year', The Observer (London), 16 February 1983, p. 16.

Koestler, Arthur. The Act of Creation. London: Pan, 1970.

Ladd, George W. 'Artistic Research Tools for Scientific Minds', American Journal of Agricultural Economics, 61, No. 1 (February 1979), pp. 1-11.

Vernon, P. E. (ed.). Creativity: Selected Readings. Harmondsworth, Middlesex: Penguin, 1970.

Unit Ten Writing to Convince

Timed Reading Passage 10: Preparing Effective Argument

Instructions

1 Some of the examples in the passage refer to the sample term paper on 'The Creative Imagination in Science'. Briefly recall the essay.

2 Preview the passage carefully, paying special attention to the words in italics. Which of them are familiar? Take time to recall what you know about them and anticipate what might be said. Get mentally set to read it with maximum efficiency.

3 At the signal, begin to read at the highest speed you can manage.

Most written assignments and class discussions, as well as many examination essays, require you to go beyond a mere summary of facts to show that you can use information both critically and creatively. Whether the product is called an argumentative essay, a debate, a coursework essay, a term paper, a library paper, a seminar paper or a research paper, the object is to examine the facts and the judgements of experts on a subject or issue, think your way to a point of view on it, and then convince others that the conclusion you have come to is the most reasonable one possible. Skill in argument proves mastery of the advanced thinking and communication skills associated with higher education and demanded by every kind of job a student of higher education is likely to aspire to. For convenience, we shall here refer particularly to the requirements for a paper written in your own time and shall refer to it as a research paper, to emphasize that it is an investigative paper based on library resources.

The controlling idea of a research paper—the conclusion you draw from your investigations—is expressed in a one sentence summary called a *thesis statement*. A good thesis statement is at the same time a commitment statement, because it not only sums up the paper but also makes a promise as to how it will be organized. All other ideas, facts and examples are organized so as to develop and support the thesis with maximum clarity and force. Your reader must be convinced by the evidence you present that your thesis is justified.

Since argument always involves judgements, the main issue—whether it is called the *thesis statement*, as in a research (term) paper, the *proposition* as in a debate, the *resolution* as in a meeting, or simply the *argument*, as in a discussion—is always an assertion either that something is or is not a fact, or that something should or should not be done. The same is true for sub-propositions: issues which must be proved in order to prove the main proposition (the *thesis*).

The structure of a sound argument is a series of *premise-conclusion* relationships, *premises* being statements accepted or demonstrated to be true and used as reasons for a conclusion. The simplest form consists of two statements, e.g. 'Much of the speaking and writing associated with university work calls for skill in argument; therefore students should learn to argue effectively.' However, most conclusions are based on more than one premise, and are often used in turn as premises for further conclusions.

A sentence outline for a research paper usually shows the structure of an extended argument: each subdivision (e.g., a, b, c) serves as a premise for the heading (conclusion) under which it comes (1, 2 or 3) which in turn becomes a premise for the heading (conclusion) at the next higher level (A, B or C), with the headings (conclusion) for the major sections (I, II and III) becoming the premises which justify the overall conclusion (the thesis).

For example, observations by creative scientists about their own ways of thinking and working have led some of them to draw conclusions about how their ideas come. Similarities in these accounts have been used as premises for conclusions about specific aspects of creativity, e.g. intuition, or about creative people in general. These conclusions can become premises for further conclusions, until the structure is strong enough to support an overall conclusion (thesis), e.g. that we can learn how to increase our own creativity by finding out how creative scientists make their discoveries.

Moving from a premise to a conclusion usually involves making an unstated *assumption*, e.g. that if other people can learn to make better use of their creative imaginations, you can too. It is important to recognize what has been taken for granted in reasoning, because an unjustified assumption can bring down a whole argument.

It is also important to distinguish among different types of premises and to be able to judge their reliability. The most reliable premises are *statements of fact*, because these are assertions which can be verified and do not depend on anyone's opinion, e.g. 'Nigeria is Africa's most populous nation' or 'Einstein claimed to see discoveries in mental pictures first'.

Inferences are conclusions based on reasoning from presumed facts (premises). *Inductive reasoning* starts with specific facts and examples and tries to form some general conclusion from them, e.g. 'Outstanding scientists tend to use intense visual imagery' is a conclusion drawn from studies of many outstanding scientists. Note that the statement is qualified, to allow for the scientists who do not use intense visual imagery. No generalization, not even a scientific law, can ever be proved with 100% certainty. While repeated experiments producing the same result make it *probable* that a statement such as 'metals expand when heated' will continue to hold true in specific instances, most everyday generalizations need careful qualifying so that you do not claim more than the evidence warrants.

Deductive reasoning starts with, or assumes, a general principle, and then notes more specific implications or instances of it, e.g. 'Metals expand when heated. Copper is a metal. Therefore copper will expand when heated.' For a deduction to be true and valid, the premises must be true and the reasoning from them correct.

Judgements go further than inferences to express an opinion or attitude, and depend on the individual's evaluation of the facts through comparing them with what he already knows. Many judgements are not suitable for serious argument, either because they are matters of personal taste, e.g. 'Biology is more interesting than chemistry', or because the wording is too loose, e.g. 'Girls are brighter than boys'. There can be no sensible argument about a value judgement unless the meaning of key terms and the criteria used in making the judgement are clear.

Most of the supporting details, examples and judgements in a library research paper are drawn from *expert testimony*: statements by presumed authorities on the subject. You are expected to choose the best-qualified and most up-to-date authorities on your subject and to present their views accurately. You should pay attention to experts who disagree with the view you favour as well as to those who agree with it, and be prepared to modify your views if the evidence warrants it.

It is often good strategy to acknowledge opposing views early in your own arguments, perhaps conceding the value or truth of particular points. The purpose is to show that you have examined all the views objectively before making a final judgement.

Effective argument is logical persuasion, carried by reason, not loudness or emotive appeals. Its preparation involves the fullest interplay of critical judgement and creative synthesis. The ideas, skilfully combined and arranged, must be amply supported by convincing evidence and reliable expert testimony, and presented in language that is precise and emotionally neutral. There should be no fallacies.

A *fallacy* is an incorrect or misleading conclusion resulting from inaccurate premises or incorrect reasoning. There are many types of fallacies. Some, called *logical fallacies*, are errors in the process of drawing a conclusion from the premises, even though the premises may be true as in this version of a famous example: 'One in every four children born in the world is Chinese. Mrs. Olatunje is expecting her fourth child. Therefore the child will be Chinese.'

However, the most common fallacies stem not from faults in logic, but from faults in the material on which a conclusion is based—the premises themselves. Sometimes known as *material fallacies*, they include verbal problems arising from undefined terms, vague and ambiguous words and emotionally slanted language: unwarranted generalizations, faulty statistics and oversimplified explanations; and a range of irrelevant emotional appeals which misrepresent or ignore altogether the question at issue.

These fallacies are serious as well as common. They can make your argument unconvincing and even worthless. Yet they can *nearly always be prevented* by careful planning and outlining before writing.

The process of thinking out a thesis statement which sums up your main idea precisely ensures you solve any verbal problems before you begin. Making a detailed outline directs your research so that you seek out the support required. By stating your conclusion clearly in the first paragraph, you make a commitment that all the rest of the paper will justify it—and can then firmly refuse space to irrelevancies. In addition, a questioning, critical attitude to what you read will help you select the most reliable facts and opinions, and the same attitude when you revise will help you detect any weak or fallacious arguments which slip into your first draft.

As in other aspects of life and learning, the real skill in argument is learning how to achieve control over what you say and do, and how to stay in control, so that you accomplish your purpose.

(1500 words)

Record your time and WPM. Go on to the questions.

1 Which ending is *not* correct? A good thesis statement for a library research paper
a states the conclusion of the investigation.
b is a deductive inference.
c is a commitment about purpose and organization.
d is a judgement suitable for argument.

2 The passage implies that you should
a decide on a point of view before you start and stick to it regardless.
b decide on a point of view before you start and pick out only the evidence that supports it.
c find out enough about a subject to come to a point of view on it, then convince the reader you have come to the right conclusion.
d read and make notes on aspects of a topic, then decide what the notes add up to and make an outline.

3 A premise is
a a statement proven to be true.
b the same thing as a conclusion.
c a statement derived from an assumption.
d a statement used as a basis for a conclusion.

4 An assumption is
a something taken for granted.
b an assertion which needs to be verified.
c a fallacy which can bring down an argument.
d an unreliable premise.

5 Reasoning which starts with a general rule and draws a conclusion from it about a particular instance
a gives a true and valid conclusion.
b is deductive.
c is inductive.
d is a generalization.

6 The statement 'All outstanding scientists use intense visual imagery' is an example of
a a deduction.
b an assumption.
c a faulty generalization.
d expert testimony.

7 Choose the true statement:
a Judgements are reliable if they are found in library sources.
b Judgements are arguable if they are clearly worded and the basis for judgement established.
c Judgements are never as reliable as inferences.
d Any judgement is arguable provided enough opinions are available.

8 Judging from the passage, which of the following does the writer consider *least* necessary in preventing fallacies?
a planning before writing
b a questioning attitude
c a sense of purpose
d a knowledge of logic.

9 Which of the following is *not* stated or implied in the passage?
a A good thesis statement gives you control over the paper's development.
b Without an outline, some points are likely to be inadequately developed.
c Writing a paper requires critical but not creative skills.
d Writing a paper requires both critical and creative skills.

10 The main purpose of the passage is to
a show the relationships between outlines and arguments.
b provide definitions of terms used in argument.
c give an overview of the principles and pitfalls of argument.
d emphasize the seriousness of fallacies.

K

WORDS PER MINUTE CHART: Timed Reading Passage 10 *(1500 words)*							
Time	WPM	Time	WPM	Time	WPM	Time	WPM
2.00	—	3.00	500	4.00	375	5.00	300
10	690	10	475	10	360	10	290
20	645	20	450	20	345	20	280
30	600	30	430	30	335	30	275
40	560	40	410	40	320	40	265
50	530	50	390	50	310	50	260

WORDS PER MINUTE CHART: Timed Reading Passage 10 (*1500 words*)							
Time	WPM	Time	WPM	Time	WPM	Time	WPM
6.00	250	7.00	215	8.00	190	9.00	165
10	245	10	210	10	185	10	165
20	235	20	205	20	180	20	160
30	230	30	200	30	175	30	155
40	225	40	195	40	170	40	155
50	220	50	190	50	165	50	150

Follow-up

A. Recall

Form brief explanations of the following for the benefit of someone who does not know what they are:

1 an assumption 2 an inference 3 a generalization
4 a value judgement 5 expert testimony 6 a fallacy

B. Connect

What are the likenesses and differences between written and oral argument, e.g. between a library research paper and participation in an organized debate or discussion?

C. Pre-writing tasks

Read the Summary of Pre-Writing Tasks for a Library Research Paper on page 170 and look at the three checklists.

1 Recall the steps in the summary.

2 Jot down or give orally as many mental connections as possible between the summary and the passage just read.

3 Spend a further two minutes making as many connections as possible between the summary and previous work in this course. Do you need to revise any topic before proceeding, e.g. reading, notemaking, outlining?

4 Compare the procedures outlined with your own working methods and make your own judgements.

A Summary of Pre-Writing Tasks for a Library Research Paper

1 Choose a limited subject and read for general background. (If the topic is set, decide your approach to it.)

2 Narrow the topic and test it for faults. (See Pre-Writing Checklist 1 below).

3 Write out a preliminary outline with a tentative thesis statement. (See Pre-Writing Checklists 2 and 3).

4 Compile a working bibliography of possible sources for your paper.

5 Work back and forth among Steps 1–4 until you have a clear idea of what you want your paper to do and what, exactly, you will need to find out.

6 Read for specific information, selectively and critically.

7 Make notes on note slips, then label and arrange them to correspond with the outline.

8 Work back and forth among all the previous steps until your purpose is clear and you have enough material to achieve it.

9 Decide on the final title, improve the thesis statement and construct the final outline. (See Checklists again.)

10 Set aside a block of time for writing the first draft of the paper.

Pre-Writing Checklist 1: Testing a Topic

Keep adjusting and refining the topic until you can answer Yes to each of these questions:

1 Am I really interested in this topic?

2 Is there enough written material available to me on it?

3 Does it avoid these faults?

Too big	Too vague
Too technical	Too emotional

4 Does it allow scope for using the library, sifting evidence, interpreting facts and making reasoned judgements?

5 Will a paper on this topic interest other people?

Pre-Writing Checklist 2: Testing a Thesis Statement

Keep improving your thesis statement as you work until you can answer Yes to each of these questions:

1 Is it a single sentence, with a main clause that states the controlling idea of the entire paper?

2 Does it indicate the scope and organization of the discussion?
3 Is it worded so that the meaning is unmistakably clear?
4 Does it 'match' the outline?

Pre-Writing Checklist 3: Testing an Outline

Use these questions to help you improve the outline (and thesis):

1 Will developing the major headings (I, II, III) fulfill the promise of the thesis statement?

2 Is there enough support for each main point (heading)?
a For what parts of the outline do I need more points, details, examples?
b Should any headings be combined? omitted? reworded?

3 Are the ideas and relationships clear and accurate?

4 Is the outline set out in conventional form, with standard symbols and an even left-hand margin for each level of division?

5 Are entries of the same level of importance expressed in parallel grammatical form?

6 Does this outline show in detail the content and structure of a *convincing* argument?

Related Skills

A. Limiting a topic and stating a thesis

1 Suggest ways to limit some of the general subjects listed below to specific topics. Keep restricting the topic until you have one which would be suitable for a library research paper limited to 10 pages. If possible, think of a title which would indicate the scope and approach of the paper, e.g.

Subject: Pollution
First limiting: Water Pollution
Second limiting: Effects of Water Pollution on Health
Final Topic: Better Health through Cleaner Water

Child Health
Political Systems
Universities
Birth Customs
Tourism
Women
Secondary Education
Ecology

Libraries
Appropriate Technology
Imagination
Human Rights
Newspapers
Traditional Medicine
Kinship Systems
Economic Development

2 Link two or more different subjects or interests to form a topic suitable for a research paper, e.g. agriculture, microbes and insects could be combined in the topic 'Microbial Control of Insect Pests'.

3 For any of your limited topics, make a statement which could serve as the tentative thesis. Assuming the paper would have three major sections, write possible headings for them. List subpoints for any one of the sections.

Title: Better Health Through Cleaner Water

Tentative thesis: Water pollution causes so many illnesses and deaths, especially among children, that a campaign for cleaner water, through legislation, mass education and community efforts, should be a national priority.

I. What is Water Pollution?
   A. Definition
   B. Characteristics of Polluted Water
   C. Causes of Polluted Water

II. Effects of Water Pollution

III. Ways to Improve Community Health through Cleaner Water

What subpoints would you list under III? Section III would be the longest and most important part of this paper. Would you prefer to divide its content in some way between sections II and III, moving 'Effects' to the end of section I? If so, what would your headings be?

4 Suggest statements for some of the following which could serve as the proposition in a debate. Say whether or not each would also be suitable for a research paper and explain your answer.

Multinational Companies in Developing Countries
The Creative Artist in the Community
University Education for Women
Cultural Diversity
Student Welfare
Qualifications for Political Candidates

B. Removing verbal obstacles to argument

Sensible argument on any of the following would be difficult, if not impossible, because of problems with words and meanings. Examine the statements. (Asking questions is often a useful way to start.) Identify the problem. Then, for any five of them, make a new statement that removes the obstacle to argument. What criteria would be appropriate for deciding whether to accept or reject your statement?

1 Woman's place is in the home.
(Sample questions: All women? If not, which ones? What if a woman is single? childless? professionally trained? supporting a student husband? Where is a man's place?)

2 Achebe is a better author than Ngugi.

3 Computers can think.

4 Justice is more important than Freedom.

5 Measles is a worse disease than malaria.

6 The best teaching method is the lecture.

7 The historian is a more truly educated man than the scientist.

8 Village festivals are our most important cultural activities.

9 Lack of discipline is a chief cause of falling educational standards.

10 University authorities should give students their rights.

C. Detecting fallacies of oversimplification

Some of the common ways of oversimplifying issues are listed on page 174. Read through the list so you know the kinds of problems you are looking for in this exercise. Then, for each of the following, give a brief reply or ask a question which points up the fallacy.

1 Final examinations should be abolished because they encourage cramming.

2 University students believe the only way to express their wishes is through riots and marches.

3 Lightning must cause thunder because lightning flashes before thunder roars.

4 If we had enough drugs in our hospitals, the health problems of Malaysia would be solved.

5 The reason for the continual rise in agricultural imports in this country is unused land.

6 The percentage of passes in Cambridge exams is much higher in Y state than in Z state. Y children must be much brighter.

7 The average Nigerian dies at the age of 45. Ali, who is an average Nigerian, is 42, so he hasn't long to live.

8 Just as a democratic nation selects its leaders by ballot, so should all members of a university community decide by ballot who should be the lecturers.

9 If one aspirin cures a headache in 20 minutes, then two will cure a headache in 10 minutes.

10 We would not have all these wars, strikes, riots and crimes if people would only return to religion. (NB. This is also a verbal problem.)

K 11 An investigator wished to discover the average number of days' sickness each semester among the college's students. He based his conclusions on Medical Centre records.

12 By my guess, about 60% of crimes take advantage of power failure, so the national electricity board is a major cause of crime.

13 'Education is the heart of any nation.' This quotation proves that we should be spending more money on education in Singapore.

K 14 School A produces better examination results than School B because School A had 95% passes in examinations while School B had only 70%.

15 A Student Union leader wished to determine the opinions of first year students on a certain issue and decided to consult a sample of 15%. He began with first year students in his own hostel and those in his department, and made up the rest of the 15% from other departments in his faculty.

Fallacies of Oversimplification

This list gives some of the forms of oversimplification which you should look out for. The list is by no means exhaustive!

1 Faulty generalizations occur when
- —the relative number of observed instances is too low
- —the examples are not typical or representative (*loaded sampling*)
- —an individual is assumed to possess the characteristics of a whole group (or vice versa)
- —*all* is used or implied when *some* is the case

2 Faulty causal generalizations occur when
- —there are other possible causes besides the one given as *the* cause
- —one situation is assumed to cause another simply because it precedes it in time (the *post hoc fallacy*)
- —the cause can be present without the result occurring

3 Faulty statistical generalizations occur when
- —the word *average* is used without explanation of how it was calculated
- —percentages or exact figures are used without explanation of how they were arrived at

4 Faulty analogies occur when
- —an illustrative analogy is presented as *proof*
- —the two things being compared are not alike in the respect being referred to

5 The fallacy of the false dilemma occurs when
- —two alternatives are offered as if they were the only ones possible
- —the two possibilities offered are not mutually exclusive

Five useful questions which will help you identify the fallacy:
- —How large and representative was the sample?
- —Does the so-called cause adequately explain the effect?
- —Have statistics been used fairly?
- —Are the two things being compared analogous in the crucial respect?
- —Is an either/or choice really necessary?

D. Detecting fallacies of irrelevance

Some common ways of digressing from reasoned discussion of the issue supposedly being examined are listed lower on this page. Read through the list so you know the kinds of faults you are looking for in this exercise. Then examine each of the following and explain in one sentence what is wrong with the reasoning.

1 We need not consider the views of those wild-eyed radicals in the Political Science department.

2 Since women are inferior to men, they should not receive equal pay for equal work.

3 It is un-Nigerian to have anything to do with foreign ideologies.

4 I failed the exam because the lecturer was prejudiced against me.

5 The Prime Minister himself believes in corporal punishment.

6 There is no reason why polygamy should be considered unfair to women. Women in monogamous homes with husbands who beat them are no better off.

7 The Governor announced that he would be setting up a Women's Rights Office to eliminate all discrimination against women in his government and said he would put the best man he can find in charge of it.

8 The most scientific toothpaste of them all . . . Enriched with new Formula II . . . Contains activated chlorophyll.

9 Housewives say that colds clear up 11% faster with X . . . Prescribed by doctors for over two decades.

10 I know I don't deserve to pass. But it will break my parents' hearts if you fail me.

Fallacies of Irrelevance

Digression from the point being argued into irrelevancies may be a deliberate attempt to distract attention from the real question by using emotional appeals and tricks of suggestion; that is why they are sometimes called *psychological fallacies*. Just as often in student work, however, these fallacies result from a lack of planning and purpose. Whether deliberate or unintentional, irrelevancies are a major cause of poor marks on exams and essays. They also appear frequently in advertisements, political speeches and everyday discussions. These are some of the ways in which issues are evaded. Look out for them.

1 Misrepresenting the question (e.g. by misquoting) or shifting to a different question.

2 Appealing to 'authority', but in an irrelevant field.

3 Appealing to tradition, precedent or 'the majority' when these are irrelevant.

4 Appealing to hidden fears, desires or prejudices, usually through emotive words (*slanting*).

5 Attacking or praising the person who holds the idea instead of examining the idea itself.

6 Refusing to apply the same standards to one's own case as to that of others.

7 Rationalizing: giving a seemingly good reason when it is not the real one.

8 Presenting arguments in support of an opinion arrived at before further facts were available, and ignoring the new evidence (*closed mind*).

9 *Begging the question* or *arguing in a circle*: assuming as a premise the conclusion which is to be proved or simply repeating the premise, in different words, as the conclusion.

10 Seeking to impress with word magic, number magic or science magic, e.g. big words, statistics or reference to 'scientific experiments', instead of tackling the issues.

E. Writing a first draft

Read the Hints for Writing a First Draft below. Then suggest what the reasons might be for:

1 Beginning each new paragraph of the draft on a new sheet of paper.

2 Not stopping to worry about spelling or grammatical points (except for verbs and tenses).

3 Inserting the (foot)notes right in the text as you go.

4 Writing the introduction last.

5 Putting the paper aside for a time before you reread and revise it.

In what ways does this advice resemble the advice for a first reading of a chapter?

Hints for Writing a First Draft

1 Put the thesis and outline, your note slips (arranged in the order you will use them), your bibliography slips, and a supply of paper in front of you. Think of your purpose: to prove the thesis to your reader.

2 Start with the first main point and develop it as if you were writing an essay with this heading as the topic. Concentrate on one aspect of the topic at a time (A, B, C) paying attention to relationships.

3 Begin each new paragraph on a new sheet of paper. Write on one side of the paper only, on alternate lines, with ample margins (so you can revise without unnecessary recopying). Treat each paragraph like a mini-essay: a main idea with enough details, examples or evidence to clarify, reinforce or prove it.

4 Get the ideas down steadily and fairly rapidly, blending the notes from sources into your own writing as smoothly as possible. Save any checking on spelling or grammatical points until later. Move over difficult sections and return to them later. Keep the thought moving forward. Clip any quotation note slips to the appropriate page. This saves time and avoids the risk of inaccurate recopying.

5 Insert your (foot)notes as you go, right into the text, like this:

Jean Floyd, _Study Skills for Higher Education: A Use of English Course_ (London: Collins, 1984), p. 142

You can number and move them to their proper places later.

6 Control verbs and tenses.
a Choose Present or Past as your main tense and stick to it unless the meaning demands another one.
b Make each verb agree with its subject in number and person.
c Prefer active verbs to passive constructions.

7 Aim for clear, relevant sentences, mostly short ones, each following logically from the one before. Do not spend too long working on individual sentences now, however. Keep pushing ahead.

8 Imagine your reader as you write. Picture his or her reactions to what you are writing. If he is bored, confused, lost, or annoyed, what can you do about it? Keep on telling the reader what you think he wants (or needs) to know until you have developed the whole outline, however roughly.

9 Write the conclusion. Then write the introduction, which should gain interest immediately and let the reader know exactly what to expect. It is usual to state the thesis at or near the end of the introductory paragraph.

10 Put the paper aside, preferably for several days, at least overnight.

Practice in Criticism and Essay Revision

A. Passage for summary and criticism

Read the following untitled passage. Then

1 Sum up the main point of each paragraph in the form of a 'rule' of five words or less.

2 Give the passage a title.

3 Make mental connections between the passage and earlier parts of this unit.

4 Judge the extract as a piece of writing and give reasons for your opinion.

To avoid the various foolish operations to which mankind is prone, no superhuman genius is required. A few simple rules will keep you, not from all errors, but from silly error.

If the matter is one that can be settled by observation, make the observation yourself. Aristotle could have avoided the mistake of thinking that women have fewer teeth than men, by the simple device of asking Mrs. Aristotle to keep her mouth open while he counted. He did not do so because he thought he knew. Thinking that you know when in fact you don't is a fatal mistake, to which we are all prone. I believe myself that hedgehogs eat black beetles, because I have been told that they do; but if I were writing a book on the habits of hedgehogs, I should not commit myself until I had seen one enjoying this unappetizing diet. Aristotle, however, was less cautious. Ancient and medieval authors knew all about unicorns and salamanders; not one of them thought it necessary to avoid dogmatic statements about them because he had never seen one of them.

Many matters, however, are less easily brought to the test of experience. If, like most of mankind, you have passionate convictions on many such matters, there are ways in which you can make sure of your own bias. If an opinion contrary to your own makes you angry, that is a sign that you are subconsciously aware that you have no good reason for thinking as you do. If someone maintains that two and two are five, or that Iceland is on the equator, you feel pity rather than anger, unless you know so little of arithmetic or geography that his opinion shakes your own contrary conviction. The most savage controversies are those about matters for which there is no good evidence either way. Persecution is used in theology, not arithmetic, because in arithmetic there is knowledge, but in theology there is only opinion. So whenever you find yourself getting angry about a difference of opinion, be on your guard; you will probably find, on examination, that your belief is going beyond what the evidence warrants.

A good way of ridding yourself of certain kinds of dogmatism is to become aware of opinions held in social circles different from your own. When I was young, I lived much outside my own country—in France, Germany, Italy and the United States. I found this very profitable in diminishing the intensity of insular prejudice. If you cannot travel, seek out people with whom you disagree, and read a newspaper belonging to a party that is not yours. If the people and the newspaper seem mad, perverse and wicked, remind yourself that you seem so to them. In this opinion both parties may be right, but they cannot both be wrong. This reflection should generate a certain caution.

Be very wary of opinions that flatter your self-esteem. Both men and women, nine times out of ten, are firmly convinced of the superior excellence of their own sex. There is abundant evidence on both sides. If you are a man, you can point out that most poets and men of science are male; if you are a woman, you can retort that so are most criminals. The question is inherently insoluble, but self-esteem conceals this from most people. We are all, whatever part of the world we come from, persuaded that our own nation is superior to all others. Seeing that each nation has its characteristic merits and demerits, we adjust our standard of values so as to make out that the merits possessed by our nation are really the important ones, while its demerits are comparatively trivial. Here, again, the rational man will admit that the question is one to which there is no demonstrably right answer. It is more difficult to deal with the self-esteem of man as man, because we cannot argue out the matter with some non-human mind. The only way I know of dealing with this general human conceit is to remind ourselves that man is a brief episode in the life of a small planet in a little corner of the universe, and that, for aught we know, other parts of the cosmos may contain beings as superior to ourselves as we are to jelly-fish.

(Bertrand Russell, *Unpopular Essays*)
(720 words)

B. Essay revision

Return to the essay you wrote on your preferred African novel.

1 Judge the essay as if it were someone else's, applying what you have learned in this unit to your evaluation. Check again that you have fulfilled the requirements of the instructions.

2 Improve the essay. (There are some revision hints in the next unit.)

3 Exchange papers with a classmate to get a reader's reaction. What faults did you overlook? What grade is your paper worth? Discuss suggestions for improving the essays further.

Assignments

A. Continue or repeat previous assignments

e.g. revision timetable, essay plans.

B. Continue the library investigation

Apply the information and advice in this unit to the investigation you began as Assignment 2 in Unit 9. Plan, sketch outline, read, make notes, improve the outline and thesis and write a first draft. If you are working with others, you will need to discuss the overall plan thoroughly to ensure that the part you draft fits into the whole.

C. Record examples of fallacies

Collect some examples of fallacies you encounter. Newspapers, speeches and campus talk are only three of many potential sources.

D. Apply your skills to work outside this course

Adapt and apply the information and advice in this unit to assigned writing in other courses.

Unit Eleven Presenting Written Assignments

Timed Reading Passage 11: Improving Content and Style

Instructions: Instead of answering multiple choice questions on this passage, you will be asked to test your recall in other ways. Keep this in mind as you preview, anticipate and get mentally set to read with maximum efficiency. On the signal, begin to read Part A for comprehension at the fastest possible rate.

Part A: Revising the First Draft

Any good piece of writing has been rewritten. Professional writers often revise their work many times before submitting it for publication. Student writers who give too little time to the vital revision stage deprive themselves of full credit for the time and effort invested in earlier stages. Revising the content, polishing the style, checking documentation and proofreading the final version are all essential parts of the academic writing process.

The first revision task is to evaluate critically what you have said. Having put the first draft aside for a time, you should be able to reread it more objectively, as if it were someone else's. Read it right through to judge the total impact. If its purpose is to convince, for example, you need to react to the ideas, look for irrelevancies and flaws in the reasoning, and judge the adequacy of supporting evidence so that you can make the argument more complete, sound and forceful.

If you have built up your outline carefully, the basic structure should need few changes. A reading of topic sentences should confirm that they follow a logical order which matches points and subpoints in the outline. You will probably decide, however, that some points are inadequately developed or that some paragraphs or sentences within paragraphs need reordering to make the thought flow more smoothly. Paragraphs which have been written on separate sheets are easy to reorder and if you are splitting a paragraph so as to develop each part of it more fully, you can save time by simply cutting the page. Since any footnotes are with the material they document and are not yet numbered, there is no risk of muddling them during the rearrangement and no nuisance of continually renumbering them. Any paragraph or sentence which makes no contribution to your purpose should, of course, be firmly cut out. Be particularly critical of your introduction so that you waste no words in getting started.

It is just as important to include everything necessary as to exclude everything irrelevant. A firm outline, critical reading and the rooting out of irrelevancies make it easier to detect symptoms of inadequate development. Vague terms, unexplained basic premises and unsupported generalizations are symptoms, as are assumptions, opinions or quotations treated as if they were fact or 'proof'. Other indicators are unbalanced treatment of the different sections, overdependence on one source of information or an uneven style resulting from poor blending of source material. For this reason, evaluating the use of sources is a necessary part of revising the content. Quotations must be accurate. Summaries must be fair. References must be reliable. You jeopardize the credibility of everything you say if you can be caught out even once.

When you are satisfied with what your paper says, and have made any adjustments needed in the outline, you can turn your critical attention to the way you have expressed your ideas. Many problems will have been eliminated in the process of improving the content, but a variety of weaknesses and errors will remain.

Do not underestimate your ability to deal with language faults. Research has shown that 'students can reduce their grammatical and mechanical errors—including spelling and capitalization—more than half by learning how to correct errors before submitting their papers'.[1]

Most language faults can be detected by constantly asking three simple questions which can be referred to as the *sense test*, the *word test* and the *verb test*. The three questions are: Does this sentence make sense? Is this word's meaning clear? and Is this verb in the correct tense and form?

The three basic questions lead naturally to others, e.g. Does this sentence say what I mean? Could I say this more effectively? Is this the best word to use here? What is the subject of this verb? Do subject and verb agree? Should an active verb replace this passive one?

The most common faults of grammar and style include superfluous words, sentence fragments or run-on sentences, lack of agreement between subject and verb or between pronoun and antecedent, incorrect or inconsistent tenses, unnecessary shifts in person or number, faulty pronoun references, dangling and misplaced modifiers, faulty parallelism, improper subordination of one idea to another, problems with numbers and quantities, wrong or misspelled words and faulty punctuation. Each of these faults can usually be detected by applying one or another of the three tests.

Detection will be easier if you read the paper out loud. The sound and rhythm (or lack of it) will tell you when to find a better transition, recast a sentence or correct the punctuation. Problems with commas, for example, can often be solved by noting where the pauses come in reading aloud. If you are prone to a particular kind of error, such as incorrect verb endings, you will find it worthwhile to go through the paper once to discover and deal with instances of this error alone.

Having left wide margins and written on alternate lines, you have plenty of room to make changes and corrections on your draft, accomplishing maximum revision with minimum confusion and recopying.

(870 words)

Record your time for Part A. Recall the main points. Watch for a convenient time to start Part B.

Part B: Preparing the Final Paper

A second draft is always desirable and usually necessary for a major writing assignment. Besides incorporating all the improvements to the first draft, a second draft includes all the parts required for the final presentation, in the correct order and form. It gives you the chance to find out what the 'new' paper looks and sounds like and to try it out on other readers before you prepare the version which will be marked. Sometimes the final paper is not returned to students and the second draft must serve as your copy.

There are several preparatory tasks before you write out the second draft. The first is to recheck any instructions as to parts required, length, margins, format and so forth, and the second is to assemble in front of you everything you will need: instructions, final outline, revised draft, bibliography slips and dictionary.

Next, check the footnotes. The first time a source is mentioned, full details must be

[1] Reported in Wilga M. Rivers and Mary S. Temperley, *A Practical Guide to the Teaching of English as a Second or Foreign Language* (New York: Oxford University Press, 1978), p. 323.

given, but thereafter the author's name and the relevant page numbers are usually enough. If there is any risk of confusion, include a short form of the title as well. Modern practice does not use Latin terms. Having checked the content of the notes, go through the draft and number them consecutively, placing matching superscripts (raised numbers) at the end of each item to be documented and in front of the note itself. When you finish, arrange in alphabetical order the bibliography slips for the sources you have actually used in the paper and ensure that they too are complete, accurate and correct in form—ready for copying onto your bibliography page.[2]

Read each section of your revised draft again before you transfer it so that you are clear about the changes to be made. Check any headings. Usually major headings, without symbols, are sufficient. Decide whether any long paragraphs need dividing. The length and the number of paragraphs needed to develop an idea will of course vary but, for the reader's sake, you should aim to have two or three logical breaks per page. Make sure any quoted material is introduced smoothly and enclosed in quotation marks, unless it is several lines long. In that case, instead of using quotation marks, you will set it off from the main text by indenting it and skipping a line above and below. If you still have any doubts about a word's meaning or spelling, look it up now.

When you have noted your decisions about all these things on the first draft, you are ready to write out the second draft. Unless the paper is being typed, you will single-space this time, and you will move the notes either to the bottom of the appropriate pages or to a page headed Notes at the end of the paper. It is important to keep critically alert throughout the writing so that you miss no opportunities to make further small improvements as you go.

Instead of putting the second draft away for a day or so, try to find one or two friends who will read it, perhaps by offering to read their papers in return. Comments like 'I'm not convinced on this point' or 'What is this supposed to mean?' can lead to useful further revision.

Preparing the final version is not a mindless copying exercise. It requires the utmost attention to detail. You want the presentation to create a favourable impression. Keep alert by imagining the reactions of the marker to what you are putting on paper.

There is one more very important task: proofreading. The time it takes will be a very small fraction indeed of the total time you have spent on the paper yet it will probably influence the impression the paper makes on your lecturer more than anything else you could accomplish in the same amount of time.

Proofreading is one job for which faster reading techniques are inappropriate. Every part of the paper, from the title page to the bibliography, should be subjected to slow and thorough scrutiny. All careless slips, such as omitted words or word endings, or faulty punctuation, should be caught. The object is to remove every error you are capable of detecting so that you will earn full credit for all the time, energy and thought you have invested in the paper.

(735 words)

Record your time for Part B. Average the two scores. Then recall the entire passage as completely as you can, making a mental pattern or outline of it.

---

[2] The notes and list of references (bibliography) for the sample paper, pp. 163–4, illustrate acceptable forms of documentation.

WORDS PER MINUTE CHART: Timed Reading Passage 11
(870 and 725 words)

Time	WPM 11A	WPM 11B	Time	WPM 11A	WPM 11B	Time	WPM 11A	WPM 11B	Time	WPM 11A	WPM 11B	Time	WPM 11A	WPM 11B
1.00	—	725	2.00	435	365	3.00	290	240	4.00	220	180	5.00	175	—
10	745	620	10	400	335	10	275	230	10	210	175	10	170	—
20	650	545	20	375	310	20	260	220	20	200	170	20	165	—
30	580	485	30	345	290	30	250	210	30	195	160	30	160	—
40	520	435	40	325	270	40	235	200	40	185	155	40	155	—
50	475	395	50	310	255	50	225	190	50	180	150	50	150	—

Follow-up

A. Testing comprehension

1 Using either pattern or outline form, give ten main points or subpoints made in the passage.

2 Check the completeness and accuracy of your recall and give yourself a comprehension score out of 10.

3 Add to the pattern or outline. Then think of as many links as possible between Passage 11 and previous work in this course. Attach the most important of these related ideas to the pattern or outline.

4 If there was a significant difference in speed between parts A or B, or between this passage and Passage 10, try to account for it.

B. Framing questions

1 Asking questions is as much of a skill as answering them, and one worth practising. Make up five questions which would test a reader's comprehension of the passage. Make two of them multiple choice questions with four choices each. Pay careful attention to the wording of all the questions.

2 Form a small group to evaluate the questions you have each made up. One way to begin is by trying to answer the questions. Improve the questions, e.g. by removing any ambiguities.

C. Using and documenting sources

1 Look more closely at the quotation in the passage (Part A, para 6, p. 181). Note how it is integrated with the surrounding text. Observe that the exact words quoted are enclosed in single quotation marks and that the second mark has been placed before the full stop.

2 Examine the two footnotes. Note particularly the arrangement and punctuation of the first one, which is a *reference* footnote. The second is a *content* footnote. What is the difference?

3 Examine the notes for the sample paper (pp. 163–4). You will see that some of them combine the function of reference and content notes.

4 Recall what you know about footnote and bibliography forms, referring to Unit 6 and the sample paper on pages 158–64 if necessary. Then state the differences between footnote and bibliography forms as to purpose, numbering, arrangement on a page, the order of parts and punctuation.

(K)

5 The forms used in this book are widely used. However, preferred forms do differ from one discipline, journal or lecturer to another, in such details as capitalization, punctuation and the position of the date of publication. Examine the most important journals in your field and note their practices. Find out the preferences of your lecturer for this course or any other which requires a library-based paper. The most important thing is to be *consistent* in form. When in doubt, model your notes and bibliography on the specimens in this book.

D. Presenting a final paper

1 Examine the format for a library research paper, outlined below. Compare it with the patterns appropriate for other types of writing assignment. Discuss with others the requirements for different types of written work. Then spell out the details for any one of them, e.g. a technical report, a business letter.

2 A lecturer in facetious mood compiled the list of hints on 'How to Annoy a Lecturer (and Lower your Grade)' on page 185. Read the list, then imagine and record some additional ways of lowering your grades on written work for this or some other course.

3 Test your recall of the list and your ability to adapt what you read by listing things to check if you want to *improve* your grades on written work instead of lowering them.

Typical Format for a Library Research Paper

Title The final title should be apt, descriptive and unambiguous.

Thesis and outline The thesis states, in a single sentence, the central idea of the entire paper. The outline shows exactly how this idea will be developed and how all the parts are related.

Introduction The purpose of the introduction is to gain attention and make the purpose clear. The thesis statement is normally the last sentence of the first paragraph and should accurately foretell the main sections of the paper.

Major point 1 The topic idea of the first main section should be stated concisely and developed by subpoints (normally three) which are in turn supported by facts, examples, expert testimony and illustrative details. This section often includes background information and clarification of key terms necessary for understanding the argument.

Major Point 2 This too should be concisely stated and adequately supported. It should lead naturally from Point 1 and into Point 3. This middle section often examines the various views on an issue or the possible courses of action so that the reader will understand the basis for subsequent decisions or conclusions.

Major Point 3 The final section builds on and unites the previous sections to give the most important argument—the one which should persuade the reader of the thesis.

Conclusion The ending should be brief but it should do more than merely repeat the thesis statement or the main points. An effective conclusion may predict future developments, state implications, make recommendations, suggest further lines of research or present the thesis in a new and memorable way, e.g. by means of an apt quotation.

Notes This page cites sources for specific information in the text, according to a particular format. It is also possible to put each note at the foot of the page on which reference to it occurs, in which case the notes are referred to as *footnotes*.

Bibliography A list of sources used in the paper is given at the end with entries alphabetized by authors' surnames and presented in a conventional bibliographic form. In some fields, such as the sciences, the term *List of References* is used instead.

Hints on How to Annoy a Lecturer (and Lower your Grade)

These time-tested methods of irritating a lecturer and persuading him or her to deduct marks from your essays are guaranteed to work for you too. How many of the methods do you already use?

1 Omit all clues of identification, e.g. your name, your exam number, the course title, the question number, the essay title.

2 Ignore completely any instructions about the length, number of paragraphs, type of essay, etc.

3 Use any bits of paper you can find. If you need a second sheet, make it a different size.

4 Write across both margins so the lecturer has no space for comments.

5 Write illegibly. Omit necessary words, letters and endings here and there.

6 Either make the entire essay one long paragraph *or* make each sentence a paragraph on its own.

7 Do not stick to the point. (Don't even say what the point is.) Wander about. Bring in various irrelevancies.

8 Obscure your meaning. Waffle, use plenty of jargon, use vague and abstract words.

9 Do not reveal the source of any of your information.

10 Do not bother to provide transitions and signal words.

11 Include plenty of clichés and show off the biggest words you can find. (The meaning doesn't matter.)

12 Either run sentences together *or* write sentence fragments *or* alternate the two forms.

13 Keep shuffling back and forth between present and past tenses, even within the same sentence.

14 Do not allow subjects and verbs to agree in number.

15 Shift your point of view frequently: *I, you, he, they, one.*

16 Make sure your pronouns do not refer to anything or anyone in particular.

17 Dangle modifiers.

18 Sprinkle commas everywhere.

19 Do not do any revising or proofreading. (This would be sure to raise the grade.)

20 Hand the paper in late.

Related Skills

A. Detecting faults of grammar and style

1 By this time you should be quite familiar with the Writer's Reference section because most of the problems dealt with there have been referred to in previous units. Check now to make sure you have covered all of it and tried all the exercises.

2 Make an honest assessment of your language competence now, as compared with your competence at the beginning of the course. Which faults do you still commit? Which have lecturers criticized most often in your work? Which could be dealt with through more careful revision and proofreading? Where might you get the help you need for any major problems which remain?

3 List specific steps you intend to take to reduce still further the number of faults in your written work.

B. Making a revision checklist

1 Look again at the Pre-Writing Checklists in Unit 10 for testing a topic, a thesis and an outline.

2 Make up suitable questions for a Revision Checklist by which to evaluate how well you have accomplished what you set out to do in a particular piece of written work. Use these headings and subheadings to guide you:

I. Structure

II. Text
- A. Treatment of the topic
- B. Paragraphs
- C. Sentences
- D. Spelling and mechanics

III. Documentation
- A. Footnotes
- B. Bibliography.

Revision and Proofreading Practice

A. Use your checklist

Use the checklist you have just made to help you revise the essay you began in Unit 9 or a major piece of writing assigned in another course. You will probably find yourself making changes to improve the checklist as well.

B. Revise and proofread a paper

Return to some written work that has been graded. Note the lecturer's comments and decide how they might help you do better next time. If the lecturer has not taken time to write out the reasons for the grade, see if you can work them out for yourself. Give the paper the full revision and proofreading treatment, noting how many errors you missed when you prepared it for submission. Would it deserve a higher grade now?

C. Criticize and advise

Choose any completed writing assignment and exchange papers with another student. Play the role of critic/advisor for one another, making constructive suggestions for improving the papers.

Assignments

A. Continue or repeat previous assignments

e.g. revision timetable, essay plans, finding examples of fallacies.

B. Make up exam questions

Make up three questions which might reasonably appear on a final examination for this course. They should be questions which require answers demonstrating your mastery of some major topic or skill. Make sure you can answer the questions.

C. Judge your language skills

On page 186, A.2, you considered the kinds of errors you tend to make in your writing and what you might do about them. Write out a brief assessment of your most serious problems in writing English, together with a plan for dealing with them.

D. Improve your checklist

Improve your checklist for revising written work (p. 186, B.2) and present it in a clear and useful form. Include it in your course file together with any piece of work revised with its help.

E. Practise writing an examination essay

1 Make up (or ask someone to set for you) a question whose answer requires mastery of a topic you need to know well for any of your subjects. Plan the answer by making a pattern. Then put the pattern aside and do something else.

2 Later, set yourself a time limit and write the essay, using the pattern to guide you. Take a short break, then revise the essay and set it aside.

3 Later, read the essay critically, as if it were someone else's. Judge what you have said and how you have said it. Search for careless errors. What grade is the essay worth, and why?

Unit Twelve Assessing Progress

Outline Summary: How to Deal with Examinations: Part II

Instructions: If you have followed the advice in Part I of the outline 'How to Deal with Examinations' (Unit 7) you will know enough about the subject matter of your courses for examination purposes. The advice in Part II should help you make the most of what you know when you come to write the examination. Use the reading and study skills you have learned in this course to help you understand, remember and use the examination techniques that follow. This reading will not be timed.

II. EXAMINATION TECHNIQUES

A. **Arrive early:** at least 20 minutes before the examination is scheduled to begin.
1. It is assumed that you have
    a) revised systematically.
    b) confirmed the time and place of the examination.
    c) collected all the necessary materials the night before.
    d) had a good night's sleep.
    e) got up in good time, so as to arrive early.
2. Avoid talking with other candidates about your prospects before the examination. One of them may say something to undermine your confidence, which should remain as high as possible.
3. Once in your seat, get out the equipment you will need: at least two pens, a pencil, a ruler, etc.
4. Adopt a fatalistic attitude about what you do not know. Concentrate on using all you do know to the best advantage.
5. If you cannot help thinking about the forthcoming paper, make your thoughts specific, e.g. organize in your mind an answer to one possible question.

B. **When you get the question paper, think PQRST.**
The mnemonic should help you remember that the first five steps in dealing with any type of examination are:
Preview, **Q**uestion, **R**eread, **S**elect and **T**hink.
The five steps should all be worked through before you write a single word on your answer paper.
1. **P**review the entire paper.
    a) Read all the instructions and all the essay questions.
    b) Skim passages and individual items in true-false or multiple choice questions.
2. **Q**uestion the instructions so that you are clear about what you must do, where, and within what period of time.
    a) Is the paper divided into sections? How many questions must be answered from each? (If you answer more than the required number of questions, the extra ones will not be marked.)
    b) Are any questions compulsory?
    c) How much time is allowed for the paper?
    d) How many marks are awarded for each question?

e) Where are the answers to be written? (on the question paper? in an answer booklet? each question in a separate booklet?)

Every year there are students who fail examinations because they have not answered the compulsory question, or they have chosen two questions from one section instead of one question from each section, or they discovered too late that two and not three hours were allowed. Do not be among these students.

3. **R**eread the directions for each question very carefully.
   a) Make sure you understand *precisely* what each question requires you to do.
   Pay special attention to key verbs, e.g. *circle, underline, compare, criticize, define, evaluate . . .*
   (A list of key verbs used in essay questions is given on page 195 together with a definition for each.)
   b) Be sure also about what the question does *not* ask you to do.
   If you write a full essay when the question asks you to 'make a brief numbered list', you lose in three ways:
      i) you lose time which should be spent working on another question;
      ii) you lose marks for failing to follow directions;
      iii) you lose the goodwill of the marker whose time you are wasting.
   c) Do not misread the questions, or twist any of them into the question you wish had been asked instead. To do so amounts to throwing marks away.
4. **S**elect the questions you feel most able to answer.
   a) For objective questions, decide which section of the examination can be done most easily and quickly. You will do this one first, then the next easiest, etc. If there are choices within the sections, note what they are.
   b) When selecting essay topics, remember that there are no marks for bravery. There is little point in trying to impress the lecturer by choosing a very difficult topic when you know you can write a good answer on an easier one.
   c) Decide which essay will be easiest to write and mark it *1*. Put a *2* by your next choice, and a *3* by the question which seems least difficult of the ones remaining. You should work on the essays in this order.
   d) Make your selections carefully but quickly; then stick to your choices. Procrastination steals time as well as confidence. If you keep dithering about the essay choices, you are likely to have as much difficulty with the eventual choices as you would have done with the original ones; you may have *more* difficulty because you will be more tense and anxious.
5. **T**hink how to make the best use of your time.
   You now know enough about the over-all task ahead of you to plan your strategy with intelligence. Do not worry if those around you are now writing furiously, while you still read and think. The extra minutes spent planning your work and budgeting your time will save you time and worry later by increasing your efficiency—and therefore your mark.

C. Use the ABCDE of examination time-planning.

1. **A**llocate a specific amount of time to each question or section.
   a) Use the number of marks available for each question as a guide to the relative amount of time to spend on it.
   b) Allow for time spent on your initial PQRST and for revision time (at least 15 minutes) at the end.
2. **B**reak up large tasks, (e.g. a complete essay question) into smaller ones (e.g. planning, writing, revising), and sub-divide the time allocation.

As you work your way through the tasks, the feeling that you are in control will build up a morale-boosting sense of accomplishment and progress.

3. **C**hange your activity at planned intervals (e.g. from planning Essay 3 to writing Essay 2 to revising Essay 1).
   a) By switching deliberately from one task to another, you keep renewing your ability to concentrate. A change of activity is the next best thing to a planned break away from your desk.
   b) Changing also ensures maximum help from your subconscious. When you leave an essay plan to work on another question, your subconscious goes right on working on the plan. By the time you are ready to write the essay, new associations and examples will be waiting for you.
4. **D**elay the difficult questions.
   Schedule the easiest questions first. By the time you have done them, you may find you can cope with the 'difficult' ones after all. Again, your subconscious mind has had time to work for you.
5. Give **E**qual time for equal marks.
   a) Especially on essay examinations, give roughly equal time for equal marks. Excessive length on one question will not compensate for neglect of another. Two half answers or two plans will nearly always earn more marks than one brilliant answer and one omitted one.
   b) It might be possible to shorten the time spent on an easy essay in order to have more time to spend on thinking out a difficult one, however.

Study the following plan for an examination requiring three essays in three hours, when the essays are worth equal marks. Try to think out the reasons for using such a plan:

1. Read *all* the questions carefully. Select three. (9 min.)		
2. Plan Essay 1 (10 min.) (easiest)		
3. Plan Essay 2 (12 min.)	4. Write Essay 1 (40 min.)	
5. Plan Essay 3 (14 min.) (most difficult)	6. Write Essay 2 (40 min.) 8. Write Essay 3 (40 min.)	7. Check Essay 1 (5 min.) 9. Check Essay 2 (5 min.) 10. Check Essay 3 (5 min.)

Total preparation time:	9 min. + 36 min. =	45 min.
Total writing time:	40 min × 3 =	120 min.
Total checking time:	5 min × 3 =	15 min.
		180 min. or 3 hrs.

Decide what you think about a) the sequence of tasks and b) the allocation of time. (You will be asked about your conclusions later in this unit.)

D. Begin with objective and short answer questions.

Tactics for dealing with objective and short answer questions should take into account these facts:

a) While some questions require only recall or recognition of words or facts, other demand that knowledge be applied to a new situation or used to reason out the likely answer.
b) The most frequent reasons for failure on objective examinations are:
   i) failure to read and interpret the questions correctly;
   ii) failure to reason with what is known.
c) Collecting some marks early in the examination builds confidence and encourages better performance in later questions.
d) Your subconscious is able to continue working on an unsolved problem or incomplete answer while you move on to another question.

You wish to be a *high scorer*. The word SCORER provides a mnemonic for remembering how to deal with objective questions:

1. **S**chedule your time.
   a) Note again how much time you can afford to allow for the different sections. Write down the time by which you should be finished with each section.
   b) When you begin to work through the questions, set a steady pace. Answer all the ones you can answer easily. Do not worry about the rest at this stage. Just keep moving.
   c) You should finish well within the time limit, which allows time for going back to the omitted questions later to try again.
2. Use **C**lue words. You have already noted the clues in the instructions, e.g. *circle, underline, write in a word.* Now look for clue words in the individual questions or statements.
   a) In a true-false or multiple choice test, such words as the following indicate that the statement must be absolutely true to be true at all:
      all, always, every, invariably, never, none
      e.g. *All squares have four sides.*
      (True. The 'four sides' are part of the definition.)
      Politicians are always dishonest.
      (False, we hope. The statement means that there has never been an honest politician.)
   b) Other clue words are qualifiers which indicate a limited range of truth:
      few, many, most, some;
      often, seldom, sometimes, usually.
   c) Note how the clue words affect the meaning of these statements:

All men are taller than *all* women.	False
Some men are taller than *some* women.	True
Men are *never* taller than women.	False
Men are *sometimes* taller than women.	True

3. **O**mit the difficult questions on the first attempt.
   a) Remember that you are trying to earn as many marks as you can, as quickly as you can. Answering the easy questions first sets you moving with confidence.
   b) Each time you pass over a question, make a mark in the margin (--) to indicate that you should return to the question later.
   c) On the second round, change the – to a + if you answer the question this time. Add a second mark (––) if you omit it again.
   d) After you have passed over a difficult question to work on an easier one, your mind will carry on searching for clues and trying various solutions—with no effort on your part. You may well discover that when you return to the 'impossible' question, the answer is suddenly there. How well this process works will depend on:
      i) how much information you stored while studying;
      ii) how free you can keep your mind from anxiety, e.g. by steadily accumulating marks for what you can answer easily;
      iii) how confidently you expect to find an answer;
      iv) how much 'soaking time' you allow.
4. **R**ead carefully.
   a) Read all of the question. There may be something at the end which changes the meaning,
      e.g. *Students are advised to omit difficult questions/the first time through.* True or False?

      Note that the four words following the mark / change the statement from False to True.

b) Read the statement logically. If the statement has several parts, all parts must be true if the statement is to be true.
e.g. *Chlorine gas is a greenish, poisonous, foul-smelling, very rare gas used in water purification.*

Although chlorine gas is greenish, poisonous and foul-smelling, and is used in water purification, it is not 'very rare' and therefore the statement is false.

5. **E**stimate the answer when you do not positively know it.
This means to evaluate the worth of each possible answer and to eliminate the obviously untrue. An answer arrived at in this way is often called an *educated guess.* Some questions are deliberately designed to test your ability to reason in this way.
   a) For completion or fill-in questions, part of a correct answer may give some credit. If you have any idea at all of what the answer might be, try, but think first so that your attempt is sensible.
   b) Occasionally, instructions indicate that points will be subtracted for wrong answers,
   e.g. Mark each answer T (True) or F (False). For each incorrect answer you will be penalised one point.
   If this is the case, obviously you should *not* guess on true-false questions, and you should make an educated guess on multiple choice questions only if you can narrow the possibilities down to *two.*
6. **R**eview your work.
   a) Return to the double-marked questions you found most difficult. Reread them. Look for clue words and new hints. Make an educated guess if necessary.
   b) Check the single-marked questions, e.g. those you answered on the second attempt. If you have time, also check the ones you answered on the first attempt.
   c) Do not change an answer unless you have a very good reason for doing so.
   d) Check again to make sure you have answered all the questions required.

Before you move on to the next section, stop to recall what SCORER stands for.

E. Answer the essay questions.
An examination essay question is an invitation to write the best answer possible within the time limit, not to say everything that can be said on the topic. The examiner wishes to find out whether you can do the following:
   a) interpret questions accurately;
   b) recall main ideas and significant details of the course content;
   c) reorganize, recombine and apply what has been learned;
   d) reason correctly with what you know;
   e) form generalizations and support them with relevant facts and details;
   f) organize ideas effectively and express them clearly.

Your job is to prove in your essay that you can do these things.

Complete all the PQRST steps before you do anything else.
Pause now to recall what they are:

Every student hopes for sufficient thinking and writing power in an essay examination to do himself justice. The word POWER serves as a useful mnemonic for remembering the correct approach to essay questions once the PQRST steps have been completed:

Establish a **P**urpose,
then **O**rganize, **W**rite, **E**valuate and **R**evise.

1. Establish a **P**urpose and keep it in mind throughout. This will help you avoid the chief sins of student essay writing: irrelevance and vagueness.
   a) Ask: What, precisely, am I supposed to do? The wording of the question itself will help to determine your purpose. Pay particular attention to the key verbs.
   b) Ask: Within the limits of the question, what precisely do I want to do? e.g.
   If the essay question is *Compare and contrast Okonkwo in* Things Fall Apart *and Ezeulu in* Arrow of God *as tragic characters*, then the purpose of your essay might well be this: 'to show that while Okonkwo and Ezeulu come to a similar tragic end, Ezeulu's tragedy is the greater because . . . W, X, Y and Z'. The entire essay would attempt to justify your position by developing reasons W, X, Y, and Z.
   Keep in mind that all effective writing is controlled by the writer's purpose.
   c) Ask: *How best can I achieve my purpose*? Thinking on this question leads to the next step.
2. **O**rganize your answer before you write.
   Most of the marks allotted to an essay are given for content and organization, e.g. the number, quality, relevance and arrangement of ideas, points and supporting details.

   Up to a quarter of your time can usefully be spent on the planning stage. It is often a good idea to submit the plan even when it is not asked for. Examiners appreciate your efforts to organize.

   Pattern Planning is highly effective for most types of examination essays. Proceed this way:
   a) Write the topic (or its key words) in the middle of a blank sheet of paper and around it print key words, in capital letters, for what you consider the major sub-divsions of the topic.
   b) Choose one of these sub-divisions and start branching out with points, facts and examples which develop the main idea, reducing each to a key word or phrase.
   c) When one branch dries up, switch to another. Do not worry overmuch at this stage about the exact place for each point to go, or whether all ideas are worth including. Just recall everything your mind can think of which is related to the topic. Keep the ideas flowing and the pen moving.
   d) You will soon build up a pattern which shows at a glance which main points need further development. If you cannot think of further supporting points, try to think of further examples.
   e) When you have gone as far as you can, look at your pattern and complete its organization:
      i) Encircle each group of related ideas (each branch).
      ii) Decide in which order you will deal with the branches.
      iii) Make further linking lines. Use arrows or other means to show relationships between different parts of the pattern, or points you wish to move to a new location.
      iv) If any *main* point looks insufficiently developed, either combine it with another group, or add further detail.

v) Make sure that every main idea (every numbered group) contributes to development of the central idea.
vi) Are any ideas not really to the point? Either discard them or find a way to make them relevant.

f) Whether you make an outline from the patterned plan (or do a fresh plan) will depend on how much time is available and whether the plan is to be marked. In any case, a revised plan should not be done yet.
g) Put the pattern aside and work on something else.

3. **W**rite the essay.
When you come to write the essay, you will already know what you are going to say and in what order. You can therefore give your full attention to expressing each point clearly and effectively.
a) Put your plan in front of you again. Look at it. Use it to help you think out the *ending* of your essay: the conclusion toward which everything you say should be directed. Write out the ending, at least in rough.
b) Begin the essay directly by making clear the purpose and approach. Do not waste time recopying the question or writing a rambling introduction. *Get started.* (You should give the question number and a brief title or heading.)
c) Write the essay by taking each encircled area of your plan in turn and following the logic of the branch connections. Each time you move to a new branch or major sub-branch, begin a new paragraph. Each paragraph should begin with a commitment sentence which makes clear what the paragraph will treat and how it relates to the central idea.
d) Pay special attention to words and phrases which show the relationship between one idea and the next, e.g. *on the other hand, in addition, another reason why, despite these disadvantages, similarly, as a result . . .*
e) It often helps to think out each sentence before writing it down. Is it grammatically correct? Are there any unnecessary words? Be simple, direct and to the point.
f) Write as legibly as possible.
g) If you run out of time or get bogged down, *stop writing*. Leave a big space on your answer sheet in case you can return later. Move on to the next question.

4. **E**valuate your work and your use of time as you go along.
Keep asking critical questions, e.g.
Does this paragraph help to achieve the essay's purpose?
Are there enough facts and examples to support this statement?
Is the meaning of this sentence absolutely clear?
Is the relationship between these two ideas clear?
Evaluate your progress in relation to the time available.
a) Keep a sense of priorities. Concentrate on main ideas and add as much detail as you have time for. Make every word count: very often 50 per cent could be cut from a student's answer without losing any marks!
b) If you should miscalculate your time, so that you are left with, for example, two questions to do in 40 minutes, write two plans rather than one complete answer. Two half answers are worth more marks than one complete one.

5. **R**evise the essays.
Revising is so vital that even if you have not finished, it is better to stop and revise than to spend 3–5 more minutes on a difficult question. The revising will earn more marks for you.
a) Read over your answers critically to see that you have done and said what you intended. Do not take it for granted that your lecturer will

'know what you mean'. Since he can only grade what you actually write, make sure that you have *said* exactly what you mean.

b) Insert further examples, eliminate unnecessary words, rephrase any clumsy expressions and make such other improvements as you can without making the paper look too untidy. You may earn 5–10 percent more marks here.

c) Check for misspelled or carelessly omitted words and faulty punctuation. Make the appropriate corrections.

F. Revise the entire paper.

1. Check to make sure you have answered the correct number of questions and all necessary parts of a question. Are all answers numbered?
2. Is the required identification (e.g. examination number/name, question number) on each sheet?
3. Join the answer sheets together.
4. Use any spare minutes to look again for errors of grammar, spelling or punctuation. *Use all your time.*

G. After the examination:

1. Do not indulge in depressing post-mortems with other students. The exam is over and there is nothing further you can do about it. Omissions or mistakes remembered in retrospect tend to assume unreal proportions. Relax before thinking of the next exam.
2. Think out how you can improve your technique on the next examination.

Key Verbs and the Action Required

Analyse	Examine the essential features, showing how they are related and why they are important.
Assess	*see* Evaluate
Comment on	Discuss, criticize or explain as fully as possible.
Compare	Show the similarities and differences between.
Contrast	Compare by bringing out the differences.
Criticize	Give your judgement on the good and bad points, supporting your opinions by a discussion of the evidence. (To criticize does not necessarily mean to attack.)
Define	Give the precise meaning of the word or phrase, distinguishing it from related words.
Describe	Give a detailed account or verbal picture in logical sequence or narrative form.
Discuss	Examine in detail by argument, sifting evidence and explaining pros and cons.
Enumerate	Name and list the main ideas one by one. Number them.
Evaluate	Judge the worth, the importance or the truth of the concept, giving, e.g. advantages and disadvantages.
Explain	Make plain, interpret and account for.
Illustrate	Make clear by concrete examples, comparisons or analogies. Or, in some subjects: Use a figure or diagram to explain or clarify.
Interpret	Give the meaning, using enough explanation and examples to make it clear.
Justify	Give reasons for the statement or conclusion or decision.
List	Make a numbered list of words, sentences, ideas, reasons, etc. *See* Enumerate.

Outline	Give the main ideas or principles and the important supporting details. Emphasize the relationships among the parts. The instruction to use *outline form* could mean using conventional symbols and progressive indentation to show parts and their sub-divisions.
Relate	Show how things are connected to one another and to what extent they affect one another. Sometimes *relate* means simply to narrate.
Review	Give a survey or summary of the topic, criticizing where appropriate.
State	Describe the main points in clear, brief form.
Summarize	Give a concise account of the main points, omitting details and examples.
Trace	Follow the development or history of the subject.

Follow-up

A. Test your comprehension

Make up questions to test your comprehension of the advice on examination technique. Then team up with one or more coursemates to exchange questions and discuss the advice. Which ideas do you already use and how do they work? Which ideas are new? Which ones in particular do you intend to try on your next examinations?

B. Compare your conclusions

At the end of B5 of the outline, you were asked to think out the reasons for the sequence of tasks and time allocation recommended for a three essay examination. How many of the following reasons did you think of?

1 Planning deserves up to a quarter of the time because it is the stage when you choose and arrange the ideas, facts and examples which earn marks.

2 Once the planning is complete, you know you have done the hardest and most mark-worthy work; all that remains is to expand on the plan. You know just what work you have left to cover and can budget the remaining time efficiently.

3 Switching from one activity to another means you can keep 'starting fresh'. This helps to compensate for not being able to take a physical break during an examination.

4 Doing all the planning first gives your subconscious a chance to work for you. Your mind is likely to carry on with a train of thought even while you are writing and so may come up with fresh associations that will help you in a later stage of writing.

5 By writing all the plans at the beginning, you lessen the chances of repeating yourself from one essay to another.

6 A difficult essay needs more thinking time. A firm time plan prevents writing at excessive length on a topic you know well to the neglect of another topic. You cannot store up credit for a good answer to transfer to an inadequate one.

7 Extra marks are almost always earned by revising and proofreading what has been written. It is vital to allow time for these tasks.

Discuss possible reasons for any other advice in the outline which seemed new or strange.

C. Judge your improvement as a reader

Think about the ways in which your reading and study efficiency have improved since Unit 1. For example, how did your reading of the outline on examination technique differ from your reading of Timed Passage 1? Consider also the problems still to be overcome, the reasons why you may have improved more markedly in some skills than others, and what you could have done to progress further or faster. You may find it useful to compare notes with classmates.

Related Skills

A. Storing in the memory

Reduce all of the advice on Examination Techniques to one page. Try to do this more effectively than you did for Part I.

B. Planning examination strategy

Decide how you would plan your time and divide up the tasks on an examination taking the following form and covering about half of this course:

I. Reading and Study Skills—short answers, 25 marks
II. Applied Reading Skills—a passage with comprehension and summary questions, 25 marks
III. Writing Skills—e.g. correction of faulty sentences, 20 marks
IV. Essay with Plan—30 marks.

C. Answering the questions asked

1 What, exactly, does each of the following questions require you to do, and how might you organize each answer?

a Compare and contrast the views of Chinua Achebe and Ngugi wa Thiong'o on the role of the writer in society.

b Analyse the problems involved in providing a safe water supply to rural communities in your area.

c Relate an amusing, embarrasing, instructive or otherwise memorable experience you have had in learning English.

d To what extent do you consider the education you have received so far to have been 'relevant'?

e Explain with examples what you understand by the term 'balance of nature'.

f 'The role of a social services department is fulfilled in Nigeria by the extended family.' Discuss.

2 Make up or find examples of examination questions for your various subjects and note what each one requires you to do. If there is no key verb giving directions, decide what approach you would take to the topic.

Practice in Answering Examination Questions

The questions which follow might well be asked on an examination for this course. Use them to help you review.

Instructions
Assume that each section is part of a 3-hour examination and that each separate question is worth the number of marks (out of 100) indicated in parentheses. The number of marks for all the questions totals more than 100 as there are more questions than could appear in a single examination. For example, sections I–III might appear on a first semester examination, sections V–VII on a second semester or sessional examination and section IV on either. Before you begin a section, decide on the amount of time you should spend on it. Record this, and the amount of time you actually spend. Make sure that you do exactly what each question requires.

I. READING AND STUDY SKILLS *(total: 40 marks)*

A. For each of the following, write the number of the statement and the word which belongs in each blank. *(6 marks)*

1. ________ is a way of rapid reading when full comprehension is not required.
2. The meaning of a new word can often be inferred from the ________.
3. High reading speeds become possible when we learn to bring the ________ hemisphere of the brain into the reading process.
4. SQ3R is a ________ which stands for ________, ________, ________, ________, ________.

B. Choose any five of the following and for each list two purposes for including the exercise or assignment in this course. *(10 marks)*

1. reading upside down
2. starting a reading or study session with a high speed drill
3. compiling glossaries in your major subjects
4. making key word patterns of lectures in other subjects
5. making study and revision timetables
6. reducing the outline on 'Preparation for Examinations' to one page
7. reading two novels.

C. Choose any two of the following statements, and for each write three concise sentences which support or develop the statement. *(6 marks)*

1. In study reading, it is usually better to read a section two or three times quickly than once slowly.

2. During a study session it is advantageous to take short breaks at intervals of 20 to 40 minutes.
3. The most effective notes from a book or lecture are those which prove you have understood and which help you to remember.
4. It is good practice to try working out the meaning of a word for yourself before looking it up in the dictionary.

D. Make succinct notes on any two of the following. You may use symbols, abbreviations or any other aids which will help you convey the important points clearly and economically. *(6 marks)*

1. overcoming regression
2. previewing
3. recall after learning
4. writing summaries

E. Imagine that you are to give a talk to upper secondary school pupils on one of the skills taught in the course. Make a key word pattern which you could use during your talk to remind you of the points you intend to make. *(6 marks)*

F. Write a paragraph explaining how you have developed and made use of any one skill or routine taught in this course. Do not choose the skill selected for question E. *(6 marks)*

II. APPLIED READING SKILLS *(total: 25 marks)*

Use the various reading and study skills at your command for the purpose of understanding the passage and answering the questions which follow it. The passage is adapted from the first chapter of an undergraduate writing course. The chapter title is deliberately omitted.

---

1 When asked why we must write, most students think first of the need to communicate. Communication is so important that it is easy to overlook our other reasons for writing. We write as part of our day-to-day work: to help us to remember, to observe, to think, to plan and to organize, as well as to communicate. Above all, writing helps us to think and to express our thoughts—and anyone who writes badly is handicapped both in private study and in dealing with others.

2 By writing we can communicate with people we know who can judge us by everything that they know about us—by our writing and by our conversation, appearance and behaviour. However, when we write to people whom we have never met, they must judge us in the only way they can—by our writing. The way in which a letter of application is written, for example, may be all that an employer needs to indicate that the applicant is not suitable for the job.

3 Students are judged by their course work (essays, records of experiments, project reports and theses) and by their performance in written examinations. Only by writing well can we give a good account of ourselves as students, as applicants for employment, and as employees (writing letters, instructions, progress reports, articles and reviews, and scientific papers for publication).

4 Some students fully recognize the importance of writing in their work, whatever the subject, and take trouble over it. Others know that they write badly, but they do not

worry about it because they hold the sadly mistaken notion that writing is not particularly important if you are a geologist or biochemist, or economist, or indeed anything but an English major! Still others, thinking their writing is already satisfactory, do not consider the possibility of improvement.

5 Many people may be encouraged in their belief that their writing is satisfactory by their success in school and college examinations. However, most students would get higher marks in course work and in examinations if they were better able to put their thoughts into words. Any teacher or examiner knows how many marks are lost by students who do not show clearly whether or not they understand their work. In schools, even the most able pupils may fail to show their ability. For example, the following comments are from an examiners' report on a scholarship paper:

6 All answers included much irrelevant information. Looseness of expression and superfluous words indicated a lack of careful thought. The standard of explanation was disappointing . . . Many candidates had the knowledge but were unable to express themselves. Very few answers were comprehensive. Marks were lost through omission. Even when they knew the answer many candidates had difficulty in bringing facts together in an effective order.

7 In the universities student writing reflects insufficient instruction and practice in the elements of literary expression. Various studies have been made of the use of English in marked essays of both arts and science students. Nearly all students make spelling mistakes. Malapropisms are frequent. Confused syntax is common: dangling participles abound, plural subjects are attached to singular verbs, 'thus' is used to introduce a new idea, and tenses are changed at random. In punctuation the commonest error is the interchange of full stops and commas but some authors omit commas entirely, whilst others sprinkle them on the text as though from a watering can, making it difficult to discover the meaning at first reading.

8 Many students are clever enough to understand their work and yet unable to communicate their knowledge and ideas effectively. They need help with their writing as much as further instruction in their chosen subject. Authorities tell us that in some fields what is learned now will be out of date in ten years, but no one has been heard to say that skill in *writing* acquired today will become outdated. Weakness in writing will continue to be a handicap and skill in writing an asset in professional advancement.

9 The need for improvement is further demonstrated in the writing of scholars and scientists who presumably do their best work when they are preparing papers for publication. Yet the experienced editor of a scientific periodical claims:

10 The most important part of my editorial work consists of trying to help contributors to say clearly and concisely what they have to say . . . It is the duty of every university to see that young people are trained better than ever before in expressing themselves lucidly, concisely and with precision.

11 And another editor writes:

As I sit editing an article which may actually have something to say, beneath the ingrained verbiage, and as I try to put nouns back into verbs, passives into actives, and to remove 'isms' and 'izations' from nearly everything, I shudder to think of the amount of congested and unclear writing that the social sciences tolerate . . .

12 Despite the efforts of editors, many published papers include verbose and ambiguous sentences which indicate that many educated people either do not think sufficiently about what they wish to write, or are unable to express their meaning clearly and concisely. Unfortunately, they may be content with their standard of writing. One critic comments:

13 We are with difficulty persuaded that we have much to learn about language, or that our understanding is defective. . . . The first condition for improvement in the adult's use of language must be to disturb this ludicrous piece of self-deception.

14 Many students, particularly in the sciences, receive no formal instruction in the art of writing and when they write badly their English may not be corrected. This is why many scientists do not appreciate how important writing is in science and why they may remain unaware of their shortcomings.

15 It is not enough to teach scientists about science (or social scientists about social science). Their teachers must also help them to be effective as scientists. There is a certain irony in teaching students of science and engineering to use techniques and instruments, some of which they may never use in their working lives, and yet not teaching them to write. This is the one thing that they must do every day as students and as administrators, executives, managers, teachers, citizens and scientists. It is also amazing that the scientist who, as a matter of course, conducts his laboratory research with the greatest refinement and highest precision of which science is capable, is so often willing to dash into print without making sure that his statements are clearly expressed. Surely the scientist, of all people, is under obligation to write not only so that he may be understood but so that he cannot be misunderstood.

16 In a university which uses English as the medium of instruction, learning in all fields depends on the understanding and effective use of English. Since writing will be part of a student's work in future, skill in writing must be regarded as a professional tool, to be ranked on a par with the other knowledge and skills which comprise his or her professional qualifications.

QUESTIONS ON THE PASSAGE

1. Write a suitable title for the entire passage. *(2 marks)*
2. Write one sentence stating what you consider to be the author's purpose in writing the passage. *(2 marks)*
3. List two reasons suggested by the author for some students' lack of concern over improving their written English. *(2 marks)*
4. Use two sentences to tell how the author supports his claim that supposedly educated people often write badly. *(2 marks)*
5. Write one concise paragraph summarizing the author's various reasons for insisting that all students should learn how to write better. *(6 marks)*
6. List any six of the following and after each give another word or phrase which shows that you understand the meaning in the context of the passage. Scan to find the word in the paragraph indicated. *(6 marks)*
   a) superfluous (Para 6)
   b) malapropisms (7)
   c) confused syntax (7)
   d) at random (7)
   e) ingrained verbiage (11)
   f) ambiguous (12)
   g) defective (13)
   h) ludicrous (13)
   i) on a par (16)
7. Explain what the author means when he says (in Paragraph 15) that there is a certain *irony* in teaching students how to use techniques and instruments . . . and yet not teaching them to write. *(5 marks)*

III. ESSAY

(Plan 5 marks)
(Essay 20 marks)

Plan and write one of the following. The plan may be in either pattern or outline form. Revise and proofread the essay carefully.

1. Compare and contrast your first impressions of the college or university with your present views.

2. Describe a tradition of your culture which you think should be preserved, say why you think it should continue, and suggest steps which might be taken to ensure it does not die out.

3. If you were a presidential candidate in a national election, which would be the top priorities of your programme, and why?

IV. WRITING SKILLS *(20 marks)*

Scoring in this section will be done by deducting half marks for errors from the total marks (20) available.

A. Rewrite each of the following to give a sentence that makes sense, is grammatically correct, and has no unnecessary words.

1. You would find that lecturers here are very different from teachers in secondary school; it is very demanding.
2. The examination includes a passage for comprehension and summary, there are some questions about reading and study skills, it has some sentences with errors, and then you have to plan and write an essay.
3. Generally, my father is a polygamous one and numbers children up to nine and a pair of twins.
4. Students in a crowded classroom is like crowded plants which they must all struggle in competition for survival.
5. Anyone doing biology has to divide themselves up for labs on different days and again in seeing specimens.
6. I am male by sex and I am an Ibibio of Itam clan. An extended family. A native of Itu LGA. The last male child. Unmarried.
7. Use of English helps to prepare students on how to tackle their way out of the various kinds of academic work and enhances their inabilities.
8. Before coming here, my uncle gave me many useful informations and pieces of advice about what life would be like at university.

B. Completely rewrite the following paragraph so that it conveys clearly, correctly and concisely what you think the student should have said. Your version should contain no errors of logic, grammar, diction, punctuation or spelling.

I have discovered that most of the people in Nigeria are 95% illitrate. This class, which as said latter on had been downgraded to the background will be made to benefit from my political party because all of the hospitals make these group of people to pay exorbitant prizes for some treatments. I am having this priority in view because I believe that if voted into power the poor masses will give a sign of releif when all have been executed.

C. Rewrite the following using correct punctuation:

This is excellent exclaimed the lecturer the topic is fascinating your thesis outline and text all match your source material is well blended your quotations are apt and your footnotes and bibliography are well nigh perfect in form i can see youve revised carefully too this is a first rate piece of work its been a pleasure to read it

D. Copy the correct spelling in each case.

1. proffessor/professor/professer
2. definately/deffinately/definitely
3. pronuntiation/pronounciation/pronunciation
4. privilege/privelege/priviledge
5. embarrased/embarrassed/embarassed
6. theoretical/theoritical/theororitical
7. accomodation/accommodation/acommodation
8. sepration/seperation/separation
9. maintainance/maintenance/maintenence
10. ocassionally/occasionally/occassionally

V. LIBRARY AND RESEARCH SKILLS *(total: 25 marks)*

A. Locating information

1. Name the classification system used to organize books and journals in your college or university library. *(1 mark)*
2. Explain clearly in one sentence what is meant by the term *call number*. *(1 mark)*
3. Give the class letters or numbers for books on any two of your major subjects. Name the subjects. *(2 marks)*
4. List briefly and in order the steps you would take to locate a book on a particular subject in your library. *(3 marks)*
5. Give an example of a *location mark* in your library and say what it means. *(1 mark)*
6. Name a specific purpose for which you might go to
   a) the reference room b) the current serials room *(2 marks)*

B. Using information

1. Write one well-constructed paragraph of about four sentences explaining *plagiarism* to a student who has not heard the term before. *(4 marks)*
2. If you were giving advice on note-making for a research paper, which three hints would you consider most important? Briefly list them. *(3 marks)*
3. The three parts of this question test your knowledge of the forms used in a final bibliography and in footnoting.

   a) Extract the necessary facts from the following, then arrange and punctuate the information exactly as it should appear in the final bibliography of a term paper.

   A book titled Writing English written by D. J. Collinson was published in 1982 by Pan Books. The book has a sub-title: A working guide to the skills of written English.

b) Follow the same procedure for the following:

An article called Helping Health in Africa, by Florence Kabba-Diallo, appears in number 3382 of the weekly magazine West Africa which was published on 31 May, 1982. The article begins on page 1449 and ends on page 1451.

c) The first footnote of the research paper refers to information on page 1450 of the article by Kabba-Diallo. Write the footnote in proper form.

VI. THINKING SKILLS *(total: 30 marks)*

A. Make a one sentence comment on the assumptions in each of the following *(3 marks)*

1. The present rate of population growth means that the world's population in two hundred years will allow each person to have only one square foot of space.
2. (From a questionnaire accompanying an advance copy of a geography text on the tropics):

   Do you appreciate very much the inclusion of numerous examples taken from all over the tropical world, the vivid descriptions and beautiful illustrations in the form of sketch maps and photographs?
3. Enrol today with Exam Success. Your guarantee for a First Time Pass!

B. For any three of the following, state two items of information you would require in order to decide whether the conclusion is justified. *(6 marks)*

1. Trust Mohammed Nasir, D.P.H., M.Th., C.T., F.R.Q.S.
2. Air travel is safer than travel by road.
3. The medical course at X university is the most demanding in the country.
4. Scientific experiments have proved that our product makes your clothes whiter.
5. This report proves that the standard of English among modern students is much lower than it was a generation ago.

C. Choose any fourteen of the following examples of fallacious reasoning. For each, explain in one well-constructed sentence what is wrong with the reasoning. *(21 marks)*

1. I know my spelling is dreadful, but all the members of my family are poor spellers.
2. It would be foolish to advise the scientist in his experiment or to question the advice of the doctor. Surely then, it is best to leave the politician alone to run the government?
3. We have a high crime rate because our judges are too lenient in sentencing convicted criminals.
4. Our lab tests have shown that the drug in question has no medicinal value whatever. We conclude therefore that it cannot be sold successfully and will be a commercial failure.
5. Either you come with us tomorrow, or we'll know you're an enemy of students' rights.

6. It's not my fault my term paper is so late. I had too many other assignments.
7. Nigeria is the wealthiest nation in black Africa so it is absurd to say that poverty is a problem in Nigeria.
8. You can't accept Dr. Chan's arguments for higher salaries for university lecturers. He is a university lecturer himself.
9. How much longer are you going to waste your time in studies when you might be doing some real work in the world and contributing to the needs of society? What you lack is a sense of social responsibility.
10. Each of these books is on sale at 50 per cent off. If I buy two of them, that will be 100 per cent off, so I'll be getting them for nothing.
11. It's not fair to rusticate me for plagiarizing. I know a student at another university who did exactly the same thing last year and got away with it.
12. Statistics are unreliable as a means of determining public opinion. After careful tabulation of the answers on more than 1,000 questionnaires, I have concluded that 70 per cent of those questioned think that statistical opinion polls misrepresent public opinion.
13. There is no reason for my father to worry about lending me the money to start a business. Just as soon as the profits come in I will pay him back with interest.
14. Dr. L, who has developed a system known as Basic Spelling, declared, 'I have always ended my public lectures by asking how many people in the audience favour my reformed spelling system, and at least three quarters of them raise their hands every time.'
15. Germany, France, Sweden and other countries nearer to Britain don't use English as a lingua franca. So why should we use it as our lingua franca?
16. A good personality is the most important thing a person can have.
17. Since you are all familiar with Mr. Shen's ridiculous proposal, I need do no more than remind you of its absurdity.

VII. ESSAY *(30 marks)*

Make a plan for a well-reasoned argument for or against one of the following propositions. Write the essay. Revise and proofread it carefully.

1. There should/should not be an increase in the number of first year admissions to your college or university next session.
2. Candidates for seats in the National Assembly should/should not be required to meet minimum educational qualifications.
3. Use of English should/should not be compulsory for all students admitted to your department.

Assignments

A. Check your answers

Check your answers to the practice examination questions, (How can you do the checking without a key?) Correct or improve them, e.g. by making answers briefer and more to the point.

B. Consider possible questions

Collect examples of questions from past question papers in your various courses, and imagine other possible questions. Analyse exactly what each question requires and plan as many answers as possible. Try writing out a few answers in full, within a time limit.

C. Make up additional questions

Make up suitable questions to cover points in this course which you think are important but for which there are no sample questions.

D. Self-assessment

Return to the self-assessment questionnaire at the end of Unit 1 and go through it again. Use it, the thinking you did earlier in this Unit, and your performance on essays, tests and examinations during the session, to help you write an assessment of your progress. Your evaluation should include an analysis of successes and problems, and suggestions for achieving further improvement.

E. Write a letter of encouragement and advice

Imagine that a student who has been admitted to your department for next session has expressed the worry that he or she will not be able to cope with the academic work. Write a brief letter of encouragement and practical advice.

Writer's Reference

This appendix is a revision aid rather than a complete handbook of English. It summarizes information and offers examples, practical tips and exercises intended to help you avoid some of the most common faults in grammar, punctuation and spelling. When you realize that you need more help with any point than this book provides, use your library skills or ask your lecturer for help in locating an appropriate reference source.

A. Some common faults of grammar and style and what to do about them

You can catch most language faults by applying three simple tests repeatedly: the *sense* test, the *word* test and the *verb* test. Each can take the form of a question:

Does this sentence make sense?
Is the meaning of this word clear?
Is the verb in the correct tense and form?

The three basic questions lead to others, e.g. is this the most appropriate word? What is the subject of this verb?

SUPERFLUOUS WORDS

Be ruthless. If a word adds no meaning, cross it out. Reduce longwinded expressions to concise ones. Get rid of all inflated words, all unnecessary technical words, and all forms of jargon, replacing them with plain English. Change passive verbs and abstract nouns into active verbs wherever possible. In eliminating unnecessary words you will also cure some grammatical faults and be able to see others you might otherwise miss.

MISMADE SENTENCES

1 **Sentence fragments**

These are parts of sentences written as if they were complete ones. Checking the sense and the form of the verb will help you detect them.

Faulty: *Problems as well as blessings accruing from our many cultures.* (wrong form of verb)

Revised: *Problems as well as blessings accrue from our many cultures.*

Faulty: *To boil their instruments before and after use so as to prevent infection.* (Where is the verb? What is the subject?)

Revised: *Midwives are taught to boil their instruments before and after use so as to prevent infection.*

2 **Run-together sentences**

Run-together or fused sentences are two sentences written as one, either without any separating punctuation or connecting word at all, or with a comma where a full stop or a semicolon should be.

Faulty: *Get rid of inflated words, use plain English instead.*

Revised: *Get rid of inflated words. Use plain English instead.*

LACK OF AGREEMENT AND CONSISTENCY

1 **Lack of agreement between subject and verb**

This fault, probably the most common one of all, is nearly always avoidable if you check the verb. Identify each verb, find its true subject and see whether subject and verb agree in number and person. Practise on these examples:

Faulty: *General Studies courses has made students more aware of their national heritage.*

Faulty: *There is, in addition, a laboratory, a theatre and two classroom blocks.*

Faulty: *The solution of routine tasks require the use of memory rather than intelligence.*

2 **Lack of agreement between pronoun and antecedent**

In informal English it is normal to hear statements like this:

The lecturer told everyone to bring their books to class.

In formal written English, however, a pronoun must agree with the noun it stands for in number, gender (masculine/feminine) and case (subjective/objective).

Faulty: *A student can improve their health by exercising.*

Revised: *A student can improve his health by exercising.*

Revised: *Students can improve their health by exercising.*

3 **Incorrect or inconsistent tenses**

Time relationships must be logical. The first example below does not pass the sense test. The second violates the rule that you should stay within the same 'block' of tenses (Present or Past) unless the sense demands a change.

Faulty: *The National Youth Service Corps is for university graduates. It later included NCE holders as well.*

Revised: *The National Youth Service Corps was originally for university graduates only, but it now includes NCE holders as well.*

Faulty: *If you review your coursework regularly, you would find it easy to prepare for exams.*

Revised: *If you review your coursework regularly, you will find it easy to prepare for exams.*

Revised: *If you reviewed your coursework regularly, you would find it easy to prepare for exams.*

4 **Unnecessary shifts in person, number or voice**

As with tenses, the aim is consistency. Within a paragraph or sentence, you should not change from *he* to *they* or *one* to *you* or from active to passive without good reason. How would you deal with these?

Faulty: *If one intends to be a writer, you must first of all learn to be self-disciplined.*

Faulty: *They had known hardship at first hand, for the dangers and misery of the Civil War had been experienced by them.*

LACK OF CLARITY

1 **Faulty pronoun references**

A pronoun without an easily identified antecedent is an obstacle to understanding. You can eliminate pronoun faults by testing each word for its meaning. If you cannot point to the word or words meant by a pronoun, then replace it with a noun or recast the sentence.

Faulty: *He offered to resign, but it was refused.* (What does *it* refer to?)
Revised: *His offer to resign was refused.*

Both of the next examples fail both the sense test and the word test and need complete rewriting. Try to imagine what the student meant to say in each case and then try to say it unambiguously.

Faulty: *Gabriel Okara cannot be accused of turning his back on the cultural tradition and language of his people. This he did by writing* The Voice.

Faulty: *Misfortune can be inherited, caused by oneself or inflicted by someone else. This is what happened to Okonkwo and his community in* Things Fall Apart.

2 **Dangling and misplaced modifiers**

If you check each sentence for its sense and each *-ing* word to see if it is a verb form needing a subject, you will usually catch any dangling or misplaced modifiers. A fault can usually be corrected either by supplying a subject or by rearranging the sentence so that the modifier is next to the word it is supposed to explain.

Faulty: *After giving birth, the midwife cuts the cord.* (Is it the midwife who has given birth?)
Revised: *The midwife cuts the cord after the baby is born.*

Faulty: *Later the rats were found dead while cleaning the cage.* (The rats were cleaning the cage?)
Revised: *Later, when we went to clean the cage, we found the rats dead.*

Faulty: *The symptom was found by Oko in mice who reported that . . .* (Talking mice?)
Revised: *Oko found the same symptom in mice. He reported that . . .*

Faulty: *Automation in the end is cheapest.* (Whose end is to be automated?)
Revised: *In the end, automation is cheapest.*

3 **Faulty parallelism**

When forms for similar elements are mixed, a sentence often fails the sense text. Putting the elements in parallel grammatical form helps the reader sort out relationships accurately and thereby clarifies meaning.

Faulty: *Many West Africans are deprived of enough good food, drinking water that is safe, no electricity and they go without basic health services.*
Revised: *Many West Africans are deprived of an adequate diet, safe drinking water, electricity and basic health services.*

4 **Improper subordination of one idea to another**

Faults in relating one idea to another can also be detected by using the sense test. The main idea should be emphasized and the dependent or less important one subordinated.

Faulty: *Students belong to some committees that deal with student welfare and there is demand for greater participation.*
Revised: *Although students already belong to some committees which deal with student welfare, they are asking for greater participation.*

Faulty: *Causing Romeo and Juliet to take their own lives, a message went astray.*
Revised: *A message went astray, causing Romeo and Juliet to take their own lives.*
Revised: *Romeo and Juliet took their own lives because a message went astray.*

PROBLEMS WITH NUMBERS AND QUANTITIES

Errors in using countables and uncountables or expressions of quantity and comparison seldom cause serious communication problems, but you cannot claim full mastery of English until you can use them correctly nearly all the time. Many of the errors can be detected by applying the sense and word tests. You can improve your facility in this aspect of English usage by paying more attention to the speech and writing of native speakers:

Faulty: *There was not a single evidence in his favour.*
Revised: *There was no evidence in his favour.*
Revised: *There was not a shred of evidence in his favour.*

Faulty: *I am grateful to Dr. J. Hassan for many useful informations and pieces of advice.*
Revised: *I am grateful to Dr. J. Hassan for much useful information and advice.*

WRONG OR MISSPELLED WORDS

Many errors in word choice and spelling result from confusion between words of similar sound or meaning. Idioms and phrasal verbs cause further problems. If you apply the word test throughout a paper and look up each word of whose meaning or spelling you are uncertain, you can eliminate inappropriate words, imprecise language and misspellings. (Hints for improving spelling, and a list of commonly misspelled words, appear on pp. 213–15.) Correct the second and third examples:

Faulty: *The men students wanted to voice out their opinions too but the women oppositioned this.*
Revised: *The men students wanted to voice their opinions too but the women were opposed to this.*

Faulty: *Another way of remembering is to use pneumonics.*
Faulty: *He is a very imminent scientist.*

B. Revising faulty sentences

Study the advice and examples under A above. Then look for the faults in the sentences below.

Begin with the sense test. Go on if necessary to consider the meaning of individual words or to check the verbs. Then rewrite each sentence to say something sensible in acceptable English.

1 All the textbooks in most cases are written in English.
2 Men seem to dominate the novel, the women play minor roles.
3 The Senator has discussed the question of stocking the proposed poultry farm with his colleagues.
4 At college and university level, error in agreement arise as often through carelessness as it do through ignorance.
5 A good politician accepts the opinion of the majority of people even if they disagree with it.
6 Learning a new language is always interesting. Even in vernacular it is so.

7 Two symptoms of drug deprivation are a wet nose and the eyes are watery.

8 But traditional beliefs and habits and the availability of traditional medicine, especially in rural areas in which the vast majority of Africans still live.

9 When they repeated the experiments, the researchers had not as much problems.

10 Since a university's functions include the training of minds.

11 Malaysia's educational expansion had a rapid growth point just after independence.

12 Being convinced that they have to fight for their rights, there has been student unrest over such issues as food, water and light.

K

C. Choosing the right word

The sentences below do not say what their student authors meant them to say because words and idioms are incorrect, inappropriate or imprecise. Think of the intended meaning in each case; then completely rewrite the sentence so that it makes sense and is grammatically correct.

1 Precarious children are sometimes not challenged enough in school.

2 If everyone obeyed the rules of hygiene, there would be littler diseases.

3 Graduate teachers should be sent into the field to breed manpower.

4 The health officers should correct the people's cleanliness.

5 If this method is successful, all the mosquitoes will take to their heels.

6 Tribalism is a disruptive instrument to national unity.

7 Having pinpointed the pitfalls, the solution will not be far-fetched and loopholes can be corrected.

8 These days many children's eyes are literally glued to the TV screen.

9 In some states, the roads have not yet got off the ground.

10 As a boy, he was greatly influenced by his grandfather, so he was very cut up when the old man kicked the bucket at the age of ten.

D. Mastering punctuation

Punctuation is primarily an aid to clarity, which means that every mark used should be necessary and help the sense or the rhythm. You can learn a great deal about using punctuation marks effectively by observing how they are used in books you are reading, including this one. Find examples to illustrate each of the uses mentioned in the following summary. In your search for examples, pay special attention to the uses of commas.

THE USES OF PUNCTUATION

The full stop
The most important punctuation mark is the full stop because every sentence that is not a question or an exclamation ends with one. If you master its use and write short simple sentences you can avoid major punctuation problems. Full

stops are also used at the end of footnotes, after each main part of a bibliography entry and after some abbreviations.

, **The comma**
Commas cause the most problems. They should be used with care to make the meaning clearer and tell the reader when to pause. Their use is justified in separating items in a series, marking off introductory phrases and interrupters in longer sentences, and marking off clauses that comment but which are not essential to the sense of the sentence. When a sentence is short and its meaning clear without commas, omit them.

: **The colon**
A colon is used to introduce a list, an extended quotation or an example of what has just been discussed.

; **The semi-colon**
The most common use of the semi-colon is to replace a full stop between two sentences in order to emphasize their close relationship.

( ) **Parentheses**
Round brackets, called parentheses, are used to set off an explanation, a comment or an aside within the main text. They are also used in footnotes to enclose the place, publisher and date of a source's publication.

— **The dash**
A dash is twice as long as a hyphen. A pair of dashes may be used in the same way as parentheses, especially when the insertion is important. A dash may also be used to separate a list of items from a summing up statement about them all.

“ ” **Quotation marks**
Quotation marks indicate the beginning and end of a quotation within the text. They also enclose the titles of articles in journals and of parts of larger works, e.g. titles of chapters, encyclopedia articles. According to British practice, short quotations are placed within single quotation marks and a quotation within a quotation is placed within double quotation marks. The opposite obtains in American practice. In British practice, the final quotation mark goes last (i.e. after any other punctuation) if the entire sentence is a quotation, but inside the other punctuation if the quotation is only a part of the sentence. In American practice, commas and full stops are always placed inside the quotation marks and there are other rules for other marks. You should choose one set of rules, or find out which usage your lecturer prefers, and then stick with your choice. The important thing is to be consistent.

[ ] **Square brackets**
The main use of square brackets is to indicate that words within material being quoted are not part of the quotation but are your own interpolation.

’ **The apostrophe**
The apostrophe signals possession but it must not be used with possessive pronouns, e.g. *whose*, or possessive adjectives, e.g. *their*, *its*. Remember that *it's* is a contraction for *it is*.

- **The hyphen**
The hyphen is most often used to link together the parts of compound words. It

is also used to divide a word at the end of a line, but this should be done as seldom as possible and always between syllables.

PUNCTUATION EXERCISES

1 Remove or add commas in the following sentences so that the meaning is clear, punctuation is correct and each sentence is easy to read.
a After water proteins are the main component of the body.
b The new universities he said will all be universities of technology.
c Students, who always write with a reader in mind, tend to write clearly.
d I wish to see Dr. Abdullah who co-ordinates Nigerian History and Culture.
e Parenthetical remarks explanatory comments and other insertions, not essential to the meaning, should be set off by commas but any phrase, which is essential to the meaning, by restricting it, in some way should not be set off.

K

2 Rewrite each of the following with correct punctuation and capitalization.
a When we speak we do not use words alone the lecturer said we also express our meaning through what is sometimes called body language facial expressions gestures and postures and through variations in tone of voice speed and volume
b Which magazine do you prefer quest africa now time or newsweek
c Joseph my roommate always sees the funny side of things his laugh is famous.
d Ive just read an amusing short story called ding dong bell by Kwabana Annan a ghanaian its included in a book called modern african stories
e hand in your bibliography slips note slips and drafts as well as the final version of your research paper which should consist of title page outline text and bibliography
f The teacher looked at my friend and said you are not yourself today udo you mustnt be selfish I was very confused and upset for my friend but sir who else could he be I asked and why shouldnt he sell fish maybe he has to help his mother in the market after school he cant help it sir

K

E. Improving spelling

Use these steps to ensure that you can spell and use correctly each of the 101 commonly misspelled words listed on page 215. Make sure also that you know when and when not to use each of the commonly confused words on the second list.

1 Go through the list, ticking any words you are not sure you can spell correctly. Pass over those you know you never misspell.

2 Take a sheet of paper and list the words you have ticked, one to a line. Copy them correctly; pay attention to the letters as you write them, and to the separate parts of the word.

3 Look at each word in turn. Say it aloud with careful pronunciation; if you are not sure of the meaning, look it up in your dictionary. Then identify the trouble spot, e.g. mainTENance.

4 Write the word again, on the same line, this time with the troublesome syllable or letters in capital letters or in colour, e.g. chIEf. Shut your eyes and try to 'see' a mental picture of the word. Try to spell it. Were you correct?

5 Reinforce the mental picture by thinking up a memory aid for the word: a rule, a rhyme, an association, a phrase or sentence. Here are some possibilities:

a Does the word follow a rule? Is it an exception to a rule?
E.g. in deciding whether or not to double a consonant when adding an ending, this rule usually works: If a vowel 'says its name' don't double. If it doesn't say its name, double. Try out the rule by pronouncing these words:

writing, written, hoped, hopped, filed, filled, beginning, dining

How can you remember the spelling of these words?

K dis-satisfied, dis-appoint, mis-spell, un-necessary

What rule helps with these words?

believe, chief, niece / / receive, deceit, perceive / / freight

How might you remember these exceptions?

K counterfeit, either, forfeit, leisure, seize, weird

b Is there a related word which accents the troublesome part?

e.g. ACAdemic/ACAdemy comPLEment/comPLEte
deFINItely/deFINItion/FINIsh irriTAble/irriTAte

c Can you make up a memory aid based on some thought association?

e.g. MuM will always accoMModate you. *or* Can you recoMMend accoMModation?
An authOR should be an authORity.
APOLOgize and give him a POLO mint.
Don't beLIEve a LIE.
Is buSINess a SIN?
SCIENTists are conSCIENTious.
The two pairs of twins in embaRRaSS mean double trouble.
There's IRON in the envIRONment.
E's for ExcEllEnce.
ExaGGerate the g's.
Don't MAR your work with bad gramMAR.
An illiTERate person doesn't know his letTERs.
Is the launDRY DRY?
The double ll in parallel = parallel lines.
PasT has a T for Time; passed is the past tense of pass.
A PIEce of PIE.
Is priVILEge VILE?
Three vowels in a row make qUIEt a quiet word.
PA RATEs a sePARATE room for his office.
StationAry = StAy in one plAce. StationEry is for writing lEtters.

6 Practise remembering the word. Visualize it. Write it again and again. Keep testing yourself until you are sure you will never misspell it again.

You can eliminate virtually all of your spelling errors within a few weeks if you
—keep a record of the spelling mistakes you make;
—follow the procedure above;
—spend a few minutes each day studying and testing yourself on the words you have listed;
—form the habit of proofreading all your written work to find (and correct) any misspelled words.

101 Words Commonly Misspelled

absence
academic
accessible
accidentally
accommodation
analyse
analysis
apologize
appetizing
argument
athletics
author
beginning
belief
beneficial
benefited
biased
business
career
chief
committee
comparative
conscientious
conscious
curiosity
deceit
definitely
describe
dining
disappearance
disappointment
disease
dissatisfied
embarrassed
environment
exaggerate
excellence
existence
grammar
grievous
guardian
height
hindrance
illiterate
imagination
immediately
incidentally
inconvenience
independent
indigenous
indispensable
ineligible
influential
intention
irresistible
irritable
laundry
legitimate
leisure
lightning
literacy
maintenance
modern
negotiate
niece
noticeable
occasion
occurrence
pamphlets
parallel
perceive
perseverance
possess
precedence
prejudice
privilege
proceed
procedure
professor
prominent
pronunciation
queue
receive
referred
relief
repetition
resistance
rhythm
ridiculous
schedule
seize
separate
succeed
summary
supposed
surprise
theoretical
unnecessary
until
writing
yield

Some Words Commonly Confused

accept/except
advice/advise
affect/effect
altar/alter
bare/bear
belief/believe
berth/birth
brake/break
cease/seize
choose/chose
cite/site/sight
coarse/course
complement/compliment
decease/disease
desert/dessert
eminent/imminent
formally/formerly
guard/guide
hear/here
imply/infer
incidence/incidents
its/it's
know/no
later/latter
lead/led
loose/lose
lunch/launch
of/off
passed/past
peace/piece
plain/plane
precede/proceed
principal/principle
quiet/quite
right/write
seat/sit
stationary/stationery
super/supper
their/there/they're
threw/through
to/too/two
weather/whether
were/where
who's/whose
your/you're

Answer Key to Selected Exercises

Unit 1

Timed Reading Passage 1, p. 2

1 *b* 2 *a* 3 *d* 4 *c* 5 *b* 6 *d* 7 *b* 8 *a* 9 *c* 10 *b*

Discussion question B.1, p. 4

It is more efficient to read at 400 WPM with 70% comprehension. A 70% comprehension rate is 'normal' and often all that is required. If you need fuller comprehension, you can use the time saved by reading faster to go back and check specific points. These will be better understood because you now have a framework to fit them into.

Unit 2

Timed Reading Passage 2, p. 15

1 *c* 2 *d* 3 *c* 4 *c* 5 *b* 6 *a* 7 *b* 8 *d* 9 *b* 10 *c*

Practice in using information, p. 18

Two examples of implications: 1 You can improve reading efficiency if you learn to take in more words at a fixation. 2 Since our eyes and brain can process the material in $\frac{1}{4}$ to $\frac{1}{2}$ a second, there is no need to spend longer on a fixation. To do so may encourage mind-wandering.

Drawing inferences (passage on Helen Keller), p. 23

If you did not deduce that Helen was blind, deaf and dumb, look for the clues again. [The cause was an illness when she was about 18 months old. Thanks to a remarkable teacher, she became a very well educated woman, earning a university degree and mastering not only English but other languages. By feeling her teacher's vocal cords and trying to produce the same feel in her own, she even learned to speak.]

Unit 3

Timed Reading Passage 3, p. 35

1 *d* 2 *b* 3 *b* 4 *c* 5 *d* 6 *b* 7 *c* 8 *b* 9 *a* 10 *e*

Unit 4

Timed Reading Passage 4, p. 54

1 *b* 2 *a* 3 *c* 4 *a* 5 *c* 6 *b* 7 *c* 8 *b* 9 *d* 10 *c*

Unit 5

Timed Reading Passage 5, p. 76

1 *c* 2 *a* 3 *b* 4 *d* 5 *a* 6 *a* 7 *c* 8 *d* 9 *b* 10 *c*

Unit 6

Timed Reading Passage 6, p. 91

1 *d* 2 *c* 3 *c* 4 *b* 5 *d* 6 *d* 7 *c* 8 *a* 9 *c* 10 *b*

Scanning practice, p. 93

1 *2* 2 *6* 3 *6* 4 *3* 5 *5* 6 *10* 7 *12*

Unit 7

Timed Reading Passage 7, p. 109

1 *c* 2 *c* 3 *d* 4 *a* 5 *d* 6 *a* 7 *b* 8 *a* 9 *c* 10 *d*

Memory tests, p. 112

1 The numbers should be read in groups of two, e.g. 45, 47, 50, 54, etc. All you need to remember is that the first number is made up of 4 and $4+1=5$, that is 45, and that from then on you must keep adding one more to the previous two digit number, e.g. $45+2=47$; $47+3=50$; $50+4=54$. Can you remember them all now?

2 Sorting the items into categories gives five groups of five items each which are much easier to remember than the unsorted list, e.g.

yam, rice, maize, potato, cassava
pen, paper, ruler, pencil, notebook
soap, comb, towel, shampoo, toothpaste
fork, glass, spoon, knife, plate
mango, pawpaw, banana, orange, pineapple

Improving sentence clarity, Ex. 2, p. 114

Identification of faults and examples of correct sentences:

a ('Him' requires an antecedent.) The book was about a young girl who fell in love with a handsome young lawyer/an older man/a student from America/and then lost him.

b (Dangling modifier) The character in the book I was reading reminded me of you.

c (Misplaced modifier) I answered almost every question.

d (The three parts of the dream should be in parallel form.) My dream is to have a good job, raise a happy family and build a house in my village.

e (Give more emphasis to the insects and the effect of their eating.) The insects eat the plant off just below the soil, thereby stopping all growth. *or* By eating the plant off just below the soil, the insects stop all growth.

f ('This' needs an antecedent.) The teacher's remarks about bad behaviour referred to Inyang, but Bassey assumed they referred to him. He often made this kind of mistake.

g (Dangling modifier) The teacher wrote the word 'etiquette' on the blackboard and called on one of my classmates to say it. The boy pronounced the *qu* as in *quiet* and even the teacher laughed.

h (Misplaced modifier) During the lecture on Monday, the professor made it clear why plagiarism is wrong.

i (Lack of parallelism) Each of my courses has contributed to my being more intelligent to talk with and more efficient at learning.

j (Lack of parallelism, and clumsiness caused by use of the passive) The new English master made our lessons more lively because he knew his subject so well. *or* English lessons became more lively under our new English master because he knew his subject so well.

Unit 8

Timed Reading Passage 8, p. 129

1 *c* 2 *a* 3 *c* 4 *d* 5 *a* 6 *d* 7 *b* 8 *c* 9 *a* 10 *b*

Generalizing and drawing conclusions, pp. 131–2

Sample answers:

1 previewing aids speed and comprehension.

2 relate facts and details to principles for better retention.

3 To be effective, rereading must involve reviewing material in some new way.

4 make up questions which they expect their reading to answer and search for the answers while reading.

5 always allow time for recall after reading (because) this helps both learning and remembering.

6 Immediate recall prevents forgetting.

7 he should keep testing himself on what he has learned.

Avoiding wordiness, Ex. 3, p. 133

a more
b longer
c enough
d if
e because
f regularly
g whether
h mostly
i cannot
j try
k called
l therefore

Avoiding wordiness, Ex. 4, pp. 133–4

Sample answers:
a This course teaches basic skills such as reading, studying and using the library.
b We could see that we were surrounded.
c Summarizing can be hard work but it can be useful.
d This solution seems reasonable.
e History repeats itself.
f I have never cheated in exams.
g The subject of the paper will be the growth of Yoruba towns.
h I know many lecturers who help you as much as they can.
i The majority thought he was the better candidate.
j The teacher said that the students had been very careless.
k Many of the books I read are set in foreign countries.
l According to medical experts, human embryos can now be developed in a test tube.

Avoiding wordiness, Ex. 5, p. 134

a The English of most of the examination candidates was good.
b The theme of the novel is not obvious from its title.
c The way we speak depends on to whom we are speaking.
d At a university, students are exposed to other ways of life and new ideas through mixing with people of other ethnic groups.

Unit 9

Timed Reading Passage 9, p. 144

1 *d* 2 *e* 3 *b* 4 *c* 5 *d* 6 *a* 7 *d* 8 *b* 9 *a* 10 *c*

Problem solving through visualizing, p. 150

1 Fill the 5 litre tin. Pour this water into the 3 litre tin until it is full. Pour out the 3 litres and pour in the 2 litres remaining in the 5 litre tin. Now fill the 5 litre tin and pour from it to fill the 3 litre tin. This leaves the desired 4 litres in the 5 litre tin.

2

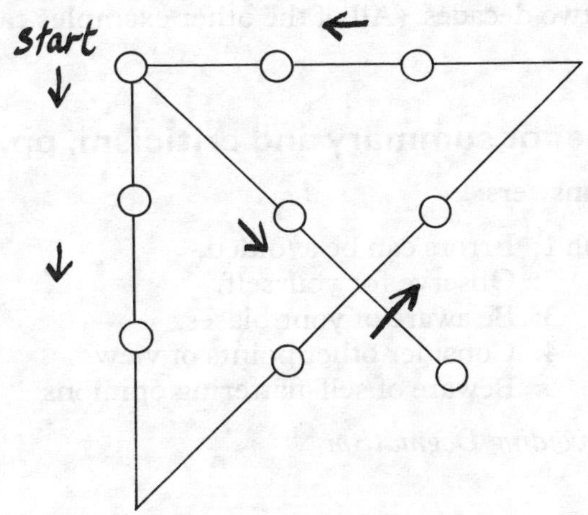

Using critical judgement, C.1, pp. 151–2

A sample title for the second passage: *Why Read Fiction*?
An acceptable summary for the second passage: *Fiction can help us understand other human beings better.*

Unit 10

Timed Reading Passage 10, p. 167

1 *b* 2 *c* 3 *d* 4 *a* 5 *b* 6 *c* 7 *b* 8 *d* 9 *c* 10 *c*

Detecting fallacies of oversimplification, pp. 173–4

Two sample answers:

11 The investigator will arrive at a distorted figure because his sample is 'loaded' and not representative of the student body as a whole. To arrive at a more reliable conclusion, he will have to include in his investigation the students who have never been sick and also those who have been sick but have not visited the Medical Centre.

14 Who was allowed to enter for the examination at each school: only those sure to pass at School A and anyone who wished at School B? How many candidates were entered altogether at each school? How many were sitting for the second time? How many distinctions were there at each school?

Detecting fallacies of irrelevance, p. 175

Sample answer:

9 We are given no reasons for believing that X will clear up colds any faster than any other medicine because we are not told which housewives were consulted, what they were asked, what they really said, whether the 11% refers just to the housewives or to their families as well, whether the 11% means the colds cleared up in eight days instead of nine, how one knows when a cold has cleared up or what proportion of doctors have prescribed it in preference to other medicines for over two decades. (All of the other examples can be answered much more briefly.)

Passage for summary and criticism, pp. 177–8

Sample answers:

1 Paragraph 1: Errors can be avoided.
2: Observe for yourself.
3: Be aware of your biases.
4: Consider other points of view.
5: Beware of self-flattering opinions.

2 Title: *Avoiding Dogmatism*

Unit 11

Using and documenting sources, Ex. 4, p. 184

Bibliography	**Footnote**
Purpose: to identify sources consulted	Purpose: to specify exactly where, within a source, the fact or idea was found
Entries not numbered	Entries numbered
Author's surname first for ease of alphabetizing	Author's names in normal order
Hanging indentation, i.e. authors' surnames project at left	Arrangement as for a paragraph
No parentheses around facts of publication	Parentheses around facts of publication
Full stops after authors' names, book titles and at end	Punctuated like sentences, with full stop only at end

Writer's Reference

Revising faulty sentences, pp. 210–11

1 Most of our textbooks are written in English.

2 Men dominate the novel; the women play minor roles.

3 The Senator has discussed with his colleagues the question of stocking the proposed poultry farm.

4 At college and university level, error in agreement arises as often through carelessness as it does through ignorance.

5 A good politician abides by the decision of the majority even if he disagrees with it.

6 Learning a new language is always interesting even when it is a local vernacular.

7 Two symptoms of drug deprivation are a wet nose and watery eyes.

8 Traditional beliefs and habits and the availability of village medicine men and midwives mean that traditional medicine is still widely used, especially in the rural areas where most Africans live.

9 When they repeated the experiments, the researchers had fewer problems.

10 One function of a university is to train minds.

11 Malaysia's educational expansion was especially rapid just after independence.

12 Convinced that they have to fight for their rights, students have demonstrated over such issues as food, water and light.

Mastering punctuation

Ex. 1, p. 213:

a After water, proteins are the main component of the body.
b The new universities, he said, will all be universities of technology.
c Students who always write with a reader in mind tend to write clearly.
d I wish to see Dr. Abdullah, who co-ordinates Nigerian History and Culture.
e Parenthetical remarks, explanatory comments and other insertions not essential to the meaning should be set off by commas, but any phrase which is essential to the meaning by restricting it in some way should not be set off.

Ex. 2, p. 213:

a 'When we speak, we do not use words alone,' the lecturer said. 'We also express our meaning through what is sometimes called "body language"—facial expressions, gestures and posture—and through variations in tone of voice, speed and volume.' (British usage)
b Which magazine do you prefer: *Quest*, *Africa Now*, *Time* or *Newsweek*? (N.B. Remember that italics in printing = underlining in handwritten or typed work.)
c Joseph, my roommate, always sees the funny side of things. His laugh is famous.
d I've just read an amusing short story called 'Ding Dong Bell' by Kwabana Annan, a Ghanaian. It's included in a book called *Modern African Stories*.
e Hand in your bibliography slips, note slips and drafts as well as the final version of your research paper, which should consist of title page, outline, text and bibliography.
f The teacher looked at my friend and said, 'You are not yourself today, Udo. You mustn't be selfish.'

I was very confused and upset for my friend. 'But Sir, who else could he be?' I asked. 'And why shouldn't he sell fish? Maybe he has to help his mother in the market after school. He can't help it, Sir!'

Improving spelling

Ex. 5a, p. 214:

Spelling rule

i before *e* except after *c*
or when pronounced *ay*
as in *neigh*bour and *weigh*

Remembering the exceptions: Make up a sentence such as

EIther forfEIt lEIsure or be sEIzed by a wEIrd counterfEIter.

Index

References are to practice exercises and assignments as well as to information. Page numbers for illustrations appear in **bold** type.